MARIAN ANDERSON

Painting by Mitchell Jamieson depicting the Marian Anderson concert on April 9, 1939, at the Lincoln Memorial. Painting hangs in the Interior Department Building in Washington, D.C. Photograph courtesy of the Marian Anderson and DAR Controversy Collection of the Moorland-Spingarn Research Center of Howard University.

MARIAN ANDERSON

AN ANNOTATED BIBLIOGRAPHY AND DISCOGRAPHY

Compiled by
JANET L. SIMS

GREENWOOD PRESS
Westport, Connecticut • London, England

Library of Congress Cataloging in Publication Data

Sims, Janet, 1945-
    Marian Anderson, an annotated bibliography and discography.

    Includes index.
    1. Anderson, Marian, 1902-   —Bibliography.
    2. Anderson, Marian, 1902-   —Discography. I. Title.
ML134.5.A5S5   016.7821'092'4   80-1787
ISBN 0-313-22559-1 (lib. bdg.)

Library of Congress Catalog Card Number: 80-1787
ISBN: 0-313-22559-1

First published in 1981

Greenwood Press
A division of Congressional Information Service, Inc.
88 Post Road West, Westport, Connecticut 06881

Printed in the United States of America

10 9 8 7 6 5 4 3 2 1

CONTENTS

FOREWORD

"Marian Anderson, the contralto, is the youngest singer of first rank among us. She is one of the most phenomenal, both in the rapidity of ascent, and in the excellence of her performance. . . . Her public has praised and has sung her triumph, and ardently comes to her praise again. Her hold upon all lovers of the Art will be continually intensified by the talent and art which is hers." So wrote Penman Lovinggood (*Famous Modern Negro Musicians*) of this great American artist in 1921. His judgement has been vindicated and his prophecy has been fulfilled many times over in the years between 1935, the year of Marian Anderson's Town Hall debut, and 1978, the year in which President Carter presented to her a special gold medal. She has become a symbol of achievement in America, and, long after her retirement from public life, her public still "ardently comes to her praise again."

This bibliography is a guide to the record of her achievement as it has been documented in newspapers, books, and magazines. Of obvious value as a source of references to one of the most outstanding American performers, the volume is especially timely in view of the awakened interest in the research and documentation of the Afro-American presence in music and in view of the even more recent interest in studies about women. Marian Anderson is more than a great singer: she is a great American woman whose humanitarian interests have led her to the United Nations and have stimulated her many efforts toward the betterment of mankind.

Inevitably the record of Marian Anderson's career as a singer is also a record of race relationships in the United States. The American concertgoer of the late nineteenth and the early twentieth centuries tended to applaud readily those artists who had received endorsement in Europe. But American audiences, having grown fond of minstrelsy, were not ready to accept the black performer of classical music. Thus, the black singer of classical music, no matter how successful abroad, found it difficult to move beyond the churches or small recital halls characteristic of black communities. In this regard, Marian Anderson, along with Roland Hayes before her, was a pioneer. She concertized in America far beyond the bounds of the black community, and after 1935 she was managed by Sol Hurok, a major impresario. Yet she had to face many instances of racial prejudice.

The most dramatic such instance took place in 1939 in Washington, D.C. The Howard University School of Music was trying to arrange for a concert by Marian Anderson as part of its concert series for which she had appeared regularly since the 1933-34 season. When the theater that was to be used for the 1939 recital was destroyed by fire, the use of white Central High School's capacious auditorium was sought. The School Board, following the pattern of racial segregation characteristic of the city, denied the request. In like manner, the Daughters of the American Revolution refused to allow the use of Constitution Hall. Finally, Marian Anderson accepted the invitation of Secretary of the Interior Harold Ickes to sing outdoors at the Lincoln Memorial. On Easter Sunday, 1939, Howard University and associated sponsors presented Marian Anderson to an audience of seventy-five thousand. Her triumph was complete.

The significance of the issue of racial prejudice against the artist caused this incident to be covered widely not only in American newspapers and magazines but also in the European press. References to this incident constitute the largest percentage of citations relating to a single event in this book, outnumbering the coverage for any of her honorary degrees or other prestigious awards.

Janet L. Sims, reference librarian at the Moorland-Spingarn Research Center and an experienced bibliographer, has grouped the references according to stages in the singer's life and career. One is therefore able to select easily the references that outline the earlier and later stages of her career, the awards that she made to young singers, and the honors and awards that she herself received. Without question, most readers will bring to this volume an already strong sense of the position of Marian Anderson in American music history. But even the well-informed reader will be impressed by the consistent use of superlatives, the constant searching for phrases with which to convey the colors of her voice, and the almost surprised admiration for her artistry that characterize these references. Interwoven through the statements concerning her art is a remarkable esteem bestowed by the world upon the noble, dignified woman who, throughout her career, has sung with shining beauty, spoken with humility, and sought to quicken the spirit of humanity among us.

Doris Evans McGinty
Chairman, Department of Music
Howard University

PREFACE

This annotated bibliography on Marian Anderson began in 1978 as part of my biographical series on black women. As the project progressed, I came to admire Marian Anderson, not only for her musical talents, but also for her deep religious convictions.

Born in 1902 (some sources list 1908), Marian Anderson broke many barriers. She came along at a time when hotels would not accommodate blacks, when theaters would not allow blacks to perform in their facilities, when audiences were segregated, and when there was a general refusal to acknowledge that blacks made any contribution to society.

Through her faith, and without malice, Marian Anderson was able to achieve distinction as one of the world's greatest contraltos. She paved the way for other artists to perform in any theater in the country and before unsegregated audiences.

This achievement should not be forgotten. This bibliography is the first major annotated bibliography on any individual black woman to date. It is only a small measure of the success of Marian Anderson.

As in all bibliographies, some citations could not be located for inclusion. Materials from foreign language sources were not included. Included are manuscript holdings on Marian Anderson and a discography of some of her recordings. I hope that this bibliography will help those doing scholarly research on the illustrious life and career of this famous contralto.

ACKNOWLEDGMENTS

I would like to thank the staffs in the various libraries I visited or wrote to for assistance: the Moorland-Spingarn Research Center, the Fine Arts Library and the Channing Pollack Collection at Howard University; the Music Division of the Library of Congress; the Oxon Hill, Maryland, Branch Library; and the Martin Luther King Memorial Library. Special thanks go to Dr. Neda M. Westlake at the Van Pelt Library, University of Pennsylvania, where the Marian Anderson Collection is housed.

I want to thank Ms. Virginia L. Brown for her diligent assistance in typing my manuscript and Linda Pearce and Jeane Brooks for their proofreading assistance.

I especially want to thank Dr. Doris McGinty for writing the foreword and for offering advice and insight on Marian Anderson.

As always, I am deeply appreciative to my family for their support and encouragement.

1
PERSONAL
DATA

Marian Anderson, *left*, and Mary McLeod Bethune, *right*, at the launching of the S.S. *Booker T. Washington* in 1942. Photograph courtesy of the OWI Photograph Section of the Prints and Photographs Collection of the Moorland-Spingarn Research Center of Howard University.

AUTOBIOGRAPHY
AND BIOGRAPHICAL
AND CAREER SKETCHES

1

Albus, Harry James. The 'Deep River' Girl; The Life of Marian Anderson In Story Form. Grand Rapids: W. B. Eerdmans Publishing Co., 1949, 85p.

Although a fiction book, the author based his book on the actual life of Miss Anderson. Incidents which are fictitious are acknowledged as such by the author. It is a story of spiritual trust and courage in the face of race prejudice and discrimination.

2

Anderson, Marian. My Lord What A Morning, An Autobiography. New York: Viking Press, 1956, 312p.

This autobiography expresses the author's warm and reverent approach to her life and her music. She gives the reader an intimate view of her philosophy toward race prejudice, how she handles her fame, her family life away from the concert stage, and the problems all entertainers face.

3

_____. "My Lord What A Morning: The Autobiography of Marian Anderson." Woman's Home Companion. Vol. 83, October, 1956, pp. 33-35, 118-119, 122-128; November, 1956, pp. 58-59, 89, 91-98.

Excerpts from Miss Anderson's autobiography. She proved that talent, courage and humanity are stronger than any barriers.

4

"Anderson, Marian," in The Afro American Encyclopedia, Vol. 1. Florida: Educational Book Publishers, Inc., 1974, 304p., pp. 143-144.

Short biographical sketch.

5
"Anderson, Marian," in <u>Afro American Singers: An Index And
    Preliminary Discography of Long-Playing Recordings of Opera,
    Choral Music, and Song</u>, by Patricia Turner. Minneapolis:
    Patricia Turner, 1976, 240p., pp. 5-8.

A discography of recordings by Marian Anderson and a short
bibliography.

6
"Anderson, Marian," in <u>The American Music Handbook</u>, by Chris-
    topher Pavlaskis. New York: The Free Press, 1974, 836p.,
    pp. 64, 375, 425.

Notes that Miss Anderson served on the National Council of
The Arts, participated in the Chicago Grant Park concerts, and
gives a history of the Marian Anderson Scholarship, listing
some previous winners.

7
"Anderson, Marian," in <u>The American Negro Reference Book</u>, Vol.
    <u>II</u>, edited by John P. Davis. New York: Educational Heritage,
    Inc., 1966, 886p., pp. 94, 704, 720, 810, 812.

Brief notes on Miss Anderson's early career, her Metropolitan Opera debut, her farewell concert tours and the March on
Washington.

8
"Anderson, Marian," in <u>Arna Bontemps - Langston Hughes Letters</u>:
    <u>1925-1967</u>, edited by Charles A. Nichols. New York: Dodd,
    Mead, 1980, 529p., pp. 67, 87, 164, 190, 206, 348-349, 399,
    451.

Miss Anderson is mentioned in several letters between Bontemps and Hughes.

9
"Anderson, Marian," in <u>Baker's Biographical Dictionary of Musi-
    cians</u>, by Nicholas Slominsky. New York: Schirmer Books,
    1978 (6th edition), 1955p., pp. 36-37.

Biographical sketch on this famous contralto.

10
"Anderson, Marian," in <u>Biographical Dictionary of American
    Music</u>, by Charles E. Claghorn. New York: Parker Publishing
    Co., 1973, 491p., pp. 24.

Short biographical sketch on Miss Anderson.

11
"Anderson, Marian," in <u>Biographical History of Blacks In
    America Since 1528</u>, by Edgar A. Toppin. New York: McKay,
    1971, 499p., pp. 248.

Short biographical sketch noting that Marian Anderson

received a Rosenwald fellowship to study in Europe.   Her fame
in America came after her 1935 debut at Town Hall.

12
"Anderson, Marian," in The Black American Reference Book,
    edited by Mable M. Smythe. New Jersey: Prentice-Hall, 1976,
    1026p., pp. 74, 350, 366, 695, 820.

Brief notes on her illustrous career.

13
"Anderson, Marian," in A Concise Biographical Dictionary Of
    Singers, by K. J. Kutsch and Leo Riemens. New York: Chilton
    Book Co., 1966, 487p., pp. 13-14.

Biographical sketch on Miss Anderson.

14
"Anderson, Marian," in Current Biography, 1940. New York: H.W.
    Wilson, 916p., pp. 17-19.

Biographical sketch on Miss Anderson.

15
"Anderson, Marian," in Current Biography, 1950. New York: H.W.
    Wilson, 704p., pp. 8-10.

Biographical sketch on Miss Anderson.

16
"Anderson, Marian (Contralto)," in The Disc Book, by David
    Hall and Abner Levin. New York: Long Player Publications,
    1955, 471p., pp. 266-267, 270, 305, 389.

Olympian beauty, strength and serenity best describe Miss
Anderson's vocalism.   She was best in works of tragic grandeur.

17
"Anderson, Marian," in First And Last Love, by Vincent Sheean.
    New York: Random House, 1956, 305p., pp. 184, 187-188, 197,
    278.

Mentions highlights of Miss Anderson's career.

18
"Anderson, Marian," in Grove's Dictionary of Music and Music-
    ians, Vol. 1, edited by Eric Blom. New York: St. Martin's
    Press, 1954, 1078p., pp. 147.

Short biography notes that Miss Anderson toured for several
years in the U. S. before going to Europe.   She returned home
with praises from a dozen different countries.   She excells in
music expressive of pensiveness and humility.

19
"Anderson, Marian," in Historical Negro Biographies, by
    Wilhelmina S. Robinson. New York: Publishers Co., Inc.,
    1967, 291p., pp. 157-158.

Making her professional debut in 1924, she sang with the
New York Philharmonic in 1925. A Rosenwald fellowship allowed
her to study in Germany. Remembering her struggles, she set
up a fund for talented artists.

20
"Anderson, Marian," in The International Cyclopedia of Music
    and Musicians, edited by Bruce Bohle. New York: Dodd, Mead,
    1975 (10th edition), 2511p., pp. 70-71.

Biographical sketch on Miss Anderson.

21
"Anderson, Marian," in Living Musicians, edited by David
    Ewen. New York: H. W. Wilson, 1940, 390p., pp. 19-21.

Biographical sketch noted how Miss Anderson had to go to
Europe to gain fame. While in London, famous musicians and
critics praised her. Roger Quilter arranged for her to
appear in a concert. Sir Henry J. Wood had her as a soloist
at his Promenade Concerts.

22
"Anderson, Marian," in Music In Philadelphia, by Robert A.
    Gerson, Philadelphia: Theodore Presser, Co., 1940, 422p.,
    pp. 200, 367.

Miss Anderson is mentioned as an artist who sang with the
Philadelphia Philharmonic Orchestra. Her debut was broadcast
from the Academy of Music, January 16, 1923. Short biographical sketch is included.

23
"Anderson, Marian," in Music Since 1900, by Nicolas Slonimsky.
    New York: Scribner's Sons, 1971 (4th edition), 1595p., pp.
    688, 989, 1163.

This chronological listing of events in music history
noted that Mrs. Eleanor Roosevelt resigned from the DAR
because of the Marian Anderson controversy. Noted Miss
Anderson's Metropolitan Opera debut and her 1963 Presidential
Medal of Freedom award.

24
"Anderson, Marian," in A New Dictionary of Music, by Arthur
    Jacobs. Chicago: Aldine Publishing Co., 1961, 416p., pp.
    18.

Biographical sketch of the musical accomplishments of
Miss Anderson.

25
"Anderson, Marian," in Vocal Music, by Philip L. Miller. New
    York: Knopf, 1955, 381p., pp. 26, 50, 129, 250, 294.

    Mentions some of Marian Anderson's recordings.

26
"Anderson, Marian," in Who's Who In Colored America, edited
    by G. James Fleming and Christian E. Burckel. New York:
    Christian E. Burckel & Associates, 1950, 648p., pp. 11.

    Biographical sketch listing her many musical accomplish-
ments.

27
"Anderson, Marian," in Who's Who of American Women, 1977-1978.
    Chicago: Marquis Who's Who, 1978, 970p., pp. 19.

    Biographical sketch noting her many accomplishments in
the music field.

28
"Anderson, Marian," in Who's Who of American Women With World
    Notables, 1970-1971. Chicago: Marquis Co., 1969, 1386p.,
    pp. 27.

    Biographical sketch noting her many accomplishments in
the music field.

29
"Anderson, Marian," in Women In American Music: A Bibliogra-
    phy of Music and Literature, by Adrienne F. Block and Carol
    Neuls-Bates. Westport, Connecticut: Greenwood Press, 1979,
    302p., pp. 3, 12, 13, 14, 36, 37, 76, 104, 105, 115, 121,
    123, 127, 129, 130, 148, 160, 163, 165.

    An annotated bibliography of books and articles about women
in music. Marian Anderson is mentioned in several citations.

30
"Anderson, Marian," in Women In Music: A Biobibliography, by
    Don L. Hixon and Don Hennessee. New Jersey: Scarecrow
    Press, 1975, 347p., pp. 8.

    Brief biography and a list of reference books with informa-
tion of Miss Anderson.

31
"Anderson, Marian," in Worlds Of Music, by Cecil M. Smith.
    Westport, Connecticut: Greenwood Press, 1976, 328p., pp.
    14, 26-27, 29-30, 88, 107, 134, 135, 137.

    Marian Anderson is mentioned several times in connection
with her musical career.

32
"Black Gold." The Wilmington (Del.) Evening Journal. 7 January, 1972, pp. 29.

Biographical sketch on Marian Anderson.

33
Boatwright, Pearl. A Time To Remember. Washington, D. C.:
The Associated Publishers, Inc., n. d., 10p.

A very short biographical sketch on Miss Anderson for juvenile readers.

34
Brent, Richard. "Guiding Lights - Marian Anderson." The New York Amsterdam News. 24 August, 1938.

Short biographical sketch of this famous black contralto.

35
Bronson, Arthur. "Marian Anderson." American Mercury. Vol. 61, September, 1945, pp. 282-288.

Biographical sketch on the successful career of Miss Anderson. Notes that her voice is eminently musical in quality, rich in color, resilient, ample in range and used with skill and sure instinct.

36
Bronson, Arthur. "The Story of A Great Singer - Marian Anderson. The Negro. Vol. 4, September, 1946, pp. 1-5.

Short biographical sketch condensed from The Woman, June, 1946.

37
"Brown Thrush." Headlines. Vol. 1, March, 1945, pp. 45.

The life of Marian Anderson was featured on a national network in the Philadelphia Board of Educations' radio series. The script covered her career, from her early choir days, to when she received the Bok Award.

38
"Carnegie Hall," in Black Magic: A Pictorial History of The Negro In American Entertainment, by Langston Hughes and Milton Meltzer. New Jersey: Prentice-Hall, 1967, 375p., pp. 136-140.

In 1923 Roland Hayes broke the color bar at Carnegie Hall. It was not until 1936, after she had become world renown, did Marian Anderson sing there. She has since appeared there many times and gave her farewell concert there in 1965.

39
Davenport, Marcia. "Music Will Out." <u>Colliers</u>. Vol. 102,
    December 3, 1938, pp. 17, 40.

Biographical sketch of Marian Anderson and her musical
accomplishments.

40
"Depict Life of Marian Anderson." <u>The Afro American</u>. 27
    January, 1945.

<u>Harmony At Home</u>, a story of the life of Marian Anderson,
was broadcast over KYW in Philadelphia. Ruth A. Scott wrote
the script.

41
"Deep River of Song," in <u>13 Against The Odds</u>, by Edwin R.
    Embree. New York; Viking Press, 1944, 261p., pp. 139-152.

Biographical sketch of her early childhood and career, the
D.A.R. controversy, her worldwide concert tours, and special
appearances before famous people and royalty, her Spingarn
Medal. Notes that she is not only one of America's greatest
singers, she is one of America's favorite personalities.

42
Ewen, David. "Marian Anderson," in <u>The Negro In Music and
    Art</u>, by Lindsay Patterson. New York: Publishers Company,
    Inc., 1967, 304p., pp. 155-158.

Biographical sketch noting that Miss Anderson is one of
the greatest artists of our generation., regardless of race,
color or nationality. She brings a wealth of humanity and
culture to every song and her rendition of Negro spirituals
is a deeply personal expression. Other citations relating
to Miss Anderson's career can be found on pages 166-167, 171,
192, 195-196, 198, 239, 240, 154, 159, 162 and 194.

43
"Ex-Choir Singer." <u>Newsweek</u>. Vol. 12, December 19, 1938, pp.
    24-25.

During her childhood of poverty, Marian Anderson sang
with the Union Baptist Choir in Philadelphia. In 1925, she
won a contest and her spectacular career began. She has
traveled throughout the world.

44
"First Lady of Colored America." <u>The Negro</u>. Vol. 1, Winter,
    1943-1944, pp. 9.

Short biographical sketch of the accomplishments of Miss
Anderson.

45
Fisher, Isaac. "Marian Anderson: Ambassador of Beauty From
    Her Race." <u>The Southern Workman</u>, Vol. 65, March, 1936,

pp. 72-80.

Mr. Fisher look at Miss Anderson's early life and personality, her achievements, comparisons with other singers, esti-
mations of critics, her musicianship and interpretations of
her work, and programs she had appeared in.

46
Georgiady, Nicholas Peter. <u>Marian Anderson, American Negro
    Musician</u>. Milwaukee: Franklin Publishers, 1969, 15p.

Juvenile biography of this famous artist.

47
Goines, Leonard. "Marian Anderson." <u>Allegro</u>. November,
    1975, pp.4.

Biographical sketch of this illustrous lady.

48
"The Golden Voice," in <u>Word Pictures of The Great</u>, by Elise
    P. Derricotte, Geneva C. Turner and Jessie Hailstalk Roy.
    Washington, D. C.: Associated Publishers, 1941, 280p.,
    pp. 46-54.

Short biographical sketch on Marian Anderson written for
children. There are questions to be answered on Miss Anderson, books to read for students and teachers and selected
topics on Miss Anderson to write about.

49
Graham, Shirley. "Spirituals To Symphonies." <u>Etude</u>. Vol.
    54, November, 1936, pp. 681-692, 723.

Survey of Negro music in America and cites some of the
outstanding Black musicians, including Marian Anderson.

50
"Humbleness Before Greatness," in <u>Climbing High Mountains</u>,
    by Frank L. Peterson. Washington, D. C.: Review and
    Herald Publishing Company Associated, 1962, 144p., pp.
    86-95.

This biographical sketch notes that Miss Anderson believed
that her voice and the ability to use it in song had been her
gift from God and she wanted to share her gift with all people. Her steady pressure against discrimination was supported
by the faith and prayers of her mother. After her disappoin-
ting Town Hall concert, Miss Anderson was in despair for a
long time. She soon began to study again and decided to
seek humbleness before greatness.

51
Hunting, Harold B. "Marian Anderson, Singer," in <u>Rising Above
    Color</u>, edited by Philip H. Lotz. New York: Fleming H.
    <u>Revell</u> Co., 1943, 112p., pp. 11-17.

Biographical sketch on the life and career of Miss Anderson with questions for discussion, a special project and further reading.

52
"In Egypt Land." Time. Vol. 48, December 30, 1946, pp. 59-60, 62, 64.

The cover cites Miss Anderson as the Big Wheel moved by faith. She considers her voice a gift from God, her singing a religious experience. Notes that musicians still debate over the musical origins of spirituals which she sings with great splendor. Words from some of her spirituals are included.

53
"Internationally Popular." The East Tennessee News. 23 December, 1937.

Pictures the internationally popular Marian Anderson.

54
Kastendieck, Miles. "Marian Anderson Pauses Midway in Career to Note A Milestone." The Brooklyn Eagle. 30 December, 1945.

Reflects on the past ten years of Miss Anderson's career. She had become well known abroad and in the U. S.

55
Keiler, Allan R. "Anderson, Marian," in Encyclopedia Of American Biography, edited by John Garraty and Jerome L. Sternstein. New York: Harper & Row, 1974, 1241p., pp. 32-33.

This biographical sketch notes that Miss Anderson's act was a combination of both natural and acquired abilities. Her voice is endowed with a three-octave range. It is rich in sound and capable of unusual agility and coloristic variety. She has a keen stylistic awareness and great linguistic skill.

56
Kimbrough, Emily. "My Life In A White World." Ladies Home Journal. Vol. 77, September, 1960, pp. 54, 173-174, 176.

Miss Anderson noted that as a child she was not directly aware of the black-white differences. She talked about the discrimination she has suffered even though she is a famous contralto.

57
Kuyper, George A. "Marian Anderson." The Southern Workman. Vol. 61, March, 1932, pp. 125-127.

Miss Anderson felt that the young artist could not fully

develop in this country. In 1925 she competed and won in a
contest in N. Y. with the prize a solo appearance with the
New York Philharmonic Orchestra. She has toured throughout
the U. S., in Europe, the Scandinavian countries and France.

58
Locke, Alain. "Negro Music Goes To Par." Opportunity. Vol.
    17, July, 1939, pp. 196-200.

Dr. Locke talks about Negro folk music and noted that
Marian Anderson's art derived from the purest strain of
Negro folk music - spirituals, and she has carried that
artistic form throughout the world.

59
"Marian Anderson." The Carolina Times. 15 March, 1980, pp.
    9.

This short sketch on Miss Anderson notes that her career
spanned over thirty years. She has performed before kings,
queens, princes and presidents and had a repertoire of 1,500
songs from Negro spirituals to the works of Bach, Brahms,
Handel and Schubert. She sings in nine languages and her
concerts have taken her to every major city in the nation,
to Europe, South America and the Far East.

60
"Marian Anderson." New York Age. 22 March, 1924, pp. 7.

Lists some of the places Miss Anderson has appeared in
New York while under the management of the Donald Musical
Bureau.

61
"Marian Anderson," in The Concise Biographical Dictionary
    of Famous Men and Women, by Harriet Lloyd Fitzhugh, Percy
    K. Fitzhugh and William Morris. New York: Grossett &
    Dunlap, 1950, 830p., pp. 761.

Short biographical sketch noted that Miss Anderson found
her singing a means of helping to support her family. She
fought discrimination and went on to Europe to become famous.
She then returned to the U. S. Highlights several events in
her career.

62
"Marian Anderson," in Doers and Dowagers, by Felicia W.
    Roosevelt. New York: Doubleday, 1975, 225p., pp. 139-
    148.

This biographical sketch notes that Miss Anderson has
made more concert tours throughout the world than any other
musician and has still had time to write her autobiography,
work at the United Nations, and make lecture tours. She and
her husband live in Danbury, Connecticut.

63

"Marian Anderson," in Famous American Women, by Hope Stoddard.
    New York: Crowell, 1970, 461p., pp. 24-35.

Biographical sketch noting Miss Anderson's early singing
career.

64

"Marian Anderson," in Famous Modern Negro Musicians, by Penna
    Lovingood. New York: Press Forum Co., 1921, 68p., pp.
    38-40.

Biographical sketch noting that Miss Anderson sings in
various styles and has a strong dramatic tendency.

65

"Marian Anderson," in Famous Women Singers, by Homer Ulrich.
    New York: Dodd, Mead, 1953, 127p., pp. 97-100.

Biographical sketch noting that she is best in art songs,
especially those of Franz Schubert. She sings in nine languages and has a vast repertoire. Her character, her great
talent, and her reverent attitude are an inspiration to
others.

66

"Marian Anderson," in 50 Great Modern Lives, by Henry Thomas
    and Dana Lee Thomas. New York: Hanover House, 1956, 502p.,
    pp. 479-488.

Biographical sketch detailing her many concert appearances
and especially her experiences during her travels to foreign
countries. Gives some important dates in her career.

67

"Marian Anderson in Fifty Voices Of The Twentieth Century,
    by Emery Kelen. New York: Lothrop, Lee & Shepard, 1970,
    192p., pp. 11-12.

Marian Anderson has the inner guidance of spiritual excellence, intellect and intuition. Notes some of the highlights
of her musical career.

68

"Marian Anderson," in Great Black Americans: by Ben Richardson
    and W. A. Fahey. New York: Crowell, 1976, 344p., pp. 31-39.

Biographical sketch of Miss Anderson's early life and
struggles after the death of her father, her musical career
which included singing throughout the world, her many degrees
and awards and her retirement concert at Carnegie Hall in
1965.

69

"Marian Anderson," in Great Negroes Past and Present, by
    Russell L. Adams. Chicago: Afro-Am Publishing Co., 1963,
    182p. pp. 154.

This short biographical sketch relates that Miss Anderson
was such an exceptional contralto that the famous music
teacher, Giuseppe Borghetti, taught her for one year at no
expense.

70
"Marian Anderson," in Her Way, by Mary-Ellen Kulkin.
    Chicago: American Library Association, 1976, 499p., pp.
    10-11.

    Juvenile biographical sketch on Miss Anderson.

71
"Marian Anderson," in Men and Women Who Make Music, by David
    Ewen. New York: Merlin Press, 1949, 233p., pp. 80-89.

    Notes that Miss Anderson's success represents the triumph
of genius over race prejudice. Both as an artist and as a
human being, she holds a regal position and rare stateliness.
She has upheld the highest standards of integrity and dignity
in her artistic work and in her daily life. A short biographical sketch and accomplishments in her musical career are
highlighted.

72
"Marian Anderson," in The Music of Black Americans: A History,
    by Eileen Southern. New York: W. W. Norton, 1971, 552p.,
    pp. 422-424.

    Notes that Miss Anderson's career includes many notable
events, not all of them pleasant. By 1941, she was one of
the highest paid concert artists in the United States. Miss
Anderson's quiet dignity and tremendous talent brought down
many color barriers. In 1957, she traveled over 39,000 miles
as good-will ambassador through Asia. She had received many
awards and degrees.

73
"Marian Anderson, 1902 - ," in Musicians Since 1900: Perfor-
    mers In Concert and Opera, compiled and edited by David
    Ewen. New York: H. W. Wilson Co., 1978, 974p., pp. 13-18.

    Biographical sketch noting the many highlights and accom-
plishments of Miss Anderson's life and career.

74
"Marian Anderson," in The Negro Almanac: A Reference Work on
    The Afro American, by Harry A. Ploski. New York: Bell-
    wether Co., 1976, 1206p., pp. 850.

    Short biographical sketch on Miss Anderson's musical
career.

75
"Marian Anderson," in The Negro In American Life, by Mabel
    Morsbach. New York: Harcort, Brace & World, 1967, 273p.,

pp. 178-181, 231.

Preparing for a musical career was a problem for Miss Anderson because of lack of money and racial discrimination. While traveling, she had to use Jim Crow railroad cars and often stayed in private homes because few hotels would accommodate Blacks. Notes some of the highlights of her musical career.

76
"Marian Anderson.," in Negroes of Achievement, by James J. Flynn. New York: Dodd, Mead, & Co., 1970, 273p., pp. 249-254.

Biographical sketch on the accomplishments of Miss Anderson. Her singing can be summed up in the words of Arturo Toscanini after hearing her perform: "what I heard today, one is privileged to hear only once in a hundred years."

77
"Marian Anderson," in Our Great Americans: The Negro Contribution To American Progress, edited by Fletcher Martin. Chicago: Gamma Corporation, 1954, 96p., pp. 15-16.

Highlights the career of Miss Anderson, especially overseas. She made her debut in Paris and captured the beauty of the German and French arias, the Russian folk songs and the deep seated yearning in the Negro spirituals during her concerts. She has sung command performances for King Gustav in Stockholm and King Christian in Copenhagen. She sang before four reigning Queens. The Finnish composer, Sibelius, invited her to his home.

78
"Marian Anderson," in Portraits In Color: The Lives of Colorful Negro Women, by Gwendolyn Cherry, Ruby Thomas and Pauline Willis. New York: Pageant Press, 1962, 224p., pp. 63-71, 212-214.

Biographical sketch highlighting the musical career of Miss Anderson. Among her accomplishments was her Lincoln Memorial concert in 1939, and her world-wide tours. She won numerous awards, including the Spingarn Medal, the Bok Award and The Page One Award. She was asked to sing the "Star Spangled Banner" at the Inaguration of President Eisenhower and on this day, Albany, New York proclaimed Marian Anderson Day. A short bibliography is also included.

79
"Marian Anderson," in Profiles of Negro Womanhood, Vol. II 20th Century, by Sylvia G. L. Dannett. New York: Educational Heritage, Inc., 1966, 240p., pp. 158-171.

This biographical sketch noted that Miss Anderson's goals as both esthetic and humane: communications with others "in order to advance those things which are essential" to mankind.

80
"Marian Anderson," in They Had A Dream, Vol. 1, by George
    Reasons and Sam Patrick. California: Los Angeles Times
    Syndicate, 1969, 64p., pp. 10.

Notes that the voice of Marian Anderson has a special
richness, broad range and an emotional depth which could
move one to tears. She has been hailed as "one of the greatest singers of the century." Highlights the many accomplishments during her illustrous career.

81
"Marian Anderson," in Twentieth Century Women of Achievement,
    by Samuel Kostman. New York: Rosen Press, 1976, 178p.,
    pp. 138-154.

This biographical sketch notes that Miss Anderson has won
the hearts of men and women all over the world through her
spiritual beauty, personal dignity, and musical talent. A
picture and short bibliography are included.

82
"Marian Anderson," in Voices of Joy, Voices of Freedom, by
    Arnold Dobrin. New York: McCann, 1972, 120p., pp. 57-75.

Juvenile biographical sketch of the life and vivid career
of Marian Anderson.

83
"Marian Anderson, Celebrated Contralto," in 100 Years After
    Emancipation: History of the Philadelphia Negro, 1787-
    1963, by John A. Saunders. Philadelphia: F. R. S. Pub-
    lishing Co., 1966, 225p., pp. 176-179.

Notes the many outstanding awards received by Miss Anderson.

84
"Marian Anderson, Concert Singer," in In The Big Time: Career
    Stories of American Entertainers, by Katherine L. Bakeless.
    New York: Lippincott, 1953, 211p., pp. 91-109.

Biographical sketch noting that Miss Anderson's quality
of devotion, intensity, self-effacement, breadth and nobility
of style, simplicy of manner and honesty of her thinking have
made her one of the world's most outstanding singers.

85
"Marian Anderson (1908 -   ), Concert Singer," in Negroes of
    Achievement In Modern America, by James J. Flynn. New
    York: Dodd, Mead, 1970, 272p., pp. 249-254.

Aided by one of her teachers, Mary Saunders Patterson,
Marian Anderson developed her full potential in music. Her
school principal, Dr. Lucy Wilson, arranged for her to audition for Giuseppe Boghetti. She had one year of training paid
for by her church and one year free under Boghetti. Notes her

other accomplishments: Lincoln Memorial concert, Spingarn
Medal, Bok Award, UN appointment and her farewell concert.

86
"Marian Anderson, Contralto (1908-   )," in Famous Negro
    Entertainers of Stage, Screen, and TV, by Charlemae
    Rollins. New York: Dodd, Mead, 1967, 122p., pp. 25-31.

It was noted that Miss Anderson made her first 'public'
appearance at age eight when she sang to help her church
raise funds. She was billed as the "Baby Contralto." Miss
Anderson said that the one experience of her school girl
days which stands out was when she sang on the same platform
as Roland Hayes. Several other memorable occasions in her
illustrous career are highlighted.

87
"Marian Anderson: Famous Concert Singer," in Famous American
    Negroes, by Langston Hughes. New York: Dodd, Mead & Co.,
    1954, 147p., pp. 131-135.

Sensing her exceptional musical talent, her church paid
for lessons. She became a great success in Europe. One of
her awards was the Bok Award given to her in Philadelphia in
1941 for outstanding public service.

88
"Marian Anderson: Grace Before Greatness," in American Women
    Who Scored Firsts, by Aylesa Forsee. Philadelphia: Macrae
    Smith Co., 1958, 253p., pp. 9-35.

This juvenile biography noted that the real secret of Miss
Anderson's absence of stage fright lay in her conviction that
God gave her the gift of song and that He would direct and
guide her in the use of it. She felt that spirituals con-
veyed the hope of unity and peace and always included them
in her program. The basic reason for her success has been
her faith in God's care and her conviction that if she ad-
hered to the highest standards, the results would be right.

89
"Marian Anderson: Joyous Singer of Songs," in Famous American
    Negroes, by L. Edmond Leipold. Minneapolis: Denison, 1967,
    75p., pp. 63-68.

Short biographical sketch cites that because Miss Anderson
had to work for success, it has meant more to her.

90
"Marian Anderson: The Magnificent Voice," in Heroines of
    America, by Henry Gilfond. New York: Fleet Press, 1970,
    136p., pp. 114-118.

Short biographical sketch noting the trials and triumphs
of Miss Anderson's career, especially the 1939 refusal of
the D. A. R. to allow her to sing at Constitution Hall.

91
"Marian Anderson, Metropolitan Opera Star: Early 1900's," in
    Famous Negro Music Makers, by Langston Hughes. New York:
    Dodd, Mead, & Co., 1955, 179p., pp. 127-131.

This short biography highlights Miss Anderson's debut at
the Metropolitan Opera House on January 7, 1955. She appeared
in the Un Ballo in Maschera by Verdi. Depicts some outstanding moments in her career and the New York Times reported
"For other Negro singers, it was the opening of a big new
door to opportunity."

92
"Marian Anderson, Popular Singer," in Famous American Musi-
    cians, by L. Edmond Leipold. Minneapolis: Denison, 1972,
    80p., pp. 45-52.

Juvenile biographical sketch noting the many accomplishments of Miss Anderson and her many concerts and tours.

93
"Marian Anderson, Singer (1908-   )," in Lives of Girls Who
    Became Famous, by Sarah K. Bolton. New York: Crowell,
    1949, 343., 00. 29-41.

Juvenile biographical sketch noting that she "not only
possesses a voice of unusual range and volume, of richness
and beauty, but she endows it with deep feeling and with a
soulful interpretation and emotional understanding of the
music she is representing."

94
"Marian Anderson, Voice of Glory," in American Heroes of The
    20th Century, by Harold Faber and Doris Faber. New York:
    Random House, 1967, 179p., pp. 159-165.

Juvenile biography on this outstanding singer.

95
"Marian Anderson: The Voice of The Century (1908-   )," in
    World's Great Men of Color, Vo., II, by J. A. Rogers, New
    York: J. A. Rogers, 1947, 717p., pp. 682-686.

Using a church fund called, "the Marian Anderson future,"
Miss Anderson was able to take singing lessons under Giuseppe
Boghetti. She rapidly developed into a concert artist and
has traveled throughout the country giving concerts. She
has sung in army camps during the war. Miss Anderson has
won wide acclaim from critics and has received many awards
for her talent.

96
"Marian Anderson Humble and Eloquent." The Washington Star.
    18 September, 1958.

Brief biographical sketch of the new delegate to the U.N.

97
"Marian Anderson Rise Reads Life Fairy Story." The Philadel-
    phia Tribune.   29 April, 1937.

    Short biographical sketch of this noted singer.

98
Morrow, Sara Spratt.   "Marian Anderson: Voice of a Century."
    The Message.   Vol. 31, March-April, 1965, pp. 1, 32.

    Biographical sketch of Miss Anderson.

99
"Music and Art," in Negro Builders and Heroes, by Benjamin
    Brawley.   Chapel Hill: University of North Carolina Press,
    1937, 315p., pp. 246.

    Notes that Marian Anderson has been a success with the
Philadelphia Philharmonic Orchestra.   She has had some of her
greatest triumphs in Austria and Sweden.

100
"The Negro Sings," in For Freedom, by Arthur Huff Fauset.
    Philadelphia: Franklin Publishing & Supply Co., 1927,
    200p., pp. 129-135.

    Short paragraph citing Marian Anderson as one of the out-
standing contraltos in America.

101
Newman, Shirlee P. Marian Anderson: Lady From Philadelphia.
    Philadelphia: Westminster Press, 1965, 175p.

    This biography moves from her early singing days where
she received 50¢ a concert, to the worldwide fame she won
with her great voice and then to her farewell concerts.
Discusses the prejudices she faced due to her color: rejection into music school, refusal of service at hotels, the
ban by the D. A. R., etc.

102
"Old Worlds and New: Chicago and The Elevating Influence,"
    in The Grand Tradition: Seventy Years of Singing On
    Record.   London: Duckworth, 1974, 628p., pp. 277-279.

    In noting some recordings by Marian Anderson, her spiri-
tuals are best for capturing the special character of her
concerts.

103
" 'Once In A Hundred Years ...' ," in Impresario: A Memoir
    By S. Hurok, by Solomon Hurok with Ruth Goode.   New York:
    Random House, 1946, 291p., pp. 237-261.

    Mr. Hurok tells of how he first heard Marian Anderson sing
in a small concert hall in Paris and signed her to do several

concerts upon her return to the United States. Gives an
inside view of the many accomplishments of this great singer
plus the many discriminations she suffered because of her
color.

104
"Philadelphia Childhood," in Early Years: The Childhoods of
    Famous People, by Jacqueline Mudie. London: Purnell,
    1968, 77p., pp. 58-59.

This juvenile book tells of Marian Anderson's childhood
days in Philadelphia and how she began singing in the church
choir.

105
Pilcher, J. Mitchell. "The Negro Spiritual." Etude. Vol. 64,
    April, 1946, pp. 194, 226.

Discusses the origins of the Negro spiritual and the four
outstanding Black musicians, one being Marian Anderson, who
contributed to the development of the spiritual.

106
Piquion, Rene. Marian Anderson. Port-au-Prince: Henri
    Deachamps, n.d., 13p

Short biography in French.

107
Programs Of Recitals By Marian Anderson, Contralto. Washing-
    ton: The Library of Congress, n.d.

A collection of various program booklets for Marian Anderson's concerts.

108
Reasons, George and Sam Partick. "Marian Anderson - Once In
    A Lifetime." The Washington Star. 31 May, 1969.

Biographical sketch on Miss Anderson who won fame in Europe
and then in the U. S. She was refused an engagement at Constitution Hall by the D. A. R. She then gave an open-air
concert at Lincoln Memorial. She gave her farewell performance at Carnegie Hall in 1965.

109
Roy, Jessie H. "Pin Point Portrait of Marian Anderson." The
    Negro History Bulletin. Vol. 26, November, 1962, pp. 104.

Notes that Miss Anderson's Christian love and beauty shines
out from inside to give her the wonderful touch of divinity.
List several things to look up and answer concerning Miss
Anderson's life and career.

110
Sedwick, Ruth W. "Over Jordan." Christian Century. February
   21, 1940. pp. 245-247.

Sketch of the accomplishments of Marian Anderson.

111
Selby, John. "Marian Anderson." The Associated Press Biographical Service. Sketch #3005, December 1, 1942.

Biography and picture of this great singer.

112
"Singer and Citizen." Newsweek. Vol. 33, April 25, 1949,
   pp. 84-86.

Short sketch of the many accomplishments of this great
contralto.

113
"Singers: Roland Hayes, Jules Bledsoe, Marian Anderson, and
   Others," in The Negro Genuis, by Benjamin Bradley, New
   York: Dodd, Mead, & Co., 1937, 366p., pp. 313-314.

Marian Anderson was one of the outstanding singers of the
world. The New York Times said of her: "it is a contralto
of stunning range and volume managed with suppliness and
grace."

114
Spivey, Lenore. Singing Heart: A Story Based On The Life Of
   Marian Anderson. Largo, Florida: Community Service Foun-
   dation, 1963, 66p.

A fictional biography for children which tells of the
musical accomplishments of Marian Anderson.

115
Stevenson, Janet. Singing For The World: Marian Anderson.
   Chicago: Encyclopedia Britannica Press, 189p.

An easily read biography depicting the almost empty house
she sang to in her debut at Town Hall, the agony of racial
prejudice and the financial strains in her early career, the
D. A. R. incident, her travels throughout the world and her
farewell concerts.

116
Taubman, Howard. "Voice of A Race." The New York Times Magazine. 6 April, 1941, pp. 9, 21.

Biographical sketch of a poor girl from Philadelphia who
went to music school only through contributions from her
neighbors. She went on to become America's greatest Black
contralto. She has sung throughout the world and has helped
other young artists in their quests.

117
"This Is My America." The Negro. Vol. 4, February, 1946, pp.
    48-50.

Miss Anderson talked about her life and experiences as she
has toured throughout the world. She said the children gave
her the greatest faith in her future.

118
Thompson, Mary Helen. "Black History Week - Marian Anderson."
    The Boston Globe. 10 February, 1974.

Sketch of the brilliant career of Marian Anderson. Since
her retirement in 1965, she and her husband have managed their
estate in Danbury, Connecticut. She did not express any bit-
terness in recalling the many discriminations she faced during
her career because of her race.

119
Tobias, Tobi. Marian Anderson. New York: Crowell, 1972, 40p.

Juvenile biography on the life and accomplishments of this
famous contralto.

120
Truman, Margaret. "Triumph of Marian Anderson." McCalls. Vol.
    103, April, 1976, pp. 114, 116, 120, 124.

Biographical sketch especially noting her open-air concert
at Lincoln Memorial on Easter Sunday, 1939, after the D. A. R.
refused to let her sing at Constitution Hall.

121
Vehanen, Kosti. Marian Anderson: A Portrait. New York:
    McGraw-Hill, 1941, 270p.

Biography with an appendix of important dates in Miss
Anderson's career, reviews of some of her performances, and
two of her programs. Several photos are also included.

122
"The Voice Of A Race," in Women of Courage, by Margaret
    Truman. New York: Morrow & Co., 1976, 254p., pp. 163-179.

Noted how the faith of Marian Anderson's mother helped her
overcome several barriers during her musical career. She
would often discuss her fears with her mother and learned her
mother's way of patient trust in God. They both believed
that one would receive what is right if one was conscientious
in their faith.

123
Walker, Danton. "Stay in The Field." The Daily News. Vol. 26
    May, 1939.

Short biographical sketch of Marian Anderson.

124
Woolf, S. J. "High Priestess of Song." Negro Digest. Vol. 4,
    March, 1946, pp. 83-86.

Notes the success of one of her concerts in the U. S.
while she was still relatively unknown. Racial slurs and
indignations have left no hard feelings. She stressed that
her early hardships contributed to her musical development.

125
"World In Her Hands...Marian Anderson," in Proudly We Hail,
    by Vashti Brown and Jack Brown. New York: Houghton Mifflin,
    1968, 118p., pp. 46-51.

Biographical sketch of Miss Anderson noting how she over-
came prejudice to become the world's greatest contralto.
Known as "Baby Contralto" as a child, Miss Anderson wanted to
take singing lessons but was turned away because of her color.
She had to go to Europe to become famous.

FAMILY

AND PERSONAL LIFE

126
"Aboard Normandie." New York Amsterdam News. 26 November,
   1938.

   Miss Anderson was aboard the S. S. Normandie and was
scheduled to arrive in New York on Thanksgiving. She had
been appearing in Paris.

127
Anderson, Marian. "My Mother's Gift - Grace Before Greatness,"
   in Guideposts: Faith Made Them Champions, edited by Norman
   Vincent Peale. New York: Prentice-Hall, 1954, 270., pp.
   65-68.

   Miss Anderson felt that if she had not had her mother's
hand to guide her, her musical career would have ended long
ago. Her mother's faith was her foundation. One of her
mother's guiding precepts was "Never abuse those who abuse
you. Bear them no malice and theirs will disappear." After
her failure at Town Hall, Miss Anderson did not sing for over
a year, but her mother's constant plea for her to pray about
it finally touched her and she decided to return to music and
to seek "grace before greatness."

128
"Apartment Hunting?" The New York Amsterdam News. 26 August,
   1939, pp. 1.

   Friends said that Marian Anderson and "Razz" Fisher were
apartment hunting despite her denial that they were married.

129
"At Home with Marian Anderson." Ebony. Vol. 9, February, 1954,
   pp. 52-59.

   Shows several photos of the luxurious home Miss Anderson
and her husband (Orpheus Fisher) built in Connecticut.

130
"Brown Nightingale." The New York Amsterdam News. 7 May, 1938.

Shows Marian Anderson aboard the Normandie as she returns from her European tour.

131
"Contralto Marian Anderson Happily Tearful Upon Meeting Her
    Family at Normandie Dock." The New York Amsterdam News.
    1 January, 1938.

Miss Anderson returned to New York after her European tour and was greeted by friends and family.

132
"Contralto's Mother Dies At 89." The New York Times. 11 Jan-
    uary, 1964, pp. 23.

Mrs. Anna D. Anderson, mother of Marian Anderson, died at her home. She had been in poor health for some time.

133
"A Day At Marian Anderson's Country Hideaway." Ebony. Vol. 2,
    April, 1947, pp. 9-14.

Marianna, in Connecticut, is the 105 acre home of Marian Anderson. She calls herself a dirt farmer and tries to spend the summer months there.

134
"Entire Marian Anderson Family Joins N.A.A.C.P." The Iowa
    Bystander. 15 June, 1939.

Miss Anderson's family joined the NAACP in Philadelphia. She had contributed some of her proceeds to the organization also.

135
Epstine, Sadie C. "Home Life of Marian Anderson." The Negro.
    Vol. 6, October, 1948, pp. 1-5.

Describes Miss Anderson's home, "Marianna" and notes that she enjoys a quiet home life.

136
Fleming, G. James. "Yes, Even World's Greatest Contralto Must
    Live Somewhere When Off Stage." The Philadelphia Tribune.
    3 October, 1940.

Marian Anderson chose a home in Danbury Connecticut because of the closeness to her home in Philadelphia and her manager in New York.

137
"Greatest Triumph." The Washington Afro American. 31 December,
    1938.

Pictures the famous contralto, Marian Anderson.

138
Jasper, John. "Marian's Worst Peeve - Washing." The Afro
    American. 6 August, 1946.

Miss Anderson says her greatest moment in life was when
she was able to tell her mother she wouldn't need to take in
washing any more.

139
Johnson, Pauline Carey. "Of Tears and Toil and Laughter."
    The Brown American. Vol. 4, May, 1940, pp. 4-5.

Included in the three biographical sketches is the mother
of Marian Anderson, Mrs. Anna Anderson.

140
"La Anderson Returns For Transcontinental Tour." The Pitts-
    burgh Courier. 7 January, 1939, pp. 12.

Pictures Miss Anderson arriving home Thanksgiving day and
after her Carnegie Hall recital. She was to sing in Pittsburgh on January 22nd.

141
"Marian Anderson," in Opera Stars In The Sun, by Mary Jane
    Matz. New York: Farrar, Straus & Cudahy, 1955, 349p.,
    pp. 53.

Describes the home of Marian Anderson in Danbury, Connecticut.

142
"Marian Anderson, Famous Contralto, Earns $250,000 A Year;
    Average Audience Is 4,000 - Has Traveled Over 1,000 Miles."
    The Pittsburgh Courier. 7 January, 1939, pp. 12.

Highlights of the musical career of Ms. Anderson. During
her recent South American tour, she filled the Buenos Aires
auditorium for twelve consecutive recitals. She was booked
solid until 1940.

143
"Marian Anderson At Home." Tuesday Magazine. September, 1965,
    pp. 20-21.

Shows several pictures of Marian Anderson at her farm in
Danbury, Connecticut.

144
"Marian Anderson Attends Rites for Brother-In-Law, J. De-
    Priest." The Philadelphia Tribune. 17 October, 1942.

Miss Anderson arrived from Connecticut to attend the
funeral of her brother-in-law, James DePriest.

145
"Marian Anderson Entertains AKA's." The Afro American.   11
    June, 1938.

Miss Anderson entertained members of the AKA sorority, of
which she is an honorary member, at her home.

146
"Marian Anderson Hostess At Newspaper Folks' Luncheon." The
    New York Amsterdam News. 24 June, 1939. pp. 20.

Miss Anderson was luncheon hostess to the Metropolitan
Press.   The event was in appreciation of courtesies extended
to the artist over the past years.   Miss Anderson had just
ended her musical season and was to record for RCA Victor.

147
"Marian Anderson Ill." The New York Times. 12 November, 1945,
    pp. 16.

Miss Anderson had to postpone her recital at Carnegie Hall
because of illness.

148
"Marian Anderson In Hospital." The New York Times. 7 July,
    1948, pp. 31.

Miss Anderson was reported "doing nicely" at Jewish Hospital in Brooklyn after undergoing major surgery.

149
"Marian Anderson Is Wed." The New York Times. 19 November,
    1943, pp. 24.

Miss Anderson was married on July 17th to Orpheus H.
Fisher, a New York architect.   The ceremony took place in
Bethel, Connecticut at the Bethel Methodist Church by Rev.
Jack Grenfell.

150
"Marian Anderson May Buy New Home in South Jersey." The New
    York Herald. 17 June, 1939.

Miss Anderson was reportedly in the process of buying the
Sebbins and Collins estate as a home for her mother.

151
"Marian Anderson Robbed." The New York Times. 17 November,
    1945, pp. 19.

Miss Anderson's car was broken into on Thursday.   Articles
valued at $9,500 were stolen.

152
"Marian Anderson Spikes Rumors About Marriage." The Black
    Dispatch. 10 October, 1942.

Miss Anderson denied persistent rumors that she was to
marry soon.

153
"Marian Anderson Sued." The New York Times. 28 December, 1945,
    pp. 12.

Miss Anderson was sued after three of her dogs bit a woman
and her nephew as they walked past her estate. They were asking for $15,000 each.

154
"Marian Anderson Tells of Throat Surgery in 1948 to Save
    Voice." The Washington Star. 13 January, 1949.

Miss Anderson tells of an operation to remove a cyst from
her esophagus. The operation was so intricate that it had to
be performed through her back.

155
"Marian Anderson Weds New York Architect." The Chicago Defen-
    der. 27 November, 1943.

Miss Anderson married Orpheus H. Fisher, a New York architect on July 17th.

156
"Marian Comes Back Home For Thanksgiving." The Pittsburgh
    Courier. 3 December, 1938, pp. 20.

Miss Anderson returned from Europe on Thanksgiving. She
was scheduled to appear at Carnegie Hall on December 6.

157
"Nation's No. 1 Singer and Family Group." The Norfolk Jour-
    nal & Guide. 24 December, 1938.

Picture of Miss Anderson with her family after her concert at Carnegie Hall.

158
Neal, Steve. "Marian Anderson Today: Very Secluded, Very
    Private." The Philadelphia Inquirer. 23 February, 1975,
    pp. E1, E10.

Miss Anderson said her life today is very secluded and
private. She keeps a low profile and did not plan a come-
back.

159
Neal, Steve. "Marian Cherished Her Privacy." Biography News.
    Vol. 2, March, 1975, pp. 233.

Article from the Philadelphia Inquirer for February 23,
1975. It noted that Marian Anderson likes to keep a low profile. She lives a very private life with her husband on
their farm in Connecticut.

160
"Operation on Marian Anderson Saved Singer's Voice Last June."
    The New York Herald Tribune. 13 January, 1949.

Miss Anderson was hospitalized twelve days to have a cyst
removed from her esophagus. She had since returned to the
concert circuit.

161
"Preparing For The Season." The New York Times. 16 September
    1945, Sec. 2, pp. 4.

Shows several concert and opera stars during their off
season. Marian Anderson was pictured catching up with her
heavy recording schedule.

162
The Real Marian Anderson." Our World. Vol. 4, April, 1949,
    pp. 11-15.

Looks at Miss Anderson·at home. She lives in faded dunga-
rees and sweaters, enjoys cooking and plays hot jazz on the
piano. While on tour, she would do things for herself, not
relying on others to do for her. She loves animals, gardening
and sewing.

163
Reif, Rita. "Marian Anderson at 70, Reflecting: On A Life's
    Work." The New York Times. 28 February, 1972.

Miss Anderson observed her 70th birthday at her home in
Connecticut and reflected on her outstanding career.

164
"Report Hints Noted Singer To Wed Soon." The Chicago Defender.
    10 June, 1939.

It was rumored that Marian Anderson was planning to marry
Razel Fisher, a New York architect.

165
"Reports Say Marian Anderson Will Marry." The Afro American.
    5 October, 1940.

Reporters were trying to confirm rumors that Miss Anderson was to marry Razel Fisher, a New York architect.

166
Ryan, Bill. "Serene Marian Anderson Lives On Danbury Farm."
    The Hartford Times. 5 May, 1964.

Miss Anderson talks about her home life.

167
"Singer Settles Action." The New York Times. 26 April, 1946,
    pp. 29.

Marian Anderson paid $3,000 to a pair bitten by her dogs.
The lady and her nephew were bitten as they walked past the
Anderson estate.

168
"Singer's Earnings." The Norfolk Journal and Guide. 15 April,
   1939, pp. 2.

It was noted that Marian Anderson's net income for 1937
was $30,000. It was estimated that her gross income was
close to $150,000.

169
Wald, Richard C. "How To Live With A Famous Wife." Ebony.
   Vol. 13, August, 1958, pp. 52-54, 56.

Orpheus H. Fisher tells how he met and married Marian
Anderson. He felt that they had a good marriage because
they always consult each other. He usually traveled with
her on her concert tours.

170
"We and Marian Anderson." The New Zealand Listener. Vol. 47,
   July 13, 1962, pp. 3.

Miss Anderson talks about her life and career.

171
"What's That! Miss Anderson Plans Marriage." The New York
   Amsterdam News. 22 April, 1939, pp. 1, 12.

It was rumored that Marian Anderson was to be married in
April. She would not confirm nor deny the rumor when
questioned by reporters.

172
Woolf, S. J. "Marian Anderson's Recipe for Success." The
   New York Times Magazine. 30 December, 1945.

Miss Anderson noted that it was only through hard work
and effort that one succeeds and that when one's hard work
gains recognition, one must be deeply grateful.

INTERVIEWS

AND RECOLLECTIONS

173
Anderson, Marian. "Grace Before Greatness." Guideposts.
    April, 1976, pp. 7-9.

Excerpts from the March, 1954 article by Marian Anderson
which revealed what lies at the heart of success.

174
Anderson, Marian. "Hall Johnson, 1888-1970." The New York
    Times. 24 May, 1970, Sec. 2, pp. 17.

Obituary on Hall Johnson. Miss Anderson noted that he had
guided her to a true interpretation of folk music. Hall
Johnson taught love and brotherhood.

175
Anderson, Marian and Rose Heylbut. "Some Reflections On
    Singing." Etude. Vol. 57, October, 1939, pp. 631-632, 682.

Miss Anderson tells how she got started in music and the
value of having music teachers. She discusses vocal production, chest tones and building a repertoire.

176
Bollman, Bob. "Her Life Has Been Elevating." The Danbury
    (Ct.) News-Times. 30 June, 1974.

Marian Anderson talks about her career and life after
retirement.

177
Burroughs, Betty. "Regal, Youthful Marian Enjoys Sweet
    Success." The Wilmington (Del.) Morning News. 12 May, 1972,
    pp. 51.

Marian Anderson recalled her past achievements and remark-
ed, "I only wish I could be half the woman my mother was."

178
Cornell, George W. "Famous Influential, Powerful Share
    Common Conviction--Faith In God." The Los Angeles
    Herald Examiner. 3 January, 1970, pp. A7.

Roland Gammon interviewed several prominent people on their
personal beliefs and convictions. Marian Anderson said, "the
longer one lives on earth, the better one realizes that there
is no particular endeavor or thing that you can do alone..."

179
Heglund, Gerald. "Visits With a Star And A Satellite."
    The Jamestown (N. Y.) Post Journal. 17 July, 1965, pp. 11M.

Interview of Marian Anderson and her accompanist, Franz
Rupp. They both recalled some outstanding periods during
their career together.

180
Hertelendy, Paul. "Marian Anderson Says She's Lucky." The
    Oakland Tribune. 24 March, 1970, pp. 42.

Marian Anderson said she had no regrets about her musical
career and the obstructions because of her race. She noted
that she felt for other artists who were deprived of oppor-
tunities.

181
Hill, Roy. "Fannie Douglass. Reminiscences of Yesteryear."
    The Black Perspective In Music. Spring, 1974, pp. 54-62.

Fannie Douglass discusses her association with several
musicians, including Marian Anderson.

182
Iglauer, Edith. "We Drop In On Marian Anderson - And Behind
    The Artist Find A Woman." The Christian Science Monitor.
    26 August, 1941, woman's page.

Miss Anderson was interviewed at her home. She described
her home life, her concert tours and how she has helped
others.

183
Klaw, Barbara. " 'A Voice One Hears Once In A Hundred
    Years': An Interview With Marian Anderson." American
    Heritage. Vol. 28, February, 1977, pp. 50-57.

Marian Anderson is questioned about her childhood, how she
became a singer, her disappointments and triumphs, discriminations because of her color, what spirituals mean to her,
relationships with Sol Hurok, the DAR controversy, her Lincoln Memorial concert and Metropolitan Opera debut and her
75th birthday celebration.

184
"Miss Anderson Sees Improved Race Relations." The New York
    Herald Tribune. 31 December, 1944.

Looking back over the past ten years, Marian Anderson felt
that there had been considerable improvements in black-white
relations and believed she promoted tolerance by her concerts
in the south.

185
Neal, Steve. "A Legend Remembers The Days Of Bigotry." The
    Detroit Free Press. 11 March, 1975.

Marian Anderson was interviewed at her home and spoke of
the many discriminations she faced during her career and her
life after retirement.

186
" 'A Nice Place, Full of Nice People'." The Kalamazoo (Mich.)
    Gazette. 14 October, 1975, pp. A3.

It was remembered that on a visit to the city in 1938,
Marian Anderson had to ride the freight elevator to her
hotel room. She was in the city to visit with students at
Northglade Elementary School.

187
"1900-1936: Cloud By Day and Fire By Night," in The Negro
    Vanguard, by Richard Bardolph. New York: Rinehart & Com-
    pany, 1959, 388p., pp. 159-163.

This section noted how Marian Anderson first experienced
discrimination on a trip to the south. She went on to become one of America's most beloved singers. During her
tours, her manager took great pain to insulate her from
humiliation and she always took her meals in her room. Her
decision not to sing to segregated audiences curtailed many
of her engagements, especially in the south.

188
"Noted Singer Barred From Exclusive Club." The Chicago
    Defender." 6 May, 1944.

The Granite Club in Toronto refused to admit Miss Anderson
and her friends. This led to a storm of protests.

189
"Snubbed In Toronto: Honored By Smith." Headlines. Vol. 1,
    July, 1944, pp. 16.

Marian Anderson was snubbed at the exclusive Granite Club
in Toronto. Later she was awarded an honorary Doctor of
Music degree at Smith College.

190
"Stronger Than Death." The Saturday Review. Vol. 39, March
    24, 1956, pp. 29.

In a letter to the editor, Marian Anderson said that to
her music is the "beauty of men reaching out to comfort each
other as they struggle against a common fate." She praises
the program of The American Cancer Society and said that by
contributing to the Society all colors, races and creeds take
part in "the great symphony of helping each other."

191
"U. S. Bias Fading: Marian Anderson." The Chicago Defender.
   23 February, 1946.

In an interview in Canada, Miss Anderson felt that racial
tolerance was spreading in America and also felt that the
brotherhood engendered during World War II helped.

192
"A Voice of Velvet." African Woman. #13, January/February,
   1978. pp. 26-27.

In this interview with Barbara Klaw, Miss Anderson talks
about her experiences. She tells how she first became a
singer, the first triumph of her career, the discrimination
she suffered, especially in the south, her success in Europe,
how she approached her audiences, and the Lincoln Memorial
experience. Miss Anderson retired in 1965 and there was a
gala 75th birthday concert for her in Carnegie Hall in 1977.

193
White, Leonard. "My Father and I." The New York Times Magazine. 16 June, 1946, Sec. 6, pp. 31.

Several prominent Americans were asked to share their recol-
lections about their fathers. Marian Anderson noted that
although her father died when she was very young, she remembered his singing voice and how he always had her mother to
fix his tie.

2
CAREER
ACTIVITIES

EARLY
CAREER
APPEARANCES

National Music League Competition

194
"Marian Anderson Wins Music Contest." The New York Amsterdam
News. 8 July, 1925, pp. 9.

Miss Anderson was the only singer chosen out of 300 voca-
lists at the National Music League competition held July 1.
She was also the only Black to win. She was to appear in
several concerts sponsored by the League.

195
Perkins, F. D. "Bernard Ocks, Violinist, Achieves Success
At Stadium." The New York Herald. 26 August, 1925.

Marian Anderson was to be soloist with the Philharmonic
Orchestra at Lewisohn Stadium. Willem Van Hoogstraten was
to conduct the orchestra and William King was to accompany
Miss Anderson. She was to sing "O, Mio Fernando" and some
Negro spirituals.

196
Perkins, F. D. "Dorys Le Vene, 19, Is First Audition Soloists at Stadium." The New York Herald. 25 August, 1925.

It was noted that Marian Anderson was to appear August
26th at the Lewisohn Stadium to sing with the Philharmonic
Orchestra. She had been a winner in the auditions held
last June.

197
Perkins, F. D. "Negro Contralto Shows Remarkable Voice At
Stadium." The New York Tribune. 27 August, 1925.

About 7,500 people heard Marian Anderson sing at Lewisohn
Auditorium. She was the only singer chosen out of three
hundred when auditions were held by the National Music
League.

198
"Social Progress." <u>Opportunity</u>. Vol. 3, October, 1925, pp 317.

On August 26th, Marian Anderson appeared with the Philharmonic Orchestra in Lewisohn Auditorium. She had been
chosen over three hundred candidates by the Stadium Concert
Auditions Committee and the National Music League to appear
with the orchestra.

199
"Stadium Audition Winners Who Appear As Soloists This Week."
<u>The New York Hearld</u>. 23 August, 1925.

Pictures Marian Anderson who was one of the soloists
scheduled to appear at Lewisohn Stadium.

Salzburg Festival

200
"Festival," in <u>Between The Thunder and The Sun</u>, by Vincent
Sheean. New York: Random House, 1943, 428., pp. 25-26.

Tells of Marian Anderson's appearance at the Hotel de
l'Europe during the Salzburg festival. She did two recitals
in Salzburg: one private and one public. She sang Bach,
Schubert, Schumann, and a group of Negro spirituals. She
had done something outside of the limits of classical or
romantic music: she had frightened the audience with the
conception of a mighty suffering.

201
"Geneva Applauds Singer." <u>New York Times</u>. 4 December, 1935,
pp. 26.

Miss Anderson's concert filled the city's largest hall.
The <u>Journal de Geneva</u> said, "what can we say of this voice,
whose range stupefies, passing from the gravest to the
sharpest with disconcerting ease?"

202
"Negro Singer Says Nazis Bar Concerts In Australia." <u>New
York Times</u>. 9 July, 1935, pp. 24.

Because of her color, Marian Anderson was banned from
giving the Salzburg recital in Vienna on August 18th. The
president of the Salzburg festival committee said she was
not banned, her concert could not be fitted into the festival which had been planned months in advance.

203
Peyser, Herbert F. "Idiom of Times Sq. Rules In Salzburg."
<u>The New York Times</u>. 3 August, 1935, pp. 16.

It was noted that the ban on Marian Anderson's recital was
being reconsidered. She was to give a concert on August 28
although the event was not officially sponsored by the festival management.

204
Peyser, Herbert F. "Marian Anderson Thrills Salzburg." New
    York Times. 29 August, 1935, pp. 16.

Miss Anderson gave a well constructed program at the Salzburg festival. A private recital for leading artists,
government officials, church dignitaries and the diplomatic
corps was scheduled for later in the week.

205
Peyser, Herbert F. "Vienna Gala Weeks." New York Times. 19
    July, 1936, Section 10, pp. 5.

Tells of the festival in Vienna held during the summer.
Miss Anderson was chosen to do a solo with Burno Walter.
She learned the piece in a short time and performed without
notes.

Town Hall Debut

206
"Of Men and Music." Ebony. Vol. 6, May, 1951, pp. 49-50, 52.

20th Century-Fox released the first feature-length film
about Marian Anderson with her in the starring role. The
film begins with her historic 1935 Town Hall debut in New
York and portrays the struggle amid humble beginnings and
hard study to become a superb talent. Sixteen minutes of
the film consists of singing by the famed concert singer.

207
"Marian Anderson." New York Times. 29 December, 1935, pp. 7.

Shows a picture of Miss Anderson who was to appear at Town
Hall after a four year absence.

208
"Marian Anderson In Concert Here." New York Times. 31 Dec-
    ember, 1935, pp. 13.

Miss Anderson made her American debut at Town Hall after
a four year absence. She had been performing in Europe.
She sang with a consciousness of her ability and with a
relish of her task.

209
"Tribute To A Great American - Marian Anderson." The Negro
    Traveler. Vol. 6, June, 1950, pp. 10-12, 28.

Notes Miss Anderson first concert at Town Hall in 1935
and how she went on to become one of America's most famous
singers. Shows pictures of her home in Connecticut.

D.A.R. AND
SCHOOL BOARD
CONTROVERSY

210
"Among The Few Brave." The New York Amsterdam News. 4
March, 1939, pp. 6.

By resigning from the DAR Mrs. Roosevelt did three things:
1. she focused world wide attention on United States prejudice against Blacks, 2. she elevated the position of women,
and 3. she struck a timely blow for democracy.

211
Anderson, Marian. "Easter Sunday," in The Black Man And The
Promise of America, edited by Lettie J. Austin, Lewis H.
Fenderson and Sophia P. Nelson. Glenview, Illinois: Scott,
Foresman & Co., 1970, 523p., pp. 203-208.

An excerpt from Miss Anderson's autobiography, My Lord,
What A Morning, in which she gives an account of how she
accidently found out that the DAR would not let her perform
at Constitution Hall. She tells of how embarassing the
situation was for her. She describes the overwhelming im-
pact of seeing the multitude of people who came to hear her
at the open air concert at Lincoln Memorial and notes her
appreciation of those who stood behind her.

212
Anderson, Peggy. "I'm A Yankee Doodle Dandy." The New York
Times. 14 April, 1974, Sec. 4, pp. 15.

Recalls the 1939 ban on Marian Anderson's use of Constitution Hall by the DAR. The DAR has never maintained that they
made the wrong decision in banning the concert of the Black
artist.

213
"Anderson Affair Seen as Clever Advertising." The Washington
Daily News. 8 April, 1939.

A letter was written to the newspaper noting that Miss

Anderson's name became well-known throughout the U. S. because of the controversy over her appearance at Constitution Hall which was banned by the D. A. R.

214
"Anderson Ban Called Fascistic Viewpoint." Washington News. 1 March, 1939.

In a letter to the D. A. R., Rep. Gavagan (D-N. Y.) said their decision not to let Marian Anderson sing at Constitution Hall was "Consonant with Nazi and fascist philosophy."

215
"Anderson Ban Flayed; House Inquiry Asked." The Times-Herald. 29 March, 1939.

Rep. James McGranery (D-Pa.) called the actions by the School Board to ban Miss Anderson's concert at Central High School as not democratic. He asked that the board produce all records on the use of public school auditoriums for the past five years.

216
"Anderson Ban Is Lifted." The Washington Times. 4 March, 1939.

By a vote of 6-2 the School Board agreed to lift the ban on Miss Anderson singing at Cental High School. The board ruled the case an emergency. Also notes the refusal of the D. A. R. to allow her to sing at Constitution Hall.

217
"Anderson Ban May Result In Congressional Probe." The Norfolk Journal and Guide. 1 April, 1939, pp. 1, 10.

Declaring that Marian Anderson is a citizen of his congressional district, Rep. James J. McGranery said he would introduce a resolution for a congressional probe of the D. C. School Board's ban on Miss Anderson's use of Central High School for a concert.

218
"Anderson Ban Protested." The New York Times. 23 February, 1939, pp. 18.

William Osborn, president of the American Union for Democracy and several others protested against the DAR ban on allowing Marian Anderson to sing at Constitution Hall. The protest was a telegram sent to the DAR charging that the ban "makes a mockery of the ideals" for which Washington and Lincoln struggled.

219
"Anderson Ban To Be Reconsidered." The Washington Post. 2 March, 1939.

The School Board voted to refer the Marian Anderson ban issue to the Committee on the Community Use of Buildings.

It had received requests to reopen the case.

220
"Anderson Ban Up To School Board Today." Washington Times.
3 March, 1939.

A petition with over 3,000 names was to be presented to
the School Board on behalf of Marian Anderson. The board
had refused to allow her to sing at Central High School after
she was turned away from Constitution Hall.

221
"Anderson Case At A Glance." The Washington Afro American.
4 March, 1939, pp. 1, 2.

Gives brief details of the Marian Anderson/DAR/School
Board controversy.

222
"Anderson Case Held Challenge to Democracy." The Washington
Post. 27 March, 1939.

In a letter sent to the Marian Anderson Citizens Committee,
a group of government officials called the school board
decision on the Marian Anderson concert ban a challenge to
democracy.

223
"Anderson Concert Ban Assailed by U.F.W.A." The Washington
Daily News. 18 March, 1939.

The D. C. Council of United Federal Workers of America
condemned the action of the school board in banning Marian
Anderson's concert at Central High School.

224
"The Anderson Episode." The Washington Post. 21 February,
1939.

Editorial stated that the banning of Marian Anderson from
both Constitution Hall and Cental High School was not a
slight toward the famous black singer, but showed the need
for a municipal auditorium in the area.

225
"Anderson Ghost Stalks At Meeting." The Norfolk Journal and
Guide. 29 April, 1939, pp. 20.

At the annual meeting of the DAR in Washington, D. C.,
their president presented the DAR's side of the refusal to
allow Marian Anderson use of Constitution Hall for a recital.
She placed the blame on precedential conditions circumscribed
by local customs.

226
"Anderson Protest Set in Colored Church." The Washington
Post. 25 February, 1939.

Plans were cancelled to have a protest meeting on the
Marian Anderson ban at Mt. Pleasant Congregational Church.
Instead the meeting was to be held at a black church, The
Lincoln Congregational Church.

227
"Anderson Protests Overlooked Real Evil." The Washington
    Post. 10 March, 1939.

A letter to the paper notes that the real evil of the
Marian Anderson case was overlooked. The segregated, dual
school system was the real reason for the ban on Miss Anderson.

228
"Anderson Question Up In DAR Meet." The New York Amsterdam
    News. 22 April, 1939, pp. 12.

The Marian Anderson Citizen's Committee sent a letter to
the DAR requesting that no organization be barred from
sponsoring concerts at Constitution Hall and also asked for
available dates for the next season. A second letter was
sent asking the DAR to receive a delegation to discuss principal points of the first letter.

229
"Anderson Supporters Unsatisfied by Plan for Open-Air Con-
    cert." The Washington Star. 1 April, 1939.

Although Miss Anderson was to sing at the Lincoln Memorial,
members of the Marian Anderson Citizens Committee still felt
that the main issues of use of public halls by blacks had
not been resolved.

230
"Ask D.A.R. Lead In Moral Revival." The New York Times. 17
    April, 1940, pp. 13.

The honorary president of the DAR called for a moral
revival during their 49th congress. It was remembered that
the DAR had refused to allow Marian Anderson to use Constitution Hall for a concert in 1939.

231
"Asks D.A.R. Open Hall To Negroes." The New York Times. 17
    April, 1939, pp. 19.

As the DAR held their annual convention in Washington, D.
C., the Marian Anderson Committee asked them to open Constitution Hall to Black artists in the future. The committee
sent a letter asking them to recieve a delegation to discuss
the matter.

232
"Asks D.A.R. To Reconsider." The New York Times. 20 April,
    1939, pp. 21

Sol Hurok, manager of Marian Anderson, had asked the DAR
to reconsider their former decision and to appoint any
evening from November 15-27, 1939 for a recital by Marian
Anderson at Constitution Hall.

233
"Ballet Group Refused School Because of Profit Factor." The
Washington Daily News. 6 April, 1939.

In commenting on the school board's refusal to let the
National Ballet Perform at Roosevelt High School, Attorney
Charles Houston, of the Marian Anderson Citizens Committee,
noted that the school board is not open-minded about use of
school buildings after school hours.

234
"Ban Maintained At Constitution Hall By DAR." The Washington
Afro American. 21 January, 1939, pp. 12.

The DAR said there was a clause in their contracts that
prohibits renting Constitution Hall to Blacks.

235
"Ban on Anderson Attacked by 6000." The Washington Daily
News. 28 February, 1939.

Between five and six thousand signatures went on a petition
protesting the barring of Miss Anderson from singing at
Constitution Hall and Central High School.

236
"Ban on Singer 'Pagan', Clergymen Declare." The New York
Times. 5 March, 1939.

The pastors of the St. George's Episcopal Church stated
that the actions of the DAR in refusing to let Marian
Anderson sing at Constitution Hall was 'quite pagan' and
betrayed democracy.

237
"Ban on Singer Rescinded by School Board." The Washington
Times. 4 March, 1939.

In a situation which was called 'an emergency,' Marian
Anderson was granted permission to use Central High School
for a concert.

238
"Bans Can't Still Marian's Song." The Washington Afro American. 25 February, 1939, pp. 1, 2.

It was announced that Miss Anderson would sing at a local
church after the D. C. School Board and the DAR refused to
let her use their facilities for a concert. Several opera
stars voiced their protests that the world's leading singer
would be banned from the nation's capitol.

239
Berlack-Boozer, Thelma. "Bids For D. C. Concert Given." The
New York Amsterdam News. 8 April, 1939, pp. 1, 4.

Although it was reported earlier that Mrs. Roosevelt had
invited Bill Robinson to sit in her box at the Marian Anderson Lincoln Memorial concert, it was later learned that the
report was false. He was asked, however, to be a sponsor
for the concert. A list of sponsors is included.

240
Berlack-Boozer, Thelma. "Capitol Hill Drama." The New York
Amsterdam News. 4 March, 1939, pp. 1, 7.

Mrs. Roosevelt tendered her resignation from the DAR after
they refused to allow Marian Anderson the use of Constitution Hall for a concert. She became one of the first to
disapprove of the treatment of Miss Anderson.

241
Berlack-Boozer, Thelma. "D.A.R. Fuss Continues In Hotter
Vein." The New York Amsterdam News. 11 March, 1939, pp.
1, 7.

The DAR issued a statement saying that rules covering
leasing of Constitution Hall prohibited the hall from
being rented by a Black group. This was generally the
custom in the city. A protest broadcast over station WEVD
entitled "Marian Anderson, the D.A.R. and Democracy" was
to be hosted by opera singer Lawrence Tibbett on March 10.

242
"Board of Education Is Denounced By Pickets." The Pittsburgh
Courier. 25 February, 1939, pp. 1, 4.

The Marian Anderson Citizen's Committee met to develop
plans for picketing the D. C. School Board and for carrying
out a door-to-door canvass for picketers for signatures to
a protest petition.

243
"Board Rescinds Ban on Concert At Central." The Washington
Star. 4 March, 1939.

The D.C. Board of Education would let Miss Anderson sing
at Central High School but made it understood that the
sponsors (Howard University) would never make a similar
request. The board considered it "an emergency" request
since no other suitable hall was available.

244
"Board to Seek $22,890 for Personnel for New Classrooms."
The Washington Star. 16 March, 1939.

The status of the Marian Anderson case was brought up at
the school board meeting but was up to the administrative
officials for resolution.

245
Broun, Heywood. "It Seems to Me." The Washington News. 1
    March, 1939.

Mr. Broun felt that the DAR ban on Marian Anderson was
monstrous and suggested that Miss Anderson go on radio and
sing so the entire nation could hear her.

246
"Capital School Renews Ban on Marian Anderson." The New York
    Herald Tribune. 19 March, 1939.

When Howard University refused to accept a statement by
the D. C. School Board in not setting a precedent in the
use of a high school auditorium, they withdrew their decision
to allow Miss Anderson to sing there.

247
Carter, Elmer A. "The Ladies of the D.A.R." Opportunity.
    Vol. 17, March, 1939, pp. 67.

This editorial talks about the discourtesy of the D.A.R.
in not allowing Marian Anderson to sing at Constitution Hall.
Mr. Carter offered his sympathy and pity to the D.A.R. for
their exhibition of rudeness.

248
Carter, J. C. "The Anderson Case - Four Negative Reasons."
    The Norfolk Journal and Guide. 29 April, 1939, pp. 8.

Gives the four reasons used by the DAR in their refusal
to allow Marian Anderson use of Constitution Hall. This
editorial noted that the real issue is "what has color to
do with artistic gifts, natural or acquired?"

249
"Censoring A Golden Voice." The Richmond Times Dispatch. 1
    March, 1939.

Notes how the DAR censored Marian Anderson, a great contralto, by not allowing her to perform at Constitution Hall.

250
"Central High Parents Uphold Anderson Ban." The Washington
    News. 3 March, 1939.

The Central High School PTA supported the D. C. School
Board in its ban to have Marian Anderson sing there.

251
"Central's Auditorium Accepted for Concert by Marian Ander-
    son." The Washington Star. 12 March, 1939.

Howard University Concert Series Committee accepted the
decision to have Miss Anderson sing at Central High School
but declined to pledge that it would not make more such requests as the school board had stipulated in granting the

request.

252
Clapper, Raymond. "Prejudice Slapped Down." The Washington
    Daily News. 6 April, 1939.

Because Miss Anderson was refused a concert date where
foreign artists have performed, she would have to be heard
in an open-air concert by many who would otherwise never
have the opportunity to hear her. The DAR and the D. C.
School Board had refused to let her sing in their facilities.

253
"Close To 100,000 At Lincoln Memorial Awed In Contralto."
    The New York Amsterdam News. 15 April, 1939, pp. 17.

People from every walk of American life were present to
hear Marian Anderson's Lincoln Memorial concert. The bad
weather gave way to a sunny afternoon and the crowd almost
mobbed Miss Anderson after the concert.

254
Coleman, George M. "The Struggles of Marian Anderson." The
    Atlanta Daily World. 17 February, 1978, pp. 1, 6.

Notes the 1939 DAR incident in which Marian Anderson was
banned from using Constitution Hall.

255
"Colored College Women Assail Anderson Ban." The Washington
    Star. 9 April, 1939.

Delegates of twenty-one states attending the conference
of the National Association of Negro College Women adopted
a resolution that all tax-supported parks and buildings be
open to all citizens, regardless of race or religion.

256
"Compromise in Ban on Marian Anderson Scored." The Crisis.
    Vol. 46, April, 1939, pp. 117.

The NAACP condemned the plan of Central High School to
have Marian Anderson sing there on April 9 because they
could not accept, with honor, the conditions under which
it was stated that she could use the building.

257
"Congress May Probe 'In And Out' Policy of D. C. Schools In
    Marian Anderson Ban." The Pittsburgh Courier. 25 March,
    1939, pp. 1, 4.

A Congressional investigation may be needed to decide
whether Marian Anderson could use Central High School for
a concert. The issue in the case was community use of a
public building during a holiday season.

258
"Congress Probe Asked in Ban on Singer." The Washington Star.
27 March, 1939.

A resolution was passed by the Marian Anderson Citizen's
Committee demanding an investigation of the use of D. C.
public schools for community activities.

259
"Congress To Probe Ban on Noted Singer." The Pittsburgh
    Courier. 1 April, 1939, pp. 1, 4.

It was announced at a meeting of the Marian Anderson
Citizen's Committee that Rep. James P. McGranery was to ask
for an investigation of the D. C. School Board after they
refused to allow Marian Anderson to sing at the white Central
High School.

260
"Congressman Scores School Board, DAR." The Norfolk Journal
    and Guide. 15 April, 1939, pp. 9.

Delivering a scratching verbal statement against the DAR,
Rep. James P. McGranery of Pennsylvania said the DAR had
strayed so far afield from the ideals of its revolutionary
ancestry as to "preclude itself from further consideration
as a patriotic American society." He also stated that he
had made a resolution for an investigation of the D. C.
School Board.

261
"Convention of DAR May Be Picketed." The Hartford (Conn.)
    Courant. 17 April, 1939.

The Marian Anderson Citizens Committee planned to picket
the DAR convention.

262
Cooke, Marvel. "New Laurels For Marian Anderson." The New
    York Amsterdam News. 15 April, 1939, pp. 1, 5.

Opening her free Lincoln Memorial concert with "America"
and closing with "Nobody Knows The Trouble I've Seen",
Marian Anderson was far more effective and dramatic than
any other denunciations for the actions of the DAR and the
D. C. School Board.

263
"Crowd Sees Officials Lift Ban on Singer." The Washington
    Post. 4 April, 1939.

Shows picture of crowd as they heard the school board had
rescinded its earlier decision to ban Marian Anderson from
singing at Central High School.

264
Daly, Victor R. "Washington's Minority Problem." The Crisis.
   Vol. 46, June, 1939, pp. 170-171.

   Notes that the barring of Marian Anderson from singing
at Constitution Hall by the D.A.R. spotlighted the Jim Crow
conditions in the nation's capitol and stirred black citizens
to new heights in trying to secure their civil rights.

265
"D. A. R. - Anderson Tiff is Reopened." The Cleveland Plain
   Dealer. 17 April, 1939.

   The Marian Anderson Citizens Committee threatened to
picket the D. A. R. convention for their refusal to let Miss
Anderson use Constitution Hall for a concert.

266
"D. A. R. Backtracks Now In Marian Anderson Fuss." The New
   York Amsterdam News. 4 March, 1939, pp. 1.

   Trying to save face after they denied Marian Anderson
use of Constitution Hall, the D. A. R. issued a statement
saying that the hall had already been booked for the date
Miss Anderson needed.

267
"D.A.R. Ban Draws Ire of Senator." The Chicago Defender. 18
   March, 1939.

   Senator Robert LaFollette announced that there would be
no more lectures in the Bronson Cutting Memorial Series held
at Constitution Hall because of their ban on Marian Anderson
singing there.

268
"D. A. R. Ban On Marian Anderson Remains." The Pittsburgh
   Courier. 11 February, 1939, pp. 1.

   Despite the protests of several prominent people in the
music world, the DAR voted to uphold its ban on Marian
Anderson's use of Constitution Hall.

269
"D. A. R. Convention." The New York Times. 23 April, 1939,
   Sec. 4, pp. 2.

   The DAR was holding its 48th Continental Congress. It
was noted that their ban on Marian Anderson's use of Constitution Hall brought widespread criticism and Miss Anderson
had to sing at the Lincoln Memorial.

270
"DAR Editor's Resignation Linked With Anderson Ban." The
   Norfolk Journal and Guide. 16 December, 1939, pp. 4.

Mrs. Frances Parkinson Keyes, editor of the National Historic Magazine, resigned from the DAR. It was hinted that her resignation was the result of the Marian Anderson ban.

271
"D.A.R. Explains Action On Singer." The New York Times. 19 April, 1939, pp. 25.

In an address to the congress of the DAR, their president explained that rules excluding Black artists from appearing at Constitution Hall were adopted as a result of an "unpleasant" experience and in conformity with existing and still prevailing customs in the city. Her explanation was applauded by the 4,500 members present.

272
"D. A. R. Hall Given Up by Cutting Lectures." The Washington News. 7 March, 1939.

Because of the D.A.R. ban on Marian Anderson, the Bronson Cutting Memorial Lecture Series decided not to use Constitution Hall for further lectures.

273
"D.A.R. Hall-Singer Issue Is Reopened." The Toledo Times. 17 April, 1939.

When the D.A.R. met in Washington, a protest committee sent a letter to them asking that Constitution Hall be open to all artists.

274
"D.A.R. In Washington Insults Marian Anderson." The New York Amsterdam News. 28 January, 1939, pp. 1,2.

Friends of Marian Anderson expressed both joy and embarrassment as they reflected on her musical triumphs as contrasted to her being banned by the DAR from singing at Constitution Hall.

275
"D.A.R. Not Informed of Mrs. Roosevelt's Resignation." The Washington Star. 28 February, 1939.

The D.A.R. said that Mrs. Franklin D. Roosevelt had not sent in an official resignation.

276
"D.A.R. Receives Committee." The New York Amsterdam News. 29 April, 1939, pp. 10.

The DAR agreed to meet with representatives from the Marian Anderson Citizen's Committee to discuss their ban of Marian Anderson and other Black artists from Constitution Hall.

277
"The D.A.R. States Its Case." The Norfolk Journal and Guide.
    29 April, 1939, pp. 8.

    This editorial reprinted from the Norfolk Virginian-
Pilot states that at their annual meeting, the DAR gave the
reason for refusing to let Marian Anderson use Constitution
Hall. It was noted that this does not touch the underlying
question of the moral obligation of the DAR to set an exam-
ple of enlightened social responsibility.

278
"D.A.R. To Visit First Lady Who Quit as Member." The Washing-
    ton Post. 2 March, 1939.

    Winners of the D.A.R. nation-wide trip contest planned
to visit Mrs. Roosevelt who reportedly resigned the D.A.R.
after they refused to allow Marian Anderson to sing at
Constitution Hall.

279
"DAR's Action Puts America To Shame Before World, Says Jones."
    The Norfolk Journal and Guide. 11 March, 1939, pp. 4.

    Urban League Executive, Eugene Jones, sent a letter to
the DAR in which he said that their action against Marian
Anderson is inexcusable and puts America to shame.

280
"DAR's Ban on Singer Protested By Ickes." The Pittsburgh
    Press. 3 March, 1939.

    Interior Secretary Ickes wrote a letter of protest to
the DAR for their refusal to allow Marian Anderson use of
Constitution Hall for a concert. Mr. Ickes had been noti-
fied by Howard University president, Mordecai Johnson, of
the incident.

281
"D.A.R.'s Ban Upset; She'll Sing Easter." The New York Daily
    News. 31 March, 1939.

    In a controversy which lead to a rift between Eleanor
Roosevelt and the DAR and also threatened to end the dual
school system in Washington, D. C., Marian Anderson was
refused a singing date at both Constitution Hall and Central
High School. She was finally granted permission to sing at
the Lincoln Memorial.

282
"DAR's Block Appearance of Concert Singer." The Pittsburgh
    Courier. 28 January, 1939, pp. 24.

    The DAR cited a clause in the contract for use of
Constitution Hall which prohibits Blacks from performing
there. It was stated that Marian Anderson may appear in
one of D. C.'s school auditoriums.

283
"DARlings Crossed Him Up, Declares Singer's Manager." The
    Washington News. 24 February, 1939.

    Miss Anderson's manager, S. Hurok, said that the D.A.R.
told him Constitution Hall was booked up for the date he
wanted Marian Anderson to appear but when he tried to
book another artist, he was told the date was open.

284
"Defends Exclusion of Marian Anderson." The Washington Star.
    1 March, 1939.

    This letter by a Jeffersonian Democrat defended the
D. C. School Board decision not to allow Marian Anderson to
sing at a white school and noted that freedom of choice
was one of the fundamentals of our government.

285
"Dispute Over Negro Singer Flares Anew." The New Haven
    Journal-Courier. 17 April, 1939.

    As the DAR arrived for their 48th Continental Congress,
members of the Marian Anderson Citizens Committee planned
to picket the group for their refusal to allow Miss Anderson
to sing at Constitution Hall.

286
"Dixie Press Slaps at DAR." The Afro American. 11 April, 1939.

    Representative newspapers in the south have blasted the
DAR for their refusal to allow Marian Anderson to sing at
Constitution Hall and most noted that lines of race, creed
or nationality had no place in the music world.

287
"Domestic Policies." in The D.A.R.: An Informal History, by
    Martha Strayer. Westport, Connecticut: Greenwood Press,
    1958, 1973, 262p., pp. 82-83.

    Marian Anderson was the focal point in the DAR's first
race problem. They denied her use of Constitution Hall
which led to world-wide protests. Mrs. Roosevelt and one
honorary life member of the DAR, resigned as a result of the
incident.

288
"Dragon of Race Prejudice Keeps Singer Out." The Washington
    Afro American. 25 February, 1939, pp. 1.

    Pictures Miss Anderson, Constitution Hall and Central
High School. She had been banned from using either facility for an Easter concert.

289
"Ends Ban On Negro Singer." The New York Times. 4 March,
    1939, pp. 17.

The D. C. School Board reversed their ban on Marian
Anderson and would allow her to sing at Central High School.

290
"First Lady Indicates She Quit D.A.R. Over Ban on Negro
    Diva." The Baltimore Sun. 28 February, 1939.

Although she did not name the organization, Mrs. Roosevelt indicated that she did quit the D.A.R. because of
their refusal to allow Marian Anderson to sing at Constitution Hall.

291
Fleeson, Doris. "First Lady Hints She Quit D.A.R. Over
    Race Ban." The Washington News. 28 February, 1939.

Mrs. Franklin D. Roosevelt terminated her membership in
the D.A.R. after they refused to allow Marian Anderson to
sing at Constitution Hall.

292
"Forum to Debate on Miss Anderson's Appearance Here." The
    Washington Post. 5 March, 1939.

The United Government Employers met to recommend that
Marian Anderson give an open-air concert instead of accepting
the provisions stated for her appearance at Central High
School.

293
"Friends Press Case of Marian Anderson." The New York Times.
    1 March, 1939, pp. 19.

The D. C. School Board was going to be asked to reconsider
their ban on Marian Anderson's use of Central High School
for a concert.

294
Gauthier, Eva. "Because She is a Negro." Tac Magazine. April,
    1939, pp. 5, 30.

Ms. Gauthier felt that the D.A.R. has forgotten what
their forefathers fought for in their refusal to allow
Marian Anderson to sing at Constitution Hall because of her
race.

295
"Group to Protest Marian Anderson Hall Ban Sunday." The Wash-
    ington Post. 24 March, 1939.

Oscar Chapman, Assistant Secretary of Interior, was to
chair a mass meeting at Metropolitan AME Church to protest
the ban of the D. C. School Board to have Marian Anderson
sing at Central High School.

296
Hancock, Gordon B. "The Follow-Up On The Marian Anderson
    Affair." The Norfolk Journal and Guide. 22 April, 1939.
    pp. 8.

Although this writer opposed Miss Anderson's singing
under "second rate" circumstances, he felt that the triumph
to this occasion would be whether interracial cooperation
was accomplished.

297
Hancock, Gordon B. "Prejudice In Washington and Berlin."
    The Norfolk Journal and Guide. 8 April, 1939, pp. 8.

Noted that the Marian Anderson incident brought shame to
the nation's capital. The author felt that Miss Anderson
should not appear at the Lincoln Memorial in order to humili-
ate the city.

298
"Hans Kindler Plays Before Small Crowd." The New York Amster-
    dam News. 15 April, 1939, pp. 17.

The National Symphony Orchestra under the direction of
Hans Kindler played to a small crowd at Constitution Hall
and the Sunday evening performance was completely cancelled.
The concert was the same day that Marian Anderson sang at
Lincoln Memorial. Kindler was on the committee to sponsor
Miss Anderson's concerts and sent regrets that he would not
be there.

299
" 'Have Appeared In Almost Every Other Capitol In World ---
    Barred From My Own' ... Marian Anderson." The Pittsburgh
    Courier. 4 March, 1939, pp. 1.

Speaking in California, Marian Anderson said she was
not surprised that Mrs. Roosevelt had resigned from the
DAR. She said she was 'shocked beyond words to be barred
from the capitol of my own country after having appeared
in almost every other capitol in the world.'

300
Heifetz, 'Ashamed' D. C. Hall is Denied Marian Anderson."
    The Washington Post. 20 February, 1939.

Violinist Jascha Heifetz performed at Constitution Hall
and stated that he was ashamed that Marian Anderson had
been barred from singing there.

301
"How Can They Do It?" The New York Amsterdam News. 4 February,
    1939, pp. 6.

This cartoon by Chase shows the door of Constitution
Hall being closed in the face of Marian Anderson by the DAR.

302
"Ickes At Anderson Recital Rivals Gettysburg Address." The New York Amsterdam News. 15 April, 1939, pp. 17.

In quiet simplicity, Secretary of Interior Harold Ickes gave a subtle reprimand to the DAR for their refusal to allow Marian Anderson to sing at Constitution Hall.   In his introduction of Miss Anderson, he said, "Genius draws no color line.   She had endowed Marian Anderson with such a voice as lifts any individual above his fellows, as is a matter of exultant pride to any race.   And so it is fitting that Marian Anderson should raise her voice in tribute to the noble Lincoln, whom mankind will ever honor."

303
"Ickes Comes To Aid of Colored Singer in Controversy." The Washington Star. 2 March, 1939.

Interior Secretary Ickes expressed hope that the D. C. Board of Education would reverse its slant and allow Marian Anderson to sing at Central High School.   He also protested the DAR's action against Miss Anderson singing at Constitution Hall.

304
"Ickes Protests to D.A.R. On Miss Anderson Ban." The New York Herald Tribune. 3 March, 1939.

Secretary of Interior, Harold Ickes, protested to the D.A.R. for their refusal to allow Marian Anderson to sing at Constitution Hall.

305
"Ickes Says, 'You're Swell'." The New York Amsterdam News. 15 April, 1939, pp. 17.

Pictures Secretary of Interior Harold Ickes welcoming Marian Anderson at the Lincoln Memorial for her Easter concert.

306
"Ickes Scores The 'Too Timid'." The New York Times. 10 April, 1939, pp. 19.

In introducing Marian Anderson at her Lincoln Memorial concert, Secretary of Interior, Harold Ickes, said that "there are those who are too timid or too indifferent to lift up the light that Jefferson and Lincoln carried aloft." He did not mention the DAR by name but scored their action against Miss Anderson.

307
"Ickes Taxes D.A.R. On Barring Singer." The New York Times 3 March, 1939, pp. 26.

Harold Ickes wrote the DAR to find out their reasons for barring Marian Anderson's concert at Constitution Hall.   He wanted to know if the ban was based on an old rule.

308
"Is Denied Use of Hall in Capital." The Norfolk Journal and
    Guide. 28 January, 1939, pp. 1.

It was announced that the Daughters of the American Revolution would not permit Marian Anderson to use Constitution
Hall for an Easter concert.

309
"Jim Crow Concert Hall." Time. Vol. 33, March 6, 1939, pp.
    38-39.

Makes note of the D.A.R. refusal to allow a Black, Marian
Anderson, to sing at Constitution Hall. Protests poured
into the D.A.R., visiting violinist Jascha Heifetz said he
was ashamed to appear there, and Eleanor Roosevelt resigned
the D.A.R. in protest.

310
"Joins Protest Against Ban On Marian Anderson." The Washington
    Star. 31 January, 1939.

This letter to the editor was in protest of Marian Anderson being banned from singing at Constitution Hall.

311
Lautier, Louis. "DAR Reasons For Anderson Ban Exploded."
    The Norfolk Journal and Guide. 29 April, 1939, pp. 1, 20.

Although the DAR explained that racial segregation was
the general practice, it was learned that Constitution
Hall was the only auditorium in the city which still barred
Black artists.

312
Lautier, Louis. "Sees Tragic Irony in DAR Color Bars." The
    Afro American. 20 May, 1940.

Mr. Lautier noted that the DAR ban on Black artists appearing at Constitution Hall was ironic in light of the service
of freedmen and slaves in the Revolutionary War. DAR lineage
was supposedly based upon patroits of that war.

313
"Lesson For History Week." The Washington Afro American. 11
    February, 1939, pp. 4.

This cartoon shows some of the Black soldiers who have
fought in the nation's wars. It was a lesson to the DAR
to let them know that some 3,000 Blacks served in the armed
forces and helped to gain liberty and independence.

314
"Let 'Em Stand Up." The Washington Times. 28 March, 1939.

An outraged patron wrote to uphold the DAR ban on Marian Anderson and felt that if people really wanted to hear her to go to Howard University and if there's not enough room, her true fans wouldn't mind standing.

315
"Marian Anderson." The New York Age. 8 April, 1939. pp. 6.

Rep. James P. McGrannery of Pennsylvania announced that he was calling for an investigation into the D. C. School Board's refusal to allow Marian Anderson to use a white school auditorium for a concert. Also Congresswoman Caroline O'Day asked for sponsors for a Lincoln Memorial concert after the DAR also banned Miss Anderson from singing at Constitution Hall.

316
"Marian Anderson." The New York Times. 1 March, 1939, pp. 20.

This editorial stated that it was hard to believe that any patriotic organization in this country would approve of discrimination against so gifted an artist and so fine a person as Miss Anderson.

317
"Marian Anderson Ban Arouses Wide Protest." The Crisis. Vol. 46, March, 1939, pp. 87.

The Metropolitan Opera sent a telegram to the NAACP voicing their strong protest against the D.A.R.'s refusal to allow Miss Anderson to sing at Constitution Hall. They called the action "undemocratic and un-American."

318
"Marian Anderson Barred Again In D. C." The New York Amsterdam News. 25 February, 1939, pp. 2.

Just after the DAR's refusal to allow Marian Anderson to sing at Constitution Hall, the D. C. School Board also refused her permission to sing at Central High School. The school board cited the city's dual school system which prohibits a Black from appearing in a white school.

319
"Marian Anderson Barred in Second Washington Hall." The South Bend Tribune. 18 March, 1939.

The D. C. School Board announced that Central High School would be unavailable to Miss Anderson because the sponsors, Howard University, took exception to the statement of not setting a precedent in the use of the school.

320
"Marian Anderson Declines D.A.R. Views on Stop Here." The Washington Star. 7 April, 1939.

Miss Anderson did not speak on the ban of the D.A.R. and
the D. C. School Board in allowing her to sing in Washington.
She was in the city to visit her hospitalized accompanist.

321
"Marian Anderson in the Nation's Capitol - Managers and
    AGMA Sign." The New York Times. 9 April, 1939.

The Department of Interior hosted the occasion of Miss
Anderson's concert at Lincoln Memorial.

322
"Marian Anderson Row Breaks Out Anew." The Newark Ledger.
    17 April, 1939.

Members of the Marian Anderson Citizens Committee picketed the 48th Continental Congress of the D.A.R. for their
refusal to grant Marian Anderson a performance date at
Constitution Hall.

323
"Marian Anderson Under New Ban." The New York Mirror. 19
    March, 1939.

School Superintendent Ballou retracted the approval of
Miss Anderson to sing at Central High School when Howard
University refused to accept the provision that the D. C.
School Board not set a precedent in the use of the school.

324
"Marian Anderson Urged To Refuse School Offer." The Washing-
    ton Star. 6 March, 1939.

The United Government Employees sent a request to Miss
Anderson asking her to refuse the offer of the D. C. School
Board which would let her sing at Central High School but
that it would not set a precedent. The Employees felt that
this would prohibit future performances by Blacks there.

325
"Marian Anderson Urged To Reject Action By Schoolmen." The
    New York Amsterdam News. 18 March, 1939, pp. 5.

The NAACP urged Marian Anderson to reject the D. C.
School Board's restrictive clause in letting her sing at
Central High School. The clause stated that her appearance
should not act as a precedent for future use of a white
school by Blacks.

326
"Marian Anderson's Easter Concert Cause of Nation-Wide
    Controversy --- Principals In Demand For Fair Plan."
    The Pittsburgh Courier. 11 March, 1939, pp. 14.

Short preview of the events in the controversy of where
Miss Anderson was to perform her Easter Sunday concert.

327
"Marian Anderson's Manager Attacks D.A.R." The Pittsburgh
    Courier. 4 March, 1939, pp. 4.

In a statement attacking the DAR, S. Hurok said, "the
DAR's un-American, unconstitutional restriction upon Marian
Anderson is a plain instance of the charge that they have
not yet begun to understand the true meaning of American
democracy." Of Mrs. Roosevelt, Hurok said, "by her action,
Mrs. Roosevelt has shown herself to be a woman of courage
and excellent taste."

328
"Marian Will Not Sing In School." The Pittsburgh Courier.
    25 March, 1939, pp. 4.

Howard University, sponsors of the Marian Anderson Easter
concert, refused to accept the conditions set forth by the
D. C. School Board for use of Central High School. The
board had specified that this concert would not set a precedent for future use of the school by Blacks.

329
"Mass Meeting Tomorrow To Protest Singer's Ban." The Wash-
    ington News. 25 February, 1939.

A mass meeting to protest the Marian Anderson ban was
moved from Mount Pleasant Congregational Church to Lincoln
Congregational Church because members of the Mount Pleasant
Church questioned the use of the church for such a contro-
versial meeting.

330
"May Picket DAR Session In Capitol." The Norfolk Journal and
    Guide. 22 April, 1939, pp. 10.

The Marian Anderson Citizens Committee planned to picket
the DAR during their convention in Washington, D. C. It
noted that Mrs. Roosevelt, who resigned from the DAR, would
not be home when the delegates would visit the White House.

331
"Meeting Protesting Singer Ban Makes Auditorium Plea."
    The Washington Star. 27 February, 1939.

A mass meeting in protest of the Marian Anderson ban
at Central High School asked Congress to provide a municipal
auditorium for use by everyone.

332
"Miss Anderson and the D.A.R." The New York Times. 26 Febru-
    ary, 1939, Sec. 9, pp. 6.

This letter to the editor protests the DAR ban on Miss
Anderson's use of Constitution Hall. The letter noted some
of the discriminations Blacks have suffered and details their
many contributions to the American society.

333
"Miss Anderson Will Sing At Central High." The Washington
    Post. 12 March, 1939.

The D. C. Board of Education rescinded its decision to
let Marian Anderson sing at Central High School. The school
board termed the request an emergency situation that would
not be considered a precedent.

334
"Mrs. Roosevelt Approved." The New York Times. 19 March,
    1939, Sec. 3, pp. 4.

A poll taken after Mrs. Roosevelt resigned the DAR over
the Marian Anderson controversy. It showed that 67% approved
her decision.

335
"Mrs. Roosevelt Confirms DAR Resignation." The Pittsburgh
    Courier. 1 April, 1939, pp. 14.

Mrs. Roosevelt confirmed the report that she had resigned
from the DAR. It was speculated that she resigned because of
the DAR's refusal to allow Marian Anderson to sing at Constitution Hall.

336
"Mrs. Roosevelt Hints She Had Quit D.A.R." The Washington
    Star. 27 February, 1939.

Mrs. Roosevelt stated in her syndicated column, that she
quit an organization, which she did not name, because she
did not approve of a recent action of the group.

337
"Mrs. Roosevelt Hints 'Twas D.A.R. She Quit'." The Washington
    News. 27 February, 1939.

Mrs. Roosevelt resigned from the D.A.R. because they
refused to let Marian Anderson sign at Constitution Hall.

338
"Mrs. Roosevelt Indicates She Has Resigned From D.A.R. Over
    Refusal of Hall to Negro." The New York Times. 28 Febru-
    ary, 1939.

Mrs. Roosevelt would neither confirm nor deny that it
was the D.A.R. she had resigned from because of their refusal to allow a Black singer to perform there. She would
only admit that she did resign from an organization for
that reason.

339
"Mrs. Roosevelt Quits D.A.R." The Pittsburgh Courier. 4
    March, 1939, pp. 1, 4.

Mrs. Roosevelt hinted that she had resigned from the DAR

because they would not allow Marian Anderson to sing at
Constitution Hall. She did not name the DAR specifically
as the organization from which she had resigned but only
said the organization has policies she did not approve of.

340
"Mrs. Roosevelt Quits DAR." The Washington Afro American.
    4 March, 1939, pp. 1,2.

Mrs. Roosevelt resigned the DAR. Although she did not
state the name of the organization from which she had
resigned, she stated that she did not wish to be considered
in accord with a certain action that had been taken by the
organization. Marian Anderson said she was not surprised
at Mrs. Roosevelt's resignation.

341
"Mrs. Roosevelt Quits D.A.R. in Anderson Row." The Washington
    Post. 28 February, 1939.

At a press conference, Mrs. Roosevelt indicated she quit
the D.A.R. because of their ban on Marian Anderson singing
at Constitution Hall. She did not name the organization
specifically, but she left little doubt that it was the
D.A.R. she quit.

342
"Mrs. Roosevelt Quits D.A.R. Reports Say." The Norfolk Jour-
    nal and Guide. 4 March, 1939, pp. 1.

Mrs. Roosevelt would not state whether it was the DAR
from which she had resigned. She did say that the organization she resigned had policies which she could not approve.
She had already publicly deplored the DAR.

343
"Mrs. Roosevelt Resigns From D.A.R. Because of Snubbing of
    Negro Singer." The Statesville (N.C.) Daily. 28 February,
    1939.

Mrs. Roosevelt resigned from the D.A.R. because of their
refusal to let Marian Anderson sing at Constitution Hall,
but would not make a specific statement to that effect.

344
"Mrs. Roosevelt Won't Be Home." The Pittsburgh Courier. 15
    April, 1939, pp. 4.

Mrs. Roosevelt admitted that she resigned the DAR because
of their ban on Marian Anderson singing at Constitution Hall.
She also related that she would be out of town during the
DAR's annual reception held at the White House.

345
"Negro Singer Barred Again." The New York Telegraph. 19
    March, 1939.

The D. C. School Board retracted its decision to allow
Marian Anderson to sing at Central High School when Howard
University refused to accept the provision that the board
was not setting a precedent in use of the hall by a Black.

346
"Negro Singer Controversy Left for Ballou Decision." The
    Washington News. 16 March, 1939.

D. C. School Superintendent, F. W. Ballou, would make the
final decision on whether to allow Marian Anderson to sing
at Constitution Hall. The D. C. School Board had voted to
ban her performance.

347
"Negro Singer Partisans Still Cry: 'No Strings'!" The Wash-
    ington Daily News. 27 March, 1939.

After the D. C. School Board agreed to let Miss Anderson
sing at a white school as long as it was not a precedent,
the Howard University Music Department refused to accept
these terms, so the school superintendent declined to
issue a permit for her to sing.

348
"Negro Singer Wins Right to Appear in D.C." The Baltimore
    Sun 4 March, 1939.

The D. C. Board of Education revised its ruling on the
use of Central High School for a concert by Marian Anderson, under the condition that it did not set a precedent.
This condition was refused by Howard University who was to
sponsor the concert.

349
"Negro Singer's Recital Still An Uncertainty." The Washington
    News. 13 March, 1939.

A decision still had not been made on the Howard University request to have Marian Anderson sing at Central High
School. The board stipulated that it must be an emergency
and not a precedent for interchangable use of black and
white schools.

350
"Negroes' Use of Halls Not D.A.R. Problem Alone, Conclave
    Told." The Washington Daily News. 18 April, 1939, pp. 5.

D.A.R. president said that it did not change its policies toward Miss Anderson because of signed agreements and
customs for all similar properties in D. C. She noted that
the D.A.R. would adapt its policies in accordance when
other groups did so.

351
"New DAR Takes Shape." The Midwest (Chicago) Daily Record.
    9 March, 1939.

Some members of the D.A.R. made resolutions to end Jim Crow policies of the organization. This new group, Descendants of the American Revolution, felt the old organization to be too hide-bound and reactionary.

352
"The Obvious Moral." The Washington Post. 11 April, 1939.

In a letter to the paper, F. R. Allen noted that thanks to the D.A.R. and the D. C. School Board, over 70,000 people would be able to hear Marian Anderson sing, whereas, if she had appeared at Constitution Hall or Central High School, only a fraction of people would have heard her.

353
"1,500 To Fight School Ban on Colored Singer." The Washington Post. 27 February, 1939.

Over 1,500 people pledged to attend the meeting of the D. C. School Board to protest their ban on Marian Anderson singing at Central High School. Mrs. Eleanor Roosevelt sent a telegram to the group voicing her dissatisfaction with the ban.

354
"Opera Stars Protest Ban On Marian Anderson." The Pittsburgh Courier. 4 February, 1939, pp. 4.

Famous names in the music world, including several stars of the Metropolitan Opera, protested the action of the DAR in refusing to allow Marian Anderson to sing at Constitution Hall. Among those protesting were Lawrence Tibbett, Kirsten Flagstad, Geraldine Farrar and Leopold Stokowski.

355
"Opera Stars Protest Marian Anderson Ban." The Washington Star. 31 January, 1939

Metropolitan Opera stars and other musicians protested the refusal of the D.A.R. to allow Miss Anderson a concert date at Constitution Hall.

356
"Opera Stars Raps D.A.R. Bar on Marian Anderson." The Chicago Defender. 4 February, 1939.

Members of the Metropolitan Opera termed the D.A.R. ban on Marian Anderson's appearance at Constitution Hall as 'undemocratic and unAmerican' in a telegram to the NAACP.

357
"Points To Irony In Marian Anderson Issue." The Washington Star. 7 March, 1939.

The Chairman of the Race Relations Committee of the Washington Federation of Churches wrote that it was ironic that the nation was celebrating 150 years of democratic

freedom, but a great artist could not appear in the nation's
capitol because of her race.

358
Prattis, P. L. "Why Not Put The 'Curse of Ham' On The DAR?
    Inquires A Mississippi Reader." The Pittsburgh Courier.
    8 April, 1939, pp. 13.

A writer from Mississippi suggested that something should
be done about the organized prejudice of the DAR against
Marian Anderson. He suggested that domestic workers should
seek references from potential employers just as they require
references on the domestics.

359
"Protests Anderson Ban." The New York Times. 27 March, 1939,
    pp. 10.

Senator Wagner sent a letter to the Marian Anderson protest committee stating that "the Marian Anderson case is a
matter of foremost national and international importance."

360
"Protests On DAR Ban Against Singer Grow." The New York
    Times. 2 March, 1939, pp. 17.

Telegrams from Mayor LaGuardia and other prominent persons flowed into the DAR in protest over the Marian Anderson ban. LaGuardia said, "no hall is too good for Marian
Anderson."

361
"Race - The Past," in The Daughters: An Unconventional Look
    At America's Fan Club - The DAR, by Peggy Anderson. New
    York: St. Martin's Press, 1974, 360p., pp. 109-153.

Cited the fact that the whole truth of the 1939 Marian
Anderson controversy could not be found in one place and
some of it had been lost forever. Also, the incident could
not be considered apart from the policies governing Constitution Hall. Gives an in-depth description of the policies
of the DAR toward Black artists and noted that the real
mystery about the 1939 incident was not that they barred
Marian Anderson, but that they bound themselves to a policy
that barred all Black artists.

362
"Racial Ban Still In Effect." The Norfolk Journal and Guide.
    2 December, 1939, pp. 1, 10.

Dr. Anson Phelps Stokes made a plea to the DAR to lift
their ban on Marian Anderson. He said that "I cannot but
believe that the DAR's action in banning Miss Anderson was
immediately known in Moscow, Berlin and Rome and that it
has given aid and encouragement to the opponents of true
democracy."

363
"Rally To Protest Second Ban On Singer." The Washington
Times. 24 March, 1939.

Seventy-three organizations planned to join the Marian
Anderson Citizens Committee in a mass meeting to protest
the refusal of the D. C. School Board to let Miss Anderson
sing at Central High School.

364
"Rally Will Discuss Municipal Auditorium." The Washington
Star. 26 February, 1939.

When a rally of 1,500 sympathizers met to protest the
ban on Marian Anderson from Constitution Hall and Central
High School, they would also discuss a resolution supporting
a municipal auditorium.

365
"Reversal of Ban on Anderson Concert At Central Sought." The
Washington Star. 1 March, 1939.

With some 7,000 signatures, members of the Marian Anderson Citizens Committee met with the D. C. School Board to
seek a reversal of their ban on her concert at Central
High School.

366
"School 'Backs Down' On Ban Against Marian Anderson." The
Pittsburgh Courier. 11 March, 1939, pp. 1, 4.

The D. C. School Board rescinded its decision to ban
Marian Anderson from using Central High School for an
Easter concert provided Blacks did not use this situation
to attempt to get future dates at the school.

367
"School Ban Stands on Miss Anderson." The New York Times.
21 March, 1939.

Insisting on the provision that the Marian Anderson concert at Central High School not set a precedent, the D. C.
School Board retracted its invitation when Miss Anderson's
sponsors refused to accept those provisions.

368
"School Board Apes DAR; Bars Marian." The Washington Afro
American. 18 February, 1939, pp. 1, 2.

The D. C. School Board voted 5-1 to bar Marian Anderson
from singing at Central High School. The board stated that
the dual school system prohibited use of buildings by different racial groups.

369
"School Board Prexy Backs Anderson 'Sing'." The Washington
Daily News. 5 April, 1939.

President of the D. C. School Board, Mrs. Henry Doyle,
agreed to be an honorary sponsor of the Marian Anderson open-
air concert. Also the "new D.A.R.," The Descendents of the
American Revolution, pledged support.

370
"The School Board Received The Case." The Washington Tribune.
  25 March, 1939.

Excerpt from the proposal sent to the school board by
the Marian Anderson Citizens Committee for their reconsidera-
tion of the Marian Anderson ban at Central High School.

371
"School Board to Act Today on Singer Ban." The Washington
  Times. 3 March, 1939.

The D. C. School Board was to meet to reconsider their
ban on Marian Anderson singing at Central High School.

372
"School Board To Reconsider Ban on Singer." The Washington
  Times. 2 March, 1939.

The D. C. School Board was to meet to consider the ban
on Marian Anderson singing at white Central High School.
The two main issues were: 1. use of a public building by a
paid performer, and 2. maintenance of a dual or black/white
school system.

373
"School Board Unit Considers Anderson Controversy, Today."
  The Washington Star. 3 March, 1939.

D. C. School Board members were to meet again to consider
the ban on Marian Anderson at Central High School. The
Central High P.T.A. endorsed the refusal.

374
"School Uses For 15 Years To Be Probed." The Washington Star.
  6 April, 1939.

The D. C. School Board's Committee on Community Use of
Buildings was to make a study of past uses of school buildings after school hours and on non-school days for the past
fifteen years in the aftermath of the Marian Anderson ban
on the use of Central High School.

375
"Score 2nd Discrimination Against Marian Anderson." The
  Norfolk Journal and Guide. 25 February, 1939, pp. 1

On February 16th, the D. C. School Board announced that
Marian Anderson could not use the white Central High School
for an Easter concert. She had already been denied use of
Constitution Hall by the DAR.

376
"Sec. Wallace Protests Ban on Contralto." The Washington
Times. 26 March, 1939.

Secretary of Agriculture, Henry Wallace, along with
many educators, protested the ban of the D. C. Board of
Education on Marian Anderson singing at Central High School.

377
"Shuns Anderson Protest." The New York Times. 20 March,
   1939, pp. 12.

It was revealed that at a meeting of the New Jersey DAR,
the members rejected a resolution to condemn the national
organization for refusing to allow Marian Anderson to sing
at Constitution Hall.

378
"Singer's Ban Decision Now Up To Ballou." The Washington
   Times. 16 March, 1939.

The D. C. Board of Education gave Superintendent Frank
Ballou the right to decide on whether Marian Anderson could
use Central High School for a concert.

379
"Sponsors of Negro Singer Win Point in Fight for School
   Hall." The Baltimore Morning Sun. 2 March, 1939.

The Marian Anderson Citizens Committee scored a point
in contesting the D. C. School Board's refusal to allow
Marian Anderson to sing at white Central High School because it was a commercial venture. It was noted that other
artists had performed there and received a fee. Also lawyers
felt that after school hours, the school belonged to the community.

380
"Stars Join Mayor In Plea For Fund." The New York Times. 24
   April, 1939, pp. 4.

The Greater New York Fund presented a program broadcast
over stations WJZ, WABC and WQXR. Marian Anderson sang
"America." She was characterized as "one of the greatest
living artists in the entire world."

381
Stokes, Anson Phelps. Art And The Color Line; An Appeal Made
   May 31, 1939, To The President General and Other Officers
   Of The Daughters of the American Revolution To Modify Their
   Rules So As To Permit Distinguished Negro Artists Such As
   Miss Marian Anderson To Be Heard In Constitution Hall.
   Washington, D. C.: Marian Anderson Committee, 1939, 26p.

Outline of the statement made by Mr. Stokes on behalf
of the Marian Anderson Committee before the D.A.R. Gives

a resume of the incident, purpose of the Marian Anderson
Committee, objectives raised and answered, reactions of
public opinion, a history of D.A.R. attitudes on interracial matters and the appeal to the D.A.R. to reconsider its
decision.

382
Strayer, Martha.   "Please Leave the Room." The Washington
News. 2 March, 1939.

Although D. C. School Board meeting were suppose to be
open, they went into executive session to debate the Marian
Anderson case.

383
"Thank The D.A.R." The Washington Daily News. 10 April, 1939.

Thanks to the D.A.R., countless more people were able to
hear Marian Anderson than would have if she had sung at
Constitution Hall.

383
"This D.A.R." The Hartford Courant. 4 March, 1939.

The Rev. Moody condemned the D.A.R. for their refusal to
let Marian Anderson sing at Constitution Hall.

385
"Threaten DAR Color Ban Suit." The Washington Afro American.
11 February, 1939, pp. 1.

The NAACP was considering filing a petition to have tax
exemptions withdrawn from Constitution Hall because the DAR
refused to permit Marian Anderson sing there.

386
"To Keep Ban on Negroes." The Washington Tribune.   11 February, 1939.

Despite protests from the NAACP and the Metropolitan
Opera, the DAR ruled to uphold its ban on the use of Constitution Hall by Marian Anderson.

387
"Triumph." The Brown American. Vol. 3, January, 1940, pp. 13.

Notes the wide protest when Marian Anderson was denied
use of Constitution Hall by the D.A.R. She was honored
with the Spingarn Medal and was also asked to sing before
the King and Queen of England.

388
"Unit Opposes Picketing of D.A.R. Here." The Washington
Herald. 17 April, 1939.

The United Government Employees condemned the proposal of
the Marian Anderson Citizen's Committee to picket the D.A.R.

convention.

389
Waldrop, Frank C. "Dr. Ballou Is Not To Blame." The Washington Times. 23 March, 1939.

Author felt that School Superintendent Ballou was blamed
unfairly for the decision not to let Marian Anderson use
Central High School. Dr. Ballou was only carrying out the
policy ordered by his employers.

390
"Was The D.A.R. She Quit, Says Mrs. Roosevelt." The New York
Times. 23 March, 1939, pp. 25.

Speaking in Los Angeles, Mrs. Roosevelt said she had quit
the DAR although the DAR said her resignation had not been
received.

391
"Washington 'Fed Up' On La Anderson Indident." The Pittsburgh
Courier. 8 April, 1939, feature page.

It was felt that Washingtonians were fed up with the Marian Anderson/School Board/DAR controversy.

392
"Washington School Board's Retreat." The Norfolk Journal and
Guide. 11 March, 1939, pp. 8.

Notes the D. C. School Board's retreat on it's ban of
Marian Anderson singing at Central High School. But they
also tried to save face by saying this was an emergency
situation and should not set a precedent for future use of
school facilities by Blacks.

393
" 'We Must Hear Marian Anderson' Says Editor." The Norfolk
Journal and Guide. 11 March, 1939, pp. 9.

This article reprinted from the Washington Times Herald
noted that a petition with five or six thousand names was
to be sent to the D. C. School Board protesting their ban
on Marian Anderson's use of Central High School for a concert. The editor of the paper felt that this sort of
ruling only breeds malice, suspicion and discontent in all
citizens.

394
"Whether Marian Will Sing In D. C. School Auditorium Still
In Doubt." The Pittsburgh Courier. 18 March, 1939, pp. 18.

The D. C. School Board was to meet this week to decide
whether Marian Anderson was to use the white Central High
School for an Easter concert. If granted, this would mean
a departure from the dual school system in the city.

395
"While Lincoln Watched." The Washington Star. 10 April, 1939.

Picture of some of the crowd at the Lincoln Memorial to hear Marian Anderson's open-air concert.

396
" 'White Artists Only'," in The DAR, by Margaret Gibbs. New York: Holt, Rinehart & Winston, 1969, 244p., pp. 159-167.

Notes that the DAR is still haunted by the Marian Anderson controversy of 1939 and continues to justify their actions. In doing so, several pamphlets were released. One was Statements re Constitution Hall which was released in 1966. Mrs. Roosevelt's resignation caused almost as much public controversy as the "incident" itself.

397
"White House Fete Is Given For D.A.R." The New York Times. 22 April, 1939, pp. 19.

Mrs. Roosevelt was absent as the DAR attended a reception at the White House. It was noted that she had resigned from the DAR because of their ban on Marian Anderson's use of Constitution Hall.

398
Wilkins, Roy. "The Real D.A.R." The Crisis. Vol. 46, May, 1939, pp. 145.

Discusses the face-saving explanation the D.A.R. had to give after refusing to allow Marian Anderson to use their facilities for a concert.

399
Wilkins, Roy. "We Are Ashamed For Them." The Crisis. Vol. 46, February, 1939, pp. 49.

Editorial on the D.A.R. refusal to allow Marian Anderson to use their facilities.

400
"Wins Round 3 in Tilt With Miss Anderson." The Norfolk Journal & Guide. 14 November, 1942.

In this new issue on whether Miss Anderson could sing at Constitution Hall, she made three stipulations. The D.A.R. refused to not have segregated seating and refused to allow the concert to serve as a precedent for future concerts there.

401
Winter, Peter. "Marian Anderson." The Washington Star. 8 March, 1966.

An artist profile of Marian Anderson and the controversy over the D.A.R. refusal to allow her to sing at Constitution Hall.

LINCOLN
MEMORIAL
CONCERT

402
"Aid Anderson Concert." The New York Times. 5 April, 1939,
    pp. 30.

Lists the names of the patrons for the Marian Anderson
Lincoln Memorial concert to be held on Easter Sunday, April
9th.   Included among the patrons were Mayor LaGuardia of
New York.

403
"Anderson Affair." Time. Vol. 33, April 17, 1939, pp. 23.

Marian Anderson sang before 75,000 in a free, open-air
concert at Lincoln Memorial. She had been banned from Constitution Hall which caused dramatic protests and Eleanor
Roosevelt's resignation from the D.A.R.

404
"Anderson Concert Traffic Plan Is Announced." The Washington
    Star. 8 April, 1939.

Cars were banned from Lincoln Memorial because of the
large crowd expected at the Marian Anderson concert.

405
"The Anderson Recital." The Norfolk Journal and Guide. 22
    April, 1939, pp. 8.

Noted that the Marian Anderson recital was a notable
demonstration of how courage and ability can triumph over
persecutions and narrowness.

406
"Anderson To Rise On Easter." The Norfolk Journal and Guide.
    8 April, 1939, pp. 1, 10.

At twilight on Easter Sunday, Marian Anderson was to give
a free concert on the steps of the Lincoln Memorial.

407
"Autos Barred at Anderson Recital Site." The Washington News.
    8 April, 1939.

Parking was not allowed within the Lincoln Memorial on
Easter Sunday because of the large crowd expected for the
open-air concert by Marian Anderson.

408
"Biggest Concert Crowd Hears Noted Contralto." The Washington
    Post. 10 April, 1939.

The crowd at Lincoln Memorial to hear Marian Anderson
sing stretched from the memorial to the Washington Monument
hill.

409
"Brilliant Contralto Sings at Washington." The Wichita
    Beacon. 9 April, 1939.

Marian Anderson was to sing on the steps of Lincoln
Memorial on Easter Sunday, 1939.

410
Buchalter, Helen. "75,000 Hear Marian Anderson Sing At
    Memorial." The Washington Daily News. 10 April, 1939,
    pp. 5.

An estimated 75,000 were at Lincoln Memorial to hear
Marian Anderson give her Easter Sunday concert on April 9th.

411
"The Capital Acclaims Marian Anderson." The National Educa-
    tional Outlook Among Negroes. Vol. 2, April, 1939, pp. 6.

Remarks by Secretary of Interior, Ickes, when he introduced Miss Anderson at the Lincoln Memorial on Easter Sunday,
1939.

412
"Celebrated Contralto Thrills Notables With Her Voice." The
    Washington Post. 10 April, 1939.

Picture of some of the notables present at Marian Anderson's Lincoln Memorial concert.

413
Clark, Rocky. "Listening Post." The Bridgeport (Conn.) Post.
    8 April, 1939.

List of Easter activities for station WOR. Among them
was the concert of Marian Anderson at Lincoln Memorial
scheduled for 5 p.m.

414
"Concert at Memorial Granted to Anderson." Musical America.
    10 April, 1939.

Chief Justice and Mrs. Evans Hughes were among the sponsors of an open-air Easter Sunday concert by Marian Anderson
at Lincoln Memorial. She had been refused access to Constitution Hall and Central High School.

415
"Concert in Capitol for Marian Anderson." The New York Times.
    31 March, 1939.

Interior Secretary Ickes granted permission for Miss Anderson to sing at the Lincoln Memorial on April 9.

416
"Concert Recital." The Cincinnati Radio Dial. 15 April, 1939.

Marian Anderson and the Howard University choir appeared
at the Lincoln Memorial on Easter Sunday.

417
"Contralto Is Lauded." The New York Amsterdam News. 15 April,
    1939, pp. 17.

It was noted that Marian Anderson never sang better than
when she gave her open-air concert at the Lincoln Memorial.

418
"Depression and The New Deal," in Eyewitness: The Negro In
    American History, by William L. Katz. New York: Pitman
    Publishing Corporation, 1967, 553p., pp. 430-431.

Notes Marian Anderson's historic Lincoln Memorial concert after the D. C. School Board and the DAR refused her
permission to use their facilities.

419
"Easter Rites and Features Highlights of Radio Today." The
    Miami Herald. 9 April, 1939.

In listing Easter Sunday highlights, it noted that Marian
Anderson would sing at Lincoln Memorial.

420
"Ellender Protests Anderson Recital." The New York Times.
    8 April, 1939.

Senator Ellender of Louisiana, protested the recital of
Marian Anderson at Lincoln Memorial.

421
Eversman, Alice. "Concert by Marian Anderson Finds Artist
    at Her Best. The Washington Star. 10 April, 1939.

Miss Anderson sang to thousands at Lincoln Memorial while
at Constitution Hall, the National Symphony Orchestra performed. Miss Anderson had been banned from appearing at
Constitution Hall.

422
"Farley and Garner Refuse Sponsorships." The Norfolk Journal
    and Guide. 15 April, 1939, pp. 1.

Two presidential candidates ignored invitations to act as
sponsors for the Marian Anderson concert at Lincoln Memorial.
They were Vice President, John Nance Garner and Postmaster
General, James A. Farley.

423
Fleming, G. James. "Words Can't Describe Marian Anderson's
    Washington Recital." The Norfolk Journal and Guide. 15
    April, 1939, pp. 2.

Fleming gave a stirring account of Miss Anderson's recital
at the Lincoln Memorial. He describes her gestures as she
sings and the testimony in each of her renditions. He noted
that the scorching introduction of Miss Anderson by Interior
Secretary Harold Ickes was an epic. He felt that this performance would be remembered long after the apologies for
the actions of the DAR and the D. C. School Board were forgotten.

424
Folliard, Edward T. "Ickes Introduces Contralto at Lincoln
    Memorial; Many Officials Attend Concert." The Washington
    Post. 10 April, 1939.

Interior Secretary Ickes introduced Marian Anderson and
said it was wonderful she came to sing. Crowds gathered
early for the performance and Miss Anderson's mother and
two of her sisters were among those present.

425
Folliard, Edward T. "To Sing Encore of 1939 Concert." The
    Washington Post. 28 August, 1963.

Reprint of Mr. Folliard's April 10, 1939 story on Marian
Anderson's concert at Lincoln Memorial.

426
" 'God Made No Distinction Of Race, Creed, Color' Ickes Tells
    Concert Audience." The Pittsburgh Courier. 15 April, 1939,
    pp. 13.

Cites the text of Harold Ickes speech when he introduced
Marian Anderson during her concert at Lincoln Memorial.

427
Gunn, Glenn D. "75,000 Pack Mall to Hear Famed Singer." The
    Washington Times Herald. 10 April, 1939.

The crowd gathered two hours early to hear Marian Anderson sing at Lincoln Memorial. Some 75,000 attended the open-
air concert.

428
"Happy Ending." <u>The Washington Post</u>. 10 April, 1939.

Notes the happy ending which resulted after Marian Anderson was banned from performing at either Constitution Hall
or Central High School. The open-air concert at Lincoln
Memorial was more of a triumph because many more were able to
hear her sing.

429
"Howard University Choir Joins Negro Contralto." <u>The Youngs-
town Vindicator</u>. 10 April, 1939.

The Howard University choir performed behind Marian Anderson when she sang at the Lincoln Memorial.

430
"Ickes Introduces Contralto At Lincoln Memorial; Many Officials Attend Concert." <u>The Washington Post</u>. 10 April, 1939.

After an ugly controversy over where Miss Anderson would
give her performance, she gave an open-air concert on
Easter Sunday at the Lincoln Memorial to a crowd of 75,000
people.

431
"Ickes Scores Bigotry At Open Air Concert Of Marian Anderson."
<u>The New York Age</u>. 15 April, 1939, pp. 1.

Secretary of Interior Harold Ickes spoke over a nation-
wide radio hookup and slashed out at the intolerence and
racial prejudice which was responsible for Marian Anderson
having to sing at Lincoln Memorial.

432
"In United States." <u>The Memphis Commercial Appeal</u>. 9 April,
1939.

In listing Easter Sunday activities throughout the U. S.,
mention was made of the Marian Anderson concert at Lincoln
Memorial.

433
"Justice Hughes Backs Anderson Concern." <u>The Washington Daily
News</u>. 3 April, 1939.

Supreme Justice and Mrs. Charles Hughes became the first
sponsors of the Marian Anderson open-air concert at Lincoln
Memorial.

434
Lautier, Louis. "Lincoln Memorial Perfect Setting For Marian's
Voice." <u>The Pittsburgh Courier</u>. 15 April, 1939, pp. 1, 4.

Lincoln Memorial was a fitting setting for the Easter concert of Miss Anderson. Standing before the Great Emancipator,
Miss Anderson gave the world a lesson in tolerance.

435
Lindley, Ernest K. "Anderson Footnotes." The Washington Post.
    12 April, 1939.

Notes that the Marian Anderson concert at Lincoln Memorial
was a moving experience and thanked Oscar Chapman, Assistant
Secretary of the Interior, for thinking of the idea.

436
Lindley, Ernest K. "Voice From The Temple." The Washington
    Post. 12 April, 1939.

Tells of the moving experience of seeing Marian Anderson
at Lincoln Memorial on Easter Sunday.

437
"Marian Anderson - And After." The Pittsburgh Courier. 8
    April, 1939, editorial page.

Marian Anderson was to sing at Lincoln Memorial on Easter
Sunday. Both the DAR and the D. C. School Board had refused
to allow her to sing in their facilities.

438
"Marian Anderson In The Nation's Capitol." The New York
    Times. 9 April, 1939, Sec. 10, pp. 7.

Miss Anderson was to sing today on the steps of the Lincoln Memorial with an estimated 75,000 in attendance and
many more being able to hear her on radio. Several dignitaries, some also sponsors of the concert, would be in
attendance. For the first time in history a grand piano
would be carried up the Lincoln Memorial steps for Miss
Anderson's accompanist.

439
"Marian Anderson Snub Dismays Press." The Norfolk Journal
    and Guide. 4 March, 1939, pp. 8.

Articles from the New York Herald Tribune and the Philadelphia Record are reprinted. Both papers stated that the
Marian Anderson/DAR/School Board controversy was a disgrace.

440
"Marian Anderson Soars To New Heights At Washington Con-
    cert." The New York Amsterdam News. 15 April, 1939, pp. 1.

Pictures Miss Anderson as she sang "America" on the steps
of the Lincoln Memorial.

441
Marian Anderson Songs to be Heard A Mile." The Washington
    Daily News. 4 April, 1939.

Amplifying equipment was set up to carry Miss Anderson's
voice nearly a mile when she appeared at Lincoln Memorial.

442
"Marian Anderson Stories Taboo To Press Services." The
    Norfolk Journal and Guide. 8 April, 1939, pp. 10.

The Marian Anderson Citizens Committee reported that the
Associated Press and the International News Service would
not print any press releases on the Marian Anderson case.
One service felt that international news was more important
and the other had not printed, nor wanted to print, any
releases relating to the controversy.

443
"Marian Anderson Thrilled 75,000 in D. C. Last April." The
    Philadelphia Tribune. 4 April, 1940.

As April 9, 1940 drew near, many recalled Miss Anderson's
spectacular performance at Lincoln Memorial on Easter Sunday,
April 9, 1939.

444
"Marian Anderson Thrills America." The Norfolk Journal and
    Guide. 15 April, 1939.

A crowd estimated at 75,000 heard Miss Anderson sing at
Lincoln Memorial on Easter Sunday, April 9, 1939.

445
"Marian Anderson To Sing at Lincoln Memorial." The Chicago
    News. 30 March, 1939.

Miss Anderson would sing at a free open-air concert on
Easter Sunday at Lincoln Memorial.

446
"Marian Anderson To Sing at Memorial on Easter Sunday." The
    Washington Star. 30 March, 1939.

Interior Secretary Harold Ickes gave permission for Miss
Anderson's Lincoln Memorial performance. The concert was to
be broadcast on radio.

447
"Marian Anderson To Sing At World's Fair; At Standstill In
    Capitol City Controversy." The Norfolk Journal and Guide.
    25 March, 1939, pp. 1, 10.

Miss Anderson was to appear in a series of concerts at the
New York World's Fair. It was noted that there was still no
break-through on the controversy between the D. C. School
Board and Howard University, sponsors of the Marian Anderson
Easter concert, on whether she could use the white Central
High School.

448
"Marian Anderson To Sing In Lincoln Memorial Park." The New
    York Age. 8 April, 1939, pp. 1.

Miss Anderson was to give a free concert at the Lincoln Memorial on Easter Sunday after being denied use of Constitution Hall.

449
"Marian Anderson Will Sing In Open Air As Rebuke To DAR." The Norfolk Journal and Guide. 4 March, 1939, pp. 1.

It was noted that Marian Anderson would keep her Easter Sunday concert date in Washington by giving a free, open-air concert at the Lincoln Memorial. There was nation-wide protests when both the DAR and the D. C. School Board refused to let her use their facilities.

450
"Marian Anderson Wins Tribute of 75,000 at Concert." The Washington Star. 10 April, 1939.

Many dignataries were among the 75,000 at the Lincoln Memorial to hear Miss Anderson's free open-air Easter concert.

451
"Miss Anderson Is Expected To Draw 70,000." The Washington Post. 9 April, 1939.

Marian Anderson was to sing at Lincoln Memorial, weather permitting, at 5 p.m. Judges, cabinet members, and congressional members were expected to be among the 70,000 attending.

452
"Miss Anderson Sings Again At Memorial Today." The Washington Star. 20 April, 1952.

Marian Anderson was to pay tribute at Lincoln Memorial to the man (former Secretary of Interior, Harold Ickes) who made it possible for her to sing there in 1939.

453
"Miss Anderson To Give Free Concert Here." The Washington Times. 25 February, 1939.

The National Park Service said they didn't think there would be any objections of Marian Anderson holding an open-air concert at Lincoln Memorial.

454
"Miss Anderson To Sing at Lincoln Memorial at 5 p.m. Today." The Washington Star. 9 April, 1939.

The Lincoln Memorial concert was calculated to focus attention on the denial of Constitution Hall and Central High School to allow Marian Anderson a concert date at either facility.

455
"Miss Anderson To Sing Before Lincoln Shrine." The New York
    Herald Tribune. 31 March, 1939.

Secretary of Interior, Harold Ickes, authorized a free
outdoor concert at Constitution Hall by Marian Anderson when
the D.A.R. and the D. C. School Board refusal to allow her
to use their auditoriums.

456
"Miss Anderson To Sing Today at Memorial." The Washington
    Herald Times. 9 April, 1939.

Marian Anderson was to sing at Lincoln Memorial at 5 p.m.
She would be introduced by Interior Secretary Ickes.

457
"Miss Anderson's Concert." The New York Times. 2 April, 1939,
    Sec. 4, pp. 2.

It was announced that Miss Anderson, whose voice has been
called "the rarest of the time," was to sing classic lieder
and spirituals during her Easter Sunday concert at Lincoln
Memorial.

458
"Mrs. Roosevelt Expected To Attend Anderson Concert." The
    Washington Star. 6 April, 1939.

Mrs. Roosevelt was trying to return from the West Coast
in time for Marian Anderson's Lincoln Memorial concert.

459
Murray, Florence. "Marian Anderson Thrills America." The
    Norfolk Journal and Guide. 15 April, 1939, pp. 1, 2.

The largest crowd since Lindberg's visit to Washington
was at Lincoln Memorial to hear Marian Anderson give her
free Easter Sunday concert. She was cheered by the vast
crowd with dignitaries and laymen all mingling together. A
list of some of the notables in attendance is given.

460
"Nation's Who's Who Heard Marian Anderson On Sun." The New
    York Amsterdam News. 15 April, 1939, pp. 5.

Several outstanding figures in the political, social, and
cultural circle were present at the Marian Anderson concert
at Lincoln Memorial. Mrs. Roosevelt, who was out of town,
sent a large bouquet of flowers. A list of the sponsors was
given.

461
"Notables Attend Anderson Recital." The Norfolk Journal and
    Guide. 15 April, 1939, pp. 10.

Pictures several of the notables attending the Marian Anderson concert at Lincoln Memorial.

462
"Noted Singer Introduced By Sec. Ickes." The Washington Times Herald. 10 April, 1939, pp. 4.

Secretary of Interior, Harold Ickes, introduced Marian Anderson before her Lincoln Memorial concert.

463
Pearson, Drew and Robert S. Allen. "Washington Daily Merry-Go-Round." The Washington Times Herald. 10 April, 1939.

Notes that some presidential candidates were sent letters encouraging them to sponsor Marian Anderson's Lincoln Memorial concert but none replied. Since her performance, Miss Anderson's concert fees have doubled and she was booked solid for two years in advance.

464
"Rocks and Mountains of Hate Fade As Marian Sings." The Pittsburgh Courier. 15 April, 1939, pp. 24.

When called back during her Easter concert at Lincoln Memorial, Marian Anderson said she was so overwhelmed by the tribute paid her that she could not describe the feeling of gratitude.

465
Rouzlau, Edgar T. " 'Greatest Voice' Thrills 75,000." The Pittsburgh Courier. 15 April, 1939, pp. 1, 4.

Miss Anderson sang at Lincoln Memorial on Easter Sunday among the cheers and tears of dignitaries and the layman. Her new role as Goodwill Ambassador was touching.

466
"Secretary Ickes Urges Equal Opportunity." The Norfolk Journal and Guide. 15 April, 1939, pp. 1.

Secretary of Interior's Harold Ickes introduction speech of Marian Anderson at the Lincoln Memorial hinted of "equality of opportunity " and freedom from prejudice and indifference. The text of the speech is included.

467
"75,000 Acclaim Miss Anderson; Easter Visitors Throng Capitol." The Washington Post. 10 April, 1939.

Picture of Miss Anderson in front of Lincoln Memorial for her Easter performance.

468
"75,000 Applaud Marian Anderson's Easter Concert." The Times Herald. 10 April, 1939.

Crowds gathered two hours early to hear Marian Anderson sing at Lincoln Memorial. This great controversy over where she would sing was well known. Many notables were in the audience.

469
"75,000 Hear Marian Anderson Sing at Memorial." The Washington Daily News. 10 April, 1939.

Picture of the people around the reflecting pool at Lincoln Memorial listening to Marian Anderson perform.

470
"She'll Sing At Easter." The New York Times. 2 April, 1939. Sec. 4, pp. 2.

Pictures Marian Anderson, Secretary of Interior Ickes, and the Lincoln Memorial where Miss Anderson was to give her Easter concert. Ickes had granted Miss Anderson permission to use the Memorial after both the D. C. School Board and the DAR refused to let her use their facilities.

471
"A Singer, A Serious Man, A Standard Bearer." in Washington Tapestry, by Olive E. Clapper. New York: McGraw Hill, 1946, 303p., pp. 209-214.

One section in this chapter tells of Marian Anderson's historic Lincoln Memorial concert. The D. C. School Board and the DAR would not let her use their facilities for the concert.

472
"Thousands Gathered At Mall To Hear Famed Contralto's Easter Recital." The Washington Times Herald. 10 April, 1939.

Picture of the 75,000 people who attended the Marian Anderson Lincoln Memorial concert on Easter Sunday, April 9th.

473
"Throng Honors Marian Anderson In Concert At Lincoln Memorial." The New York Times. 10 April, 1939, pp. 19.

An audience of about 75,000, half being Black, gathered in a semi circle at the foot of the Lincoln Memorial to hear Marian Anderson give her Easter concert. Secretary of Interior, Harold Ickes, introduced her and many dignitaries were present. The tradition of not allowing photographs taken from within the sanctum where the statue stands was broken during the confusion following the concert when Miss Anderson was almost mobbed.

474
" 'To Go Or Not To Go'." The Pittsburgh Courier. 15 April, 1939, pp. 4.

Among the large audience at Lincoln Memorial to hear
Marian Anderson give her Easter Sunday concert were three
U. S. Supreme Court justices, four cabinet members, and
twenty-eight congressmen. The question of whether to attend
or not was a hot political issue in the city.

475
"Traffic Plans for Anderson Recital Ready." The Washington
    Post. 9 April, 1939.

Interior Secretary Ickes issued traffic regulations for
the open-air Marian Anderson concert at Lincoln Memorial.

476
"Voice Casts Spell Over Hushed Throng." The Washington Times-
    Herald. 10 April, 1939, pp. 4.

Marian Anderson's superb voice cast a spell over the
estimated 75,000 in attendance at her Lincoln Memorial
concert.

477
"Yesterday in Negro History. Jet. Vol. 1, April 17, 1952,
    pp. 47.

Noted that Marian Anderson gave an Easter recital at
Lincoln Memorial before an audience of 75,000. The date was
incorrectly given as April 12, 1939.

WORLD'S
FAIR
RECITAL

478
"Contralto Captivates Crowd At World's Fair." The New York
    Amsterdam News. 3 June, 1939, pp. 12.

Pictures several of the people at the capacity crowd concert of Marian Anderson at the New York World's Fair.

479
"Marian Anderson Draws Record Crowd at 'Fair' Music Hall."
    The Tribune. 3 June, 1939.

Miss Anderson sang at the Hall of Music at the New York
World's Fair.

480
"Marian Anderson Heard At Fair." The New York Times.   29
    May, 1939, pp. 19.

Over two hundred had to be turned away as the 2,375 seat
Music Hall at the New York World's Fair was filled to hear
Miss Anderson. She sang works of Schubert, Sibelius, Bach
and Beethoven and a group of Negro spirituals.

481
"Marian Anderson To Sing At World's Fair On May 28th." The
    New York Amsterdam News. 27 May, 1939, pp. 3.

Miss Anderson was to sing in the Hall of Music at the New
York World's Fair.

482
"Miss Anderson Will Sing At World's Fair." The New York
    Amsterdam News.   25 March, 1939, pp. 11.

Miss Anderson was to sing at the New York World's Fair
as part of a musical festival. The date had not been set.

WHITE
HOUSE
APPEARANCE

483
"American Songs Are Played and Sung For King and Queen."
The New York Times. 9 June, 1939, pp. 5.

The King and Queen of England heard the songs of American
life during their visit to the White House. Marian Anderson
was one of those asked to sing. She did "Ave Maria," "My
Soul's Been Anchored In The Lord," and "Tramping."

484
"Anderson To Sing Before British King." The Norfolk Journal
and Guide. 27 May, 1939, pp. 1.

Marian Anderson was to sing before King George VI and
Queen Elizabeth of England when they visited the White House.
Over two hundred invitations had been sent out.

485
"England's King, Queen Greet Marian Anderson." The Chicago
Defender. 7 June, 1939.

Marian Anderson sang before the King and Queen of England
at a state dinner at the White House.

486
"Footnote On Prejudice." The Norfolk Journal and Guide.
27 May, 1939, pp. 8.

It was noted that only a few months ago Marian Anderson
was denied use of two facilities in Washington, D. C. Now
she has been invited to the White House to sing before the
King and Queen of England. She and Lawrence Tibbett were
to give samples of the finest in American music and vocal
art.

487
Gordon, Evelyn P. "Visiting King and Queen to Hear Marian
Anderson. The Washington News. 4 April, 1939.

Notes some of the high officials who were and were not present at Marian Anderson's Lincoln Memorial concert. Miss Anderson was to sing before the King and Queen of England the next summer when they visited the White House.

488
Henegan, L. Herbert. "Miss Anderson Says She Was 'Thrilled'." The Washington Tribune. 17 June, 1939.

Miss Anderson talked of her experience of singing before the King and Queen of England at the White House.

489
"King, Queen To Hear Miss Anderson Sing." The Pittsburgh Courier. 15 April, 1939, pp. 1.

Mrs. Roosevelt announced that Marian Anderson would probably sing before the King and Queen of England when they visited the White House.

490
"Marian Anderson Gets Royal Date." The New York Amsterdam News. 27 May, 1939, pp. 1.

Marian Anderson was to sing before the King and Queen of England at the White House on June 8th. It was to be her second appearance there since Roosevelt became president.

491
"Marian Anderson May Sing At White House." The Pittsburgh Courier. 18 March, 1939, pp. 1.

It was speculated that Miss Anderson may give a "command performance" before the King and Queen of England at the White House.

492
"Marian Anderson To Sing For Royalty." The New York Daily News. 23 May, 1939.

Miss Anderson was to perform at the White House before the King and Queen of England. She was to be part of the entertainment after the official state dinner.

493
"Marian Anderson Will Sing For Royalty at White House." The Washington Star. 22 May, 1939.

Miss Anderson was to sing before the King and Queen of Great Britain at the White House.

494
"Miss Anderson Sings For King and Queen." The Norfolk Journal and Guide. 17 June, 1939, pp. 1, 10.

The East Room of the White House was the setting for Marian Anderson's recital before the King and Queen of

England. She, along with the other artists, was presented
to the King and Queen after the musicale and was given
autographed photographs of President and Mrs. Roosevelt.

495
"Mrs. Roosevelt May Ask Marian Anderson To Sing For Royalty."
    The New York Amsterdam News. 15 April, 1939, pp. 17.

   Mrs. Roosevelt indicated that she would invite Marian
Anderson to sing at the White House before the King and
Queen of England.

496
"Singer, Snubbed By D.A.R., to Sing for and Meet Royalty."
    The Norfolk Journal and Guide. 3 June, 1939, pp. 1, 10.

   Miss Anderson was to sing before the King and Queen of
England at the White House. Also, according to custom,
she would be presented to the King and Queen at a reception.

497
"This Week in Negro History." Jet. Vol. 2, June 12, 1952,
    pp. 30.

   Noted that Marian Anderson sang for the King and Queen
of England at the White House on June 8, 1939.

MARIAN ANDERSON

MURAL

498
"Announce Contest to Commemorate Singer's Famous Easter
    Concert." The Washington Tribune. 12 October, 1940.

A prize of $1,700 was to be given to the artist selected
to do the mural commemorating Marian Anderson's Lincoln
Memorial concert on April 9, 1939. The Marian Anderson
Fund Committee requested the Section of Fine Arts of the
Interior Department to sponsor the competition.

499
"Art." The New York Times. 20 October, 1940, Sec. 4., pp. 2.

A national sketching contest was launched by the Federal
Works Agency for a mural to depict Marian Anderson's Lin-
coln Memorial concert. The mural was to be placed in the
Interior Deparment.

500
"Dedicate Mural To Singer's Concert at Lincoln Memorial."
    The Norfolk Journal & Guide. 16 January, 1943.

A mural done by Mitchell Jamieson commemorating Marian
Anderson's free concert on Easter Sunday, 1939 at Lincoln
Memorial, was unveiled at the Interior Department Auditorium.

501
"For Miss Anderson Honor." The New York Times. 19 April,
    1939, pp. 25.

Secretary of Interior, Harold Ickes, agreed to sponsor
a movement for the installation of a mural of Marian Anderson to be placed in the Interior Department Building. The
project was to be sponsored by public subscription. Edward
Bruce, chief of the fine arts section of the Treasury Department and chairman of the mural committee said that "honoring
the famous contralto is a further step in the cultural development of our colored people."

502
"Honor For Negro Singer." The New York Times. 15 October, 1940, pp. 28.

A bulletin from the Fine Arts Section of the Federal Works Agency announced that a national competition had begun for a design for a mural portraying Marian Anderson's Easter concert at Lincoln Memorial. The $1,700 mural would be paid by public subscription. Sketches for the competition were to be submitted by December 2.

503
"Ickes Accepts Mural of Marian Anderson's Easter Concert." The Washington Star. 7 January, 1943.

Interior Secretary Ickes said that Miss Anderson's "voice and personality have come to be a symbol of American unity," as he accepted the mural commemorating the Marian Anderson Lincoln Memorial concert on Easter Sunday 1939. She was also to appear at Constitution Hall.

504
"Marian Anderson Mural." The Washington Post. 10 January, 1943.

A mural commemorating Marian Anderson's Lincoln Memorial concert on Easter Sunday, 1939, was dedicated at the Interior Department. Mitchell Jamieson was the artist.

505
"Marian Anderson Mural Is Endorsed By First Lady." The Norfolk Journal and Guide. 3 June, 1939, pp. 3.

In her column, "My Day", Mrs. Roosevelt expressed approval of the drive to raise money for a mural commemorating Marian Anderson's Easter concert at Lincoln Memorial.

506
"Marian Anderson Mural Presented." The Washington Star. 7 January, 1943.

Picture of Miss Anderson and Charles Houston being greeted by Interior Secretary Ickes as he accepted the Marian Anderson mural.

507
"May Put Mural of Singer In Ickes Office." The New York Amsterdam News. 22 April, 1939, pp. 12.

Secretary of Interior, Harold Ickes, had agreed to sponsor a drive to install a mural of Marian Anderson's Lincoln Memorial concert in the Interior Department. The project was to be financed by public subscription.

508
"Miss Anderson Honored." The New York Times. 30 December, 1942, pp. 12.

On January 6th, Miss Anderson was to sing at a special
ceremony in the auditorium of the Interior Department. At
this ceremony there was to be a formal presentation to the
Government of a mural depicting Miss Anderson's Lincoln
Memorial concert on Easter Sunday, 1939.

509
"Mural of Marian Anderson is Presented To The Nation." The
    Washington Post. 7 January, 1942.

The Marian Anderson Citizens Committee presented a mural
commemorating Miss Anderson's Lincoln Memorial concert in
1939.

510
"Negroes give $400 For Mural." The New York Times. 9 February,
    1940, pp. 13.

Sanitation Commissioner, William F. Carey, received a
check for $400 from the Negro Benevolent Society in his
department as their contribution to the mural commemorating
Marian Anderson's Easter concert at Lincoln Memorial.

511
"Plan Mural of Miss Anderson In Recital." The Norfolk Journal
    and Guide. 6 May, 1939, pp. 1, 10.

The Marian Anderson Citizen's Committee opened a fund
drive for a mural depicting Marian Anderson's Easter concert
at Lincoln Memorial. The project was undertaken because the
concert was a significant occasion in Black national development. The mural was to be hung at the Interior Department.

512
"Site Assured for Anderson Mural Here." The Washington Herald
    Times. 14 May, 1939.

Secretary of Interior Ickes assured that a place would be
available in the Interior Department for a Marian Anderson
mural commemorating her famous Lincoln Memorial concert.

WAR

YEARS

ACTIVITIES

War Bond Rally And Concert

513
"Anderson Recital To Sell Bonds." The New York Times. 8
    December, 1944, pp. 27.

A special war bond recital was to be given by Marian Anderson at Carnegie Hall on December 18th. Admission to the recital was to be by purchase of war bonds from $25 to $1,000.
War bonds were to go on sale at McCreery store at a special
Marian Anderson War Bond Concert booth.

514
"Conductor and Soloists of The Week At Lewisohn Auditorium."
    The New York Times. 12 July, 1942, Sec. 8, pp. 5.

Marian Anderson was pictured as one of the soloists who
was to appear at the Lewisohn Auditorium.

515
"Marian Anderson To Sing." The New York Times. 31 May, 1942,
    pp. 25.

Marian Anderson and Paul Robeson were to sing at a free
interracial war bond rally at the Lewisohn Auditorium. The
rally was being held on behalf of the Treasury Department
to dramatize the war bond appeal to all races.

516
"More Bond Buying Urged By Gen. Lear." The New York Times.
    18 December, 1944, pp. 13.

Although the 6th War Loan Campaign had closed, people
were urged to continue to buy bonds. An audience of 2,860
people who had purchased $1,529,000 of E F and C bonds
would hear Marian Anderson in concert at Carnegie Hall.

517
"Sales of E Bonds Show An Increase." The New York Times. 13
    December, 1944, pp. 9.

It was announced that war bond sales were going well.   The
Marian Anderson War Bond concert at Carnegie Hall had sold
out all $25, $50, and $100 tickets.   Some $500 and $1,000
tickets were still available.

518
"Sing For $1,679,000." The New York Times. 19 December, 1944,
    pp. 19.

The Marian Anderson War Bond concert at Carnegie Hall
brought in over $1,679,000. Miss Anderson thanked the
audience for their contributions. She sang selections of
several composers including Handel, Scurlatti, Haydn, Schubert, Williams, and Griffes, closing with Negro spirituals.

519
"Stettinius Urges More Bond Buying." The New York Times.   11
    December, 1944, pp. 14.

Secretary of State, Edward R. Stettinius, urged people
to over subscribe in the 6th War Bond drive. As part of
the many activities planned to promote war bond sales,
Marian Anderson was to appear in a concert at Carnegie Hall
with war bond buyers receiving tickets.

War Bond Painting

520
"Marian Anderson." PM 21 May, 1945.

A painting of Miss Anderson done by Paul Meltsner was one
of eight given to the Treasury Department to aid the war
bond drive. The picture sold for $200,000 in bonds and was
presented to Howard University.

521
"Marian Anderson Painting Given School." The Baltimore Even-
    ing Sun. 8 May, 1945.

An unidentified purchaser bought the picture of Marian
Anderson done by Paul Meltsner to aid in war bond sales. He
then donated the picture to Howard University.

522
"Value of Art in America." The Sparta (Ga.) Ishmaelite. 26
    July, 1945.

A painting of Marian Anderson done to aid the war bond
effort, was purchased for $2,000,000 and presented to
Howard University.

War Relief Concert

523
"Bid Accepted." The New York Times. 11 October, 1942, pp. 2.

The DAR accepted Miss Anderson's request to sing at
Constitution Hall by asking her to a war relief recital.
Miss Anderson accepted and gave thirty-three open dates
providing that there would be no audience segregation and
that the hall would be open to her for future dates.

524
"D.A.R. Bid Accepted By Miss Anderson." The New York Times.
6 October, 1942, pp. 19.

A letter was sent to the DAR accepting their invitation
for Miss Anderson to sing at Constitution Hall. It was
specified that there would be no audience segregation and
that her apperance be a precedent for future dates in her
annual tours. The letter also specified that the concert
benefit the Army Emergency Relief Fund.

525
"D.A.R. Calls off Marian Anderson Concert; Invitation Not
'Accepted As Extended'." The New York Times. 5 November,
1942, pp. 27.

A letter was sent to Marian Anderson's manager stating
that the DAR would not comply with her provisions for singing at the war relief recital. The DAR specified that an
appearance at the hall could not set a precedent for future
appearances.

526
"D.A.R. Invites Marian Anderson to Sing in Constitution Hall."
The Washington Star. 29 September, 1942.

The D.A.R. invited Miss Anderson to appear at the first
of a series of war relief benefit concerts at Constitution
Hall. This was a reversal of its refusal to permit her
to use the hall for an Easter Sunday concert in 1939.

527
"D.A.R. Now Invites Marian Anderson." The New York Times.
30 September, 1942, pp. 25.

Banned from appearing at Constitution Hall in 1939, the
DAR asked Miss Anderson to appear at the first in a series
of war aid concerts.

528
"DAR's Bid Accepted By Marian Anderson With Reservations."
The Washington Star. 6 October, 1942.

Miss Anderson accepted the invitation of the DAR to
sing at Constitution Hall under the condition that there
be no segregation in seating arrangements.

529
"Manager Assails D.A.R. Stand." The New York Times. 5 November, 1942, pp. 27.

Sol Hurok gave this statement about the withdrawal of the DAR invitation for Marian Anderson to sing for a war relief concert: "the DAR has not become one bit wiser since it was taught a lesson by public opinion on Easter Sunday in 1939."

530
"Marian Anderson Accepts D.A.R. Bid To Sing, Waiving Dispute In Order To Aid Army Fund." The New York Times. 7 November, 1942, pp. 17.

Miss Anderson accepted the invitation to sing at Constitution Hall dropping her dispute over whether her apperance would set a precedent for future dates there. According to her manager, "Miss Anderson feels that the Army should not be deprived of the financial income which would result from her singing at Constitution Hall." Since the DAR had not replied to the other issue of un-segregated audiences, Miss Anderson was of the opinion that there would be no barrier.

531
"Marian Anderson To Sing in D.A.R. Hall." Christian Century. Vol. 59, October 14, 1942, pp. 1245.

Miss Anderson was to sing at the D.A.R.'s first war relief concert. Also notes that she was to christen the cargo vessel Booker T. Washington.

532
"Miss Anderson's Return." The Washington Post. 17 December, 1942.

Miss Anderson was to appear at Constitution Hall which four years earlier had refused to let her perform. There was also to be no segregation of races at the performance.

HAROLD ICKES

MEMORIAL SERVICE

533
"Anderson To Sing At Memorial." The Washington Post. 5
    April, 1952.

Lincoln Memorial was to be the site of the Harold Ickes
Memorial Service. Miss Anderson was to sing. It was at
this same memorial that Miss Anderson sang in 1939 after
she was refused at Constitution Hall and Central High School.
Mr. Ickes had been responsible for her performance.

534
Edstrom, Eve. "Marian Anderson's Singing Thrills 10,000
    at Ickes Rites." The Washington Post. 21 April, 1952.

10,000 heard Miss Anderson at the memorial service for
former Interior Secretary, Harold Ickes, at Lincoln Memorial.

535
Gunn, Glenn D. "10,000 Honor Harold Ickes, Miss Anderson."
    The Washington Times Herald. 21 April, 1952.

In her 2nd Lincoln Memorial concert in 13 years, Marian
Anderson sang at the memorial service for the late former
Secretary of Interior, Harold Ickes. Mr. Ickes had made it
possible for her to sing at the Lincoln Memorial in 1939.

536
"10,000 at Memorial To Harold Ickes Hear Marian Ander-
    son Sing." The Washington Star. 21 April, 1952, pp. A-3.

At the Harold L. Ickes Memorial Service, Miss Anderson
sang some of the same songs she sang on Easter Sunday, 1939.
Mr. Ickes had granted Miss Anderson permission to sing at
Lincoln Memorial when Constitution Hall and Central High
School both refused her.

METROPOLITAN
OPERA
DEBUT

537
"Absent Friend." <u>Musical America</u>. Vol. 75, January 15, 1955, pp. 9.

Notes Marian Anderson's debut at the Metropolitan Opera. She had won the extraordinary victories over prejudices.

538
"Anderson 'Ball' Hottest Ticket." <u>Variety</u>. Vol. 197, December 29, 1954, pp. 52.

The announcement that Marian Anderson would appear at the Metropolitan Opera caused a scramble for tickets.

539
"Anderson Starts 'Met' Rehearsals." <u>The New York Times</u>. 25 December, 1954, pp. 6.

Pictures Miss Anderson rehearsing for her role in the Metropolitan Opera House production of "Masked Ball." At her first rehearsal she looked confident as she eyed the vocal score, humming phrases to herself. After a photograph session, everyone settled into their parts.

540
"Anderson To Sing at Met." <u>Scholastic</u>. Vol. 65, October 20, 1954, pp. 19.

Marian Anderson was to make her debut in January at the Metropolitan Opera in Verdi's <u>Masked Ball</u>.

541
"A Barrier Is Broken." <u>Musical America</u>. Vol. 74, November 1, 1954, pp. 4.

The Metropolitan Opera broke a long tradition and signed Marian Anderson to sing there. The article noted that it was time for the leading American opera house to open its doors to Black artists.

542
Bronson, Arthur. "Marian Anderson's Sock Met Debut In Histo-
     ric 'Ball' Seen As Trailblazer." Variety. Vol. 197, Jan-
     uary 12, 1955, pp. 72.

Review of Miss Anderson's Metropolitan Opera debut and
how she has paved the way for other Blacks to perform there.

543
"Critics Hail Miss Anderson's Debut With the Met Opera." The
     Washington Daily News. 8 January, 1955.

Marian Anderson was hailed as a new star for her dramatic
operatic debut at the Met. She received such an ovation that
the music was stopped. There was also an outburst of loud
applause after the act.

544
"Debut." Time. Vol. 65, January 17, 1955, pp. 68.

Notes the debut of Marian Anderson at the Metropolitan
Opera. Seats were sold-out weeks in advance. She played
her role with dignity and reserve. Critics felt her debut
was fifteen years overdue. She received eight curtain calls.
Her mother was seated in Box #35 to hear her daughter sing.

545
"A Door Opens: Marian Anderson Engaged For The Metropolitan."
     Olin Downes On Music: A Selection From His Writings During
     The Half-Century, 1906-1955, edited by Irene Downes. New
     York: Simon & Schuster, 1957, 273p., pp. 428-430.

Notes that Miss Anderson's engagement at the Metropolitan
was at least 15 years late and was a tardy tribute to her
rank and achievement as an artist of international fame.
Her engagement paved the way for other Black artists.

546
Downes, Olin. "Marian Anderson's Engagement By 'Met' Should
     Help Other Negro Singers." The New York Times. 17 October,
     1954, Sec. 2, pp. 7.

It was noted that Miss Anderson's appearance at the 'Met'
would open the way for her to sing dramatic music. There
are many Black singers who would enrich Metropolitan Opera
casts and Miss Anderson has paved the way for other artists
to sing there.

547
Downes, Olin. "Miss Anderson Sings With A Rich Voice." The
     New York Times. 8 January, 1955, pp. 11.

Miss Anderson's part as Ulrica in the "Masked Ball" is a
highly dramatic part requiring a dramatic personality and
sumptuous singing. At first her voice wavered a bit but as

she sang, her voice gained in sonority and concentrated resonance.

548
Downes, Olin. "Opera: 'Masked Ball'." The New York Times. 8 January, 1955.

Review of Verdi's Masked Ball in which Marian Anderson made her Metropolitan Opera debut. Although there was some unevenness in her voice, it was felt that she would improve with experience. She received a tremendous applause and was called back several times.

549
Eyer, Ronald. "Anderson Debut in Masked Ball Makes Metropolitan History." Musican America. Vol. 75, January 15, 1955, pp. 3, 12.

The Metropolitan Opera presented the first Black ever to sing with the Met in their 71 year existance. Marian Anderson made her debut on January 7th as Ulrica in Verdi's Un Ballo In Maschera. Her contribution to the exacting quintet was noted as was the deep penetration of the text.

550
"Here and There." Musical Courier. Vol. 150, November 1, 1954, pp. 36.

It was noted that the engagement of Marian Anderson to sing at the Metropolitan Opera House was good but it should have been done when she first returned from Europe during the 1930's.

551
Hornaday, Mary. "Historic Metropolitan First." The Christian Science Monitor. 8 January, 1955.

Marian Anderson became the first Black to sing at the Met. It was a joyous occasion for all of her race, although music critics took her performance in stride.

552
Hume, Paul. "Miss Anderson Fells A Barrier." The Washington Post. 24 October, 1954.

Marian Anderson was to make her debut at the Metropolitan Opera. She would be the first Black to sing there.

553
Kolodin, Irving. "Miss Anderson Makes History." The Saturday Review. Vol. 38, January 22, 1955, pp. 46.

Marian Anderson made history as she made her debut January 7, 1955 at the Metropolitan Opera. Mr. Kolodin felt that her portrayal of Ulrica in Verdi's Masked Ball was the best version heard at the Met recently. Her bearing was imposing and her sense of relationship to the other dramatic elements sure and sound.

554
"Marian Anderson at the Metropolitan." The Christian Science
    Monitor. 15 January, 1955.

On January 7th Miss Anderson made her debut at the Metropolitan Opera. She appeared repeatedly with other cast
members in response to prolonged applause at the close. An
ovation had greeted her on the rise of the curtain and her
voice wavered tremendously.

555
"Marian Anderson Makes Debut at Met Tonight." The Washington
    Post. 7 January, 1955.

Miss Anderson was to become the first Black to sing in a
leading role with the Metropolitan Opera. She would portray
the fortune teller in Verdi's Masked Ball.

556
"Marian Anderson Signed for Role at Metropolitan Opera." The
    Washington Star. 8 October, 1954.

Metropolitan Opera manager, Rudolph Bing, announced that
Miss Anderson had been signed to sing at the Met in early
January.

557
"Marian Anderson signs for Opera Role With Met." Jet. Vol.
    6, October 21, 1954, pp. 58.

Miss Anderson was the first black to sing with the Metropolitan Opera.

558
"Marian Anderson To Sing Ulrica At Metropolitan." Musical
    America. Vol. 74, November 1, 1954, pp. 8.

Miss Anderson was to make her debut at the Metropolitan
Opera in its opening season performance of Un Ballo in
Maschera.

559
"The Metropolitan." in Black Magic: A Pictorial History Of
    The Negro In American Entertainment, by Langston Hughes
    and Milton Meltzer. New Jersey: Prentice-Hall, 1967,
    375p., pp. 148-150.

Pictures Marian Anderson taking a curtain call after her
Metropolitan Opera debut. She was also shown with the Metropolitan director, Rudolf Bing. She had broken the color
ban at the Met and a new day in American integration had
begun.

560
"Miss Anderson 'Stops Music' in Tremendous Met Debut." The
    Washington Star. 8 January, 1955.

Miss Anderson received a tremendous ovation as she made
her debut at the Met. She was the first black to ever sing
there.

561
"Miss Anderson To The 'Met'." The New York Times. 9 October,
    1954, pp. 16.

This editorial congratulated Miss Anderson upon her contract to sing with the Metropolitan Opera. It was felt that
she has given splendid dignity to her every performance and
her presence would enlarge the Metropolitan Opera.

562
"Miss Anderson's Witchcraft." Opera News. Vol. 20, December
    5, 1955, pp. 15.

Miss Anderson returned to the Met as Ulrica in A Masked
Ball. She admitted that she had not yet made the role completely her own. She said opera was still new to her and she
had to absorb and project the role further.

563
"Negro Singer To Appear in Role at Met." The Washington Post.
    8 October, 1954.

The Metropolitan Opera signed Marian Anderson to sing there
this winter. She would play the role of Ulrica in The Masked
Ball.

564
"Now One Is Speechless." Time. Vol. 64, October 18, 1954,
    pp. 87.

Marian Anderson was signed to play the role of Ulrica in
Verdi's Masked Ball. When she was asked how she felt, she
said, "now one is speechless."

565
"Opera Dream Fulfilled." The New York Times. 13 January,
    1955, pp. 31.

Miss Anderson played the role of Ulrica in the "Masked
Ball" at the Philadelphia Academy of Music. She had played
the same role on January 7th when she made her debut with
the Metropolitan Opera. At a reception in her honor, Miss
Anderson said she had always dreamed of singing with the Met.
It was last October when she learned that she would sing with
the Met and she had enjoyed the experience.

566
"Opera's Gain." Newsweek. Vol. 44, October 18, 1954, pp. 96.

The Metropolitan Opera signed Marian Anderson to appear
as Ulrica in Verdi's Masked Ball.

567
Sargeant, Wintrop. "Musical Events; Anderson At The Met."
New Yorker. Vol. 30, January 15, 1955, pp. 94.

In noting Miss Anderson's debut at the Met, Sargeant felt
it was long overdue. The audience applauded for the principal of the event and not for the artistic contribution. Her
performance was timid and lacking in authority.

568
"Stranger At The Met." Newsweek. Vol. 45, January 17, 1955,
    pp. 50.

Marian Anderson made her debut at the Metropolitan Opera
playing Ulrica in Verdi's Masked Ball. In her role, she
moved little and let her expressive face act for her. She
received standing ovations before and after her performance.

569
Taubman, Howard. "Marian Anderson Signed To Sing At The
    Metropolitan This Season." The New York Times. 8 October,
    1954, pp. 1, 25.

Rudolf Bing, general manager of the Metropolitan Opera
House, announced that Marian Anderson would sing with the
company in the upcoming "Masked Ball." He had suggested
the idea to Miss Anderson at a supper party and she was
delighted. After rehearsing the score with conductor,
Dimitri Mitropoulos, she accepted the offer. She would be
the first Black to sing with the company.

570
Taubman, Howard. "Marian Anderson Wins Ovation In First Opera
    Role At The 'Met'." The New York Times. 8 January, 1955,
    pp. 1, 11.

The impossible childhood dream came true for Marian Anderson as she made her Metropolitan Opera debut on January
7th. She had to return several times with the other cast
to take their bows. When asked if she were ready to do a
second operatic role, Miss Anderson replied, "first, I must
learn to sing this one better." There was a small dinner
party after the performance at St. Regis.

571
"Triumph At The Met." The New York Times. 9 January, 1955,
    Sec. 4, pp. 8.

Miss Anderson's debut at the 'Met' was not only a triumph
for her but for the world of fine arts. She had broken another barrier of unthinking prejudice and her art has received the special accolade it deserves.

572
"Triumph At The Metropolitan." *America*. Vol. 92, January 22, 1955, pp. 416.

Miss Anderson made her debut at the Metropolitan with her accustomed sense of deep religious conviction and modesty.

573
" 'Un Ballo In Maschera'." *Musical Courier*. Vol. 151, January 15, 1955, pp. 15-16.

Verdi's "Masked Ball" returned to the Metropolitan Opera House after an absence of several seasons. It also marked Marian Anderson's first appearance at the Met. It was noted that she should have appeared there twenty years sooner when she was at the pennacle of her career.

574
"Un Ballo In Maschera With Marian Anderson: 'A Thunderous Ovation From The Whole House'," in *Olin Downes On Music*: Selections From His Writings During *The Half-Century, 1906-1955*, edited by Irene Downes. New York: Simon & Schuster, 1957, 473p., pp. 432-434.

Marian Anderson made history and fulfilled a childhood dream as she became the first Black to sing at the Metropolitan Opera. By her native sensibility, intelligence and vocal art, Miss Anderson stamped herself in the memory and lasting esteem of those who had the privilege to hear her.

575
White, Al. "Marian Smiles and the World Changes." *The Pittsburgh Courier*. 8 January, 1955.

Miss Anderson was in New York rehearsing for her January 7th debut with the Metropolitan Opera.

576
"Wild Ovation Given Marian Anderson." *The Washington Post*. 8 January, 1955.

Miss Anderson fulfilled a childhood dream when she appeared at the Metropolitan Opera.

577
"Yesterday in Negro History." *Jet*. Vol. 25, January 9, 1964, pp. 11.

On January 7, 1955, Miss Anderson made her debut at the Metropolitan Opera. She was the first Negro singer signed by the company.

BOOK
REVIEWS

578
Biancolli, Louis. "Marian Anderson's Story." The New York
    Telegram. 8 December, 1956, pp. 9.

Review of Miss Anderson's autobiography.

579
Epstein, Dena J. "Briefly Noted." Notes. Vol. 14, March,
    1957, pp. 267.

Book review of Marian Anderson's autobiography. She wrote
in a sober, pleasant style and emerged as modest, reserved,
and devoted to her music and loyal to her people.

580
Friedberg, Gertrude. "Books For The Music Minded." Music
    Clubs Magazine. Vol. 36, November, 1956, pp. 18-19.

Book review of Marian Anderson's autobiography. Simply
and modestly, she tells the trivia of a traveling artist and
the rebuffs because of her race.

581
Hume, Paul. "Marian Anderson Tells A Story Full Of Hope."
    The Washington Post. 28 October, 1956.

Review of the autobiography of Miss Anderson, My Lord What
A Morning.

582
Hutchens, John K. "Book Review." The New York Herald-Tribune.
    25 October, 1956.

Review of Miss Anderson's autobiography.

583
"Marian Anderson Tells Her Story." Musical America. Vol. 76,
    December 1, 1956, pp. 28.

Book review of Miss Anderson's autobiography, <u>My Lord,</u>
<u>What A Morning</u>.

584
"The Musician's Bookshelf." <u>The Musical Times</u>. Vol. 99,
   February, 1958, pp. 83.

Book review of Miss Anderson's autobiography. It was
noted that she did not discuss the problem of her art, but
instead, engaged in naive chattiness.

585
North, Sterling. "Marian Anderson: Poverty and Race No Bar
   To Nobility." <u>The New York World Telegram</u>. 25 October,
   1956.

Book review of Miss Anderson's autobiography. Notes her
perceptive insight on life.

586
Peterson, Melva. "Books." <u>Pan Pipes of Sigma Alpha Iota</u>.
   Vol. 50, January, 1958, pp. 31, 32.

Book review of Marian Anderson's autobiography.

587
Poore, Charles. "Books of The Time." <u>The New York Times</u>.
   25 October, 1956, pp. 31.

Book review of Marian Anderson's autobiography, <u>My Lord,</u>
<u>What A Morning</u>. She goes into detail about her tours, family
life in rural Connecticut and her favorite hobbies.

588
Schonberg, Harold C. "Book Reviews." <u>Musical Courier</u>. Vol.
   154, December 1, 1956, pp. 39.

Reviews Marian Anderson's autobiography, <u>My Lord, What A</u>
<u>Morning</u>. The dignity in her own life is carried over in
her book. Without rancor, she tells of her struggles,
encounters with race prejudice and gives her musical philosophy.

589
Schubart, Mark. "The Heart Must Be Happy." <u>The New York</u>
   <u>Times Book Review</u>. 11 November, 1956.

Review of the Marian Anderson autobiography, <u>My Lord</u>
<u>What A Morning</u>.

590
Van Vechten, Carl. "Soft Voices of Feeling." <u>Saturday Review</u>.
   Vol. 39, November 3, 1956, pp. 22.

Book review of Miss Anderson's autobiography. Notes that
her manner is modest and unassuming.

"THE LADY FROM
PHILADELPHIA"

591
"Bigger Audience." Newsweek. Vol. 51, January 20, 1958, pp.
46.

The telecast of "The Lady From Philadelphia" on See It Now
has won acclaim throughout the country. The State Department
ordered 120 prints of the telecast to distribute in 79 countries with USIA posts. It was the first time any television
show had been so honored.

592
Gould, Jack. "TV's Singing Ambassador." The New York Times.
31 December, 1957, pp. 35.

Miss Anderson's Asian tour was televised on See It Now.
The reception accorded her in each country left no doubt of
her success as a cultural ambassador.

593
Hughes, Allen. "Something Eternal." Musical America. Vol.
79, February, 1959, pp. 13, 34, 212.

Notes Miss Anderson's trip to the Far East which was seen
on See It Now. Also notes one incident at the UN General
Assembly on the disposition of petitions submitted by the
British and French Cameroons. She was criticized as un-
feeling of the African Nations. Hughes felt that Miss Anderson reminded people that something is "eternal" good and
worth believing in.

594
"Lady From Philadelphia." Ebony. Vol. 13, March, 1958, pp.
31-32, 34, 36.

Miss Anderson's eleven week tour of the Far East was telecast by See It Now. She sang and acted as a spokesperson
with her eloquent speeches.

595
"Lady From Philadelphia." The Washington Post. 1 January
    1958.

Editorial on Edward R. Murrow's documentary on Marian
Anderson's tour of Viet Nam, the Philippines, Bruma, and
other countries.

596
Laurent, Lawrence. "Marian Anderson Tour Is a TV Treat
    Tonight." The Washington Post. 30 December, 1957.

See It Now planned a tv program on Miss Anderson, entitled
The Lady From Philadelphia. The program showed her on tour in
Korea, the Philippines, Viet-nam, Burma, India and Thailand.

597
"Marian Anderson's ANTA Global Tour As "See It Now" Seg."
    Variety. Vol. 207, August 28, 1957, pp. 23.

Miss Anderson was to go on tour around the world in
behalf of the State Department and the American National
Theater and Academy. Her trip was to be televised on See
It Now.

598
"Marian Wins Top TV Award." The Philadelphia Tribune. 18
    April, 1959.

The television program Lady From Philadelphia broadcast
on See It Now won the American Film Festival honors as best
film on international relations.

599
"Members In Distinguished Roles: Marian Anderson, A Great
    Ambassador." Pan Pipes of Sigma Alpha Iota. Vol. 50,
    March, 1958, pp. 6-7, 47.

Talks about the famous "Lady From Philadelphia" which was
seen on See It Now.

600
"Philadelphia Lady." Musical America. Vol. 78, January 15,
    1958, pp. 18.

Notes Miss Anderson's tour of the Far East. She traveled
over 40,000 miles into 12 countries. She sang for troops in
Korea, at the Gandhi Memorial shrine in India, with the Bombay Symphony. She was often asked about the racial tensions
in the U. S. The trip was filmed for See It Now.

601
"Secret Weapon." Newsweek. Vol. 50, December 30, 1957, pp.
    63-64.

While on her tour of the Far East, Marian Anderson was
asked several times about the racial problems in Little Rock,

Arkansas. Her comments were heard on the See It Now presentation of "Lady From Philadelphia." Gen. Alfred Gruenther stated that the U. S. needed more Marian Anderson's and called her our "secret weapon."

602
"See It Now." The New York Times. 29 December, 1957. Sec. 2, pp. 11.

Edward R. Murrow and Marian Anderson prepared for the telecast of Miss Anderson's tour of seven Asian countries.

603
Shanley, J. P. "Singing Diplomat." The New York Times. 29 December, 1957, pp. X-11.

Marian Anderson's concert tour of Asia was to be televised on See It Now. She was often asked about the racial violence in Little Rock, Arkansas which was happeining while she was on tour.

604
Shayon, Robert Lewis. "Lady From Philadelphia." The Saturday Review. Vol. 41, January 18, 1958, pp. 57.

Miss Anderson's tour of the Far East was a propaganda trip used to show off the virtues of the United States. Her trip was "a cry for freedom, a national anthem, a morality lesson and a Christian hymn." In the television program one could see the overtones of the diffusion, challenge and potentials of unique civilizations.

605
"To Telecast Far East Tour of Miss Anderson." The Afro American. 26 November, 1957.

CBS announced plans to telecast the Far East tour of Marian Anderson on December 30th.

606
"Voice for America." The Washington Post. 3 January, 1958.

Letters to the editors complimenting CBS and Edward R. Murrow for the program on Marian Anderson.

UNITED

NATIONS

DELEGATE

607
Barron, John. "Miss Anderson Praises U. N. As Bulwark." The
    Washington Star. 24 October, 1958.

Speaking at the Shoreham Hotel, Marian Anderson said she
found the U. N. to be a bulwark against fear.

608
"Brief Review of The Progress of Trust Territories." U. S.
    Department of State Bulletin. Vol. 39, December 22, 1958,
    pp. 1027-1030.

Statement by Marian Anderson, U. N. delegate, on the progress of those involved in talks on trust territories. Notes
the work being done in Togoland, the Cameroons, Tanganyika,
and Ruanda-Urundi, and the Pacific Trust Territories.

609
"Briefing." The New York Times. 17 September, 1958, pp. 12.

Pictures Secretary of State, John Foster Dulles, as he
discusses procedures with some members of the U. S. delegation to the U. N.

610
"Diplomat Role For Marian Anderson, U. N. Delegate." Pan
    Pipes of Sigma Alpha Iota. Vol. 51, March, 1959, pp. 4.

Notes the appointment of Marian Anderson as U. N. delegate. She would return to concert work after the session
ended in January, 1959.

611
"Dulles and Distaff Delegates." The Washington Post. 19
    September, 1958.

Secretary of State, John Foster Dulles, greeted two U. S.
women delegates to the U. N. They were Mrs. Oswald B. Lord

and Miss Marian Anderson.

612
"Famed Singer Named With 6 To U. N. Post." The New York
Daily News. 24 July, 1958, pp. 44.

President Eisenhower named six to be delegates to the
United Nations. Marian Anderson was one of those chosen.

613
"Future of Togoland: Statement, November 14, 1958." U. S.
Department of State Bulletin. Vol. 39, December 29, 1958,
pp. 1073-1074.

In this statement, Marian Anderson, U. N. delegate, noted
that her committee would support any resolution to end trusteeship and accession of Togoland to independence.

614
Hemming, Roy. "Voice of The Century at The U. N." Senior
Scholastic. Vol. 73, October 31, 1958, pp. 16.

President Eisenhower named Marian Anderson as an Alternate Delegate to the United Nations for 1958-1959. She
was to combine her singing career and her duties at the
U. N. Her personal motto is "do not let hate or fear re-
strict you from being a big person."

615
Hornaday, Mary. "Emerging Africans Stirred." The Christian
Science Monitor. 28 November, 1958.

Marian Anderson became a heroine to Africans with her
personal intervention to speed UN delivery of statehood
to the British and French Cameroons.

616
James, Michael. "Marian Anderson Dissents at U. N." The New
York Times. 26 November, 1958, pp. 1.

Miss Anderson said the U. S. opposed a special session
of the U. N. General Assembly to discuss problems of the
Cameroons, but indicated that she disagreed with this position. Many delegates took Miss Anderson to task for making
the statement.

617
"Marian Anderson Appointment." The New York Times. 19 August,
1958, pp. 26.

This letter to the editor congratulated President Eisenhower on his appointment of Marian Anderson as U. N. delegate. The letter noted that she is a Christian with a
"deep sense of humility and a firm belief in the universal
brotherhood of man."

618
"Marian Anderson Named By Ike." The New York Mirror. 24
    July, 1958, pp. 27.

Miss Anderson was named as a delegate to the United
Nations General Assembly by President Eisenhower.

619
"Marian Anderson New Delegate to UN." Musical Courier. Vol.
    158, October, 1958, pp. 5.

On September 16, Marian Anderson began a new role as
alternate delegate to the United Nations. She was assigned
to the Trusteeship Committee which was concerned with the
welfare of the inhabitants of territories under trusteeship
to the UN.

620
"Marian Anderson To Be U.N. Delegate." The New York Times.
    24 July, 1958, pp. 4.

President Eisenhower named Marian Anderson as one of
seven new members of the U. S. delegation to the 13th session
of the U. N. General Assembly.

621
"Marian Anderson: U. S. Alternate Delegate, United Nations -
    1958-1959," in Negroes In Public Affairs and Government,
    Vol. 1, edited by Walter Christmas. New York: M. W.
    Lads, 1966, 352p., pp. 46-49.

When the 13th session of the United Nations convened in
September, 1958, Marian Anderson was on the Human Rights
Committee. She had been named one of the alternate delegates by President Eisenhower. Highlights her Lincoln Memorial concert, her Far East tour, and her many honors, including the Presidential Freedom Medal. In 1964, she became the only living American Black to have a rose named
for her. "The Marian Anderson Rose," a cherry-red grandi-
flora, was developed by Dr. Walter Lemmerts. Lists the
many other accomplishments of this great contralto and
humanitarian.

622
"Marian Anderson's New Role." The New York Times. 25 July,
    1958, pp. 18.

This editorial noted with pride the appointment of Marian
Anderson as a delegate to the U. N. She has shown that she
knows how to speak the language of our common humanity with
a singular eloquence.

623
"Miss Anderson Named U. S. Delegate To U. N." The Washington
    Star. 24 July, 1958.

Marian Anderson was named by President Eisenhower as a
member of the American delegation to the U. N. General
Assembly.

624
"Miss Anderson Resolves U. N. 'Teapot Tempest'." The Washing-
    ton Post. 27 November, 1958.

As a U. N. delegate, Marian Anderson resolved a controversy on the approval of a compromise resolution on the
British and French Cameroons. The U. N. session was extended to attend to the problem.

625
"New Voice At The U. N." Marian Anderson." The New York
    Times. 18 September, 1958, pp. 4.

It was noted that Miss Anderson had cancelled her concert
tours during the meeting of the U. N. General Assembly. As
a delegate, she was assigned to the Trusteeship Committee
which handles matters relating to the status and well-being
of inhabitants of territories under U. N. trusteeship.
Through her concert tours, Miss Anderson has become a symbol
to the peoples of the world.

626
"A Newer Voice." Downbeat. Vol 25, September 4, 1958, pp. 9.

Marian Anderson was nominated by President Eisenhower
to serve as a delegate to the United Nations General Assembly. She would do no more concerts until her appointment
ended. She wanted her assignment to be connected with the
Far East.

627
Schonberg, Harold. "The Other Voice of Marian Anderson." The
    New York Times Magazine. 10 August, 1958, Sec. 6, pp. 17,
    38-39.

Marian Anderson has reached a new medium as delegate to
the U. N. General Assembly. Her UN duties would include
dealing with social, humanitarian and cultural problems.
Her job was simply another form of communication which she
had also accomplished on her worldwide tours.

628
Strayer, Martha. "It Absorbs Your Entire Life." The Washing-
    ton Daily News. 24 October, 1958.

Marian Anderson spoke about the U. N. as an alternate
member of the U. S. delegation.

629
Summers, Eileen. "UN Absorbs Her Whole Life, Says Singer."
    The Washington Post. 24 October, 1958.

Speaking at a luncheon, Marian Anderson noted her first week as an American delegate to the U. N.

630
"U.N. Delegate List Approved In Senate." The New York Times. 31 July, 1958, pp. 2.

The Senate confirmed President Eisenhower's delegates to the U. N. Marian Anderson will be one of the five alternate delegates.

631
"U.N. Session Asked On The Cameroons." The New York Times. 27 November, 1958, pp. 32.

The U. N. called for a special session of the General Assembly to discuss the future of the British and French Cameroons. Marian Anderson expressed pleasure in the changes that had been made in the resolution.

632
"U. S. Delegation Sworn." The New York Times. 13 September, 1958, pp. 6.

Seven persons, including Marian Anderson, were sworn in as members of the U. S. delegation to the U. N. General Assembly.

633
"United States Delegates in Cheerful Huddle at UN." The Christian Science Monitor. 17 September, 1958.

Three UN delegates are pictured. They were Secretary of State John Foster Dulles, Marian Anderson, and Mrs. Oswald B. Lord.

634
"Well-Bestowed Honor." Musical America. Vol. 77, August, 1958, pp. 4.

President Eisnehower appointed Marian Anderson to the UN General Assembly. It was a symbol of the government's awareness of the real power of cultural forces and of the people who represent them. Miss Anderson expressed the hope that her UN appointment would be connected with Asia.

636
Zegrf, Armando. "Song and Statesmanship." Americas. Vol. 11, February, 1959, pp. 28-31.

Miss Anderson talked about her role with the United Nations General Assembly, some of her concerts abroad and her future plans.

FAREWELL
CONCERT TOUR

637
"Arrives For Concert Tonight." The Jamestown (N.Y.) Post
Journal. 8 July, 1965, pp. 19

Pictures Marian Anderson arriving for her farewell concert to be held at Chautauqua.

638
Banks, Dick. "Marian Anderson's Farewell A Throaty Drama Of
Emotion." The Charlotte (N.C.) Observer. 5 November, 1964.

Miss Anderson gave her farewell concert at Ovens Auditorium.

639
"The Beacon." Newsweek. Vol. 65, April 26, 1965, pp. 87-88.

Marian Anderson was to give her farewell concert and
spoke of the things she and her husband planned to do,
which included traveling and working on their farm. It
was stated that "she has been a beacon, a kindly light,
that has penetrated across a nation, across oceans, every-
where. There is no place where Marian Anderson does not
belong."

640
Breslin, Jimmy. "Miss Anderson: The Audience Is Still
Applauding You." The Boston Globe. 19 April, 1965, pp. 2.

Short sketch on the life of Miss Anderson as she did her
farewell concert at Carnegie Hall.

641
"Farewell, Marian Anderson." Ebony. Vol. 20, June, 1965, pp.
39-40, 42-44.

Follows Miss Anderson on her farewell concert tours. In
each city there was standing room only and she received

standing ovations and did several encoures. Notes some of
the highlights of her career and how she faced discrimination
but still received worldwide acclaim.

642
"First Lady of Song Sings Farewell." The San Francisco Chro-
    nicle. 7 March, 1965, pp. 30.

Miss Anderson was to do her farewell concert at the Opera
House.

643
Grady, Mary Elayne. "Farewell Tour." Seattle Times. 21 March,
    1965.

Marian Anderson was to give her farewell concert at the
Opera House in Seattle.

644
Grondahl, Helmar. "Marian Anderson Thrills In Farewell City
    Recital." The Oregonian. 9 March, 1965, pp. 13.

Miss Anderson gave her farewell recital at the Public
Auditorium.

645
Hawkins, William. "Marian Anderson Says Farewell." Musical
    America. Vol. 84, September, 1964, pp. 8-11.

Discusses Miss Anderson's career and her plans for world
farewell concert tours. She also discussed how she perceiv-
ed the world around her.

646
Hawkins, William. "Retirement? - No. Says Farewell." Negro
    Digest. Vol. 14, March, 1965, pp. 93-97.

An interview with Miss Anderson as she was preparing to
leave the concert world. She recalled the ups and downs of
her career. Reprinted from Musical America, September, 1964.

647
Holt, Nora D. "Marian Anderson's 'Farewell' Concert Will
    Echo Forever." The New York Courier. 24 April, 1965,
    pp. 1,2.

Marian Anderson enthralled the audience with the beauty
of her song and the richness of her voice during her farewell concert.

648
"Homage To Marian From Her Home Town." The Danbury (Ct.)
    News-Times. 19 April, 1965, pp. 1.

Over 200 friends and neighbors were at Carnegie Hall for
Marian Anderson's farewell concert. They occupied a bloc
of reserved seats in the orchestra section.

649
Hume, Paul. Marian Anderson Tour Closes Out Memorable
    Career." The Washington Post. 18 October, 1964.

Miss Anderson was to bring her career to a close with a
farewell tour beginning at Constitution Hall and notes that
no tribute to Miss Anderson could be too large.

650
Klein, Howard. "Marian Anderson Will Retire In 1965 After
    Tour of World." The New York Times. 13 December, 1963,
    pp. 40.

Marian Anderson called a press conference to announce
her upcoming retirement and a world concert tour.

651
Kolodin, Irving. "Anderson's Farewell, Ricter's Return."
    Saturday Review. Vol. 48, May 1, 1965, pp. 32.

Marian Anderson sang her farewell concert in Carnegie
Hall on Easter Sunday. She performed her characteristic
program of Schubert, Haydn, Handel, some American songs and
spirituals. The author felt that this farewell concert
should have come five years sooner.

652
Kolodin, Irving. "Music To My Ears; Anderson's Farewell."
    The Saturday Review. Vol. 48, May 1, 1965, pp. 32.

When Miss Anderson gave her retirement concert at Carnegie
Hall, she paused a long time to reflect over the past years.
Her voice was no longer at its best but the audience gave
her fervorous response.

653
Kriegsman, Alan M. "Miss Anderson Touching." The San Diego
    Union. 17 March, 1965.

Marian Anderson sang at the final concert of the International Artists series at the Civic Theater. It was also
part of her farewell tour. She performed with warmth,
compassion and sympathetic understanding.

654
"Lady From Philadelphia." The Crisis. Vol. 72, May, 1965,
    pp. 28.

Salute to Marian Anderson as she retired. She gave a
farewell concert at Carnegie Hall which was a sold-out
affair. Notes how this great artist served her people and
her nation and through her music and personality, she has
won friends for the causes of equality.

655
"A Lady of Quiet Dignity Applauds Selma Heroes." The Van-
    couver Times. 23 March, 1965.

Marian Anderson was in Vancouver for her farewell concert and praised the marchers in Selma, Alabama.

656
Landry, Robert J. "Marian Anderson: A Symbol." Variety. Vol. 238, April 21, 1965, pp. 64.

Noted how superb Miss Anderson was in her farewell concert at Carnegie Hall.

657
Lawrence, Robert. "Marian Anderson," High Fidelity. Vol. 15, July, 1965, pp. 106.

Marian Anderson gave her farewell concert in Carnegie Hall on April 18. There were standing ovations at the beginning and end of the recital.

658
Leith, Henrietta. "Marian Anderson Bows Out in Song." The Washington Post. 19 April, 1965.

Miss Anderson sang a triumphant farewell concert at Carnegie Hall. She gave many encores and received well wishes after the program.

659
"A Little Bit of Irony...Marian Anderson Begins Last Tour in Constitution Hall." The Informer. 14 November, 1964.

Miss Anderson was to begin her farewell tour concerts at Constitution Hall. Miss Anderson became more famous after the 1939 refusal of the DAR to allow her to sing at Constitution Hall. She subsequently sang at Lincoln Memorial to a crowd of 75,000.

660
Lowens, Irving. "Capital Bids Farewell to Marian Anderson." The Washington Star. 25 October, 1964.

Miss Anderson was to sing her final American concert in Constitution Hall, the same place from which she was banned from singing in 1939.

661
"Marian Anderson Due In Last City Concert." The Seattle Post Intelligencer. 21 March, 1965, pp. 12.

Miss Anderson was to give her farewell concert at the Opera House. She was to do a varied concert of classics, German songs and spirituals.

662
"Marian Anderson Retires." The New York Times. 20 April, 1965, pp. 38.

It was noted that Miss Anderson's retirement will not end

her important role in American life. Her spiral gifts
derives from a quality of person, a graciousness that is
independent of music or race. Marian Anderson will never
retire from being one of the world's greatest ladies.

663
"Marian Anderson To Retire In 1965 After Farewell World
    Concert Tour." The Philadelphia Evening Bulletin. 13
    December, 1963, pp. 46.

Miss Anderson announced her plan to retire in 1965. Her
farewell concert tour was to begin in Washington, D. C. on
October 24, 1964 and her final farewell concert at Carnegie
Hall on Easter Sunday, 1965.

664
"Marian Anderson's Farewell." The Washington Star. 24
    October, 1964.

Miss Anderson was to do a farewell concert at Constitution Hall.

665
"Marian Captures New York." The Danbury (Ct.) News-Times.
    19 April, 1965, pp. 1.

2,900 people stood, applauded and cheered as Marian Anderson ended her musical career. She had to do four encores.

666
"Miss Anderson Retires." The Virginian Pilot. 20 April,
    1965, pp. 4.

Biographical sketch of Miss Anderson.

667
"Miss Anderson Sings Upstate." The New York Times. 10 July,
    1965, pp. 14.

Marian Anderson gave her final concert in her farewell
tour at the Chautauqua Open Air Amphitheatre. About 10,000
were in attendance and gave her a standing ovation. She
sang the same program that was sung at her farewell concert
at Carnegie Hall.

668
"Miss Anderson's Farewell," in Blacks In Classical Music: A
    Personal History, by Raoul Abdul. New York: Dodd, Mead
    & Co., 1977, 253., pp. 82-89.

On the occasion of her farewell, Miss Anderson chose
songs long associated with her career. She sang compositions of Haydn, Handel, Schubert, Barber, Britten, and
Quilter. She closed with her usual group of Afro American
religious folk songs. Highlights of her career are included.

669
Mollison, John. "Marian Anderson's Last Tour." The New
    York Herald Tribune. 13 December, 1963.

Miss Anderson announced her plan to retire at a press
conference at St. Regis.

670
Nazzaro, William J. "Marian Anderson Provides An Emotional
    Experience." The Arizonia Republic. 19 March, 1965.

Miss Anderson gave her farewell concert at the Phoenix
Union High School. Her deep emotional commitment to what-
ever she sang made each song an experience.

671
"Notes From Our Correspondents - New York." High Fidelity.
    Vol. 14, October, 1964, pp. 51, 54.

Noted that Marian Anderson's farewell tour, which was to
begin in Washington, D. C., would be a sentimental journey
for millions of her listeners. RCA Victor was to release
at least five albums featuring Miss Anderson. A special
album of seldom-done spirituals was to be done and she was
to do the same spirituals on her Washington and New York
recitals.

672
Patrick, Corbin. "Marian Anderson Sings 'Farewell'." The
    Indianapolis Star. 22 January, 1965, pp. 12.

Miss Anderson sang at Clowes Hall during her farewell
concert tour.

673
"RCA Victor's Farewell Recital of Marian Anderson." The
    Negro Digest. Vol. 14, June 1965, pp. 82.

RCA Victor recorded Miss Anderson's farewell concert at
Constitution Hall. Along with the album was an illustrated
brochure with photos of the highlights of her career and an
essay by Vincent Sheean entitled "The Voice of The American
Soul" was included.

674
"Retirement." Musical America. Vol. 84, January, 1964, pp.
    16-17.

Marian Anderson called a press conference to announce her
retirement. She was to do world concert tours beginning in
October 1964 and ending April 18, 1965 at Carnegie Hall.
The tour would include Japan, the Far East, North and South
America, Europe, Israel and Africa.

675
Rich, Allan. "Critics View of Marian Anderson." The New
    York Herald Tribune. 19 February, 1965, pp. 19.

Review of Miss Anderson's farewell concert at Carnegie
Hall.

676
Rich, Alan. "Marian Anderson: She Opened The Door." The New
     York Herald Tribune. 24 January, 1965, pp. 2, 29.

As Miss Anderson prepared to retire, her accomplishments
are recalled.

677
Schonberg, Harold C. "Music: Marian Anderson." The New York
     Times. 19 April, 1965, pp. 38.

Accompanied by Franz Rupp, Marian Anderson gave her farewell concert at Carnegie Hall. It was noted that it was
Miss Anderson who paved the way for other artists. She
stood as a symbol for the emergence of the Negro. She had
unusual powers of communication. During the concert, she
took special notice of the stage audience, turning her back
to the house audience and singing two songs directly to the
people clustered behind the piano. She did several encores
and there was a half hour standing ovation to this first
rate artist.

678
Shields, Allan. "Living Legend of Artistry Sings At Farewell
     Concert." The El Cajon Californian. 17 March, 1965.

Marian Anderson gave her farewell concert at the Civic
Theater. 3,000 were in attendance.

679
"A Singer's Farewell." The New York Times. 25 April, 1965,
     Sec. 4, pp. 6.

Pictures Marian Anderson as she leaves the stage after
her farewell concert at Carnegie Hall.

680
Staff, Charles. "Great Day of Anderson Art Recalled." The
     Indianapolis News. 22 January, 1965, pp. 8.

Miss Anderson sang her farewell concert at Clowes Hall
before 1,800 people.

681
Stone, Theodore Charles. "Marian Anderson Sings A Fond
     Farewell For 3,500." The Crusader. 12 December, 1964.

As her career came to a climax, Miss Anderson gave a
farewell concert at Orchestra Hall on December 6th. Her
career spanned over thirty years and this last concert
was to a packed and appreciative audience.

682
"Ten Years Ago." The Jamestown (N.Y.) Post Journal. 12
     July, 1975.

Shows a picture of Marian Anderson taken ten years
earlier when she arrived in Jamestown for her farewell concert.

683
Ten Hoope, Karel. "Marian Anderson's Farewell." The Van-
     couver Provence. 24 March, 1965.

Miss Anderson gave her farewell concert at Queen Elizabeth Theater before a small crowd. She enthralled the
audience with her sincere and passionate interpretation
of her songs.

684
Thorp, Gerald R. "Marian Anderson In St. Louis On Her
     Farewell Concert Tour." The St. Louis Post-Dispatch.
     30 March, 1965, pp. 8C.

Miss Anderson was to appear at Kiel Auditorium on her
farewell concert tour.

685
"U. S. Singer Star In Paris Arts Festival." The Honolulu
     Advertiser. 29 September, 1965.

Marian Anderson sang her farewell concert in Paris
under the auspices of the World Festival of Negro Arts,
presided over by Seneglese President, Leopold Senghor. She
sang sixteen spirituals to a crowd who paid $500 each for
tickets. She sang in Sainte Chapelle.

686
Van Olinda, Edgar S. "A Noted Singer Comes To Town." The
     Albany (N.Y.) Times Union. 6 January, 1965, pp. 10.

Miss Anderson was to give her farewell recital at the
Emmanuel Baptist Church.

687
Webster, Daniel. "Dignity and Simplicity Mark Farewell To
     City By Marian Anderson." The Philadelphia Inquirer.
     15 January, 1965, pp. 12.

Miss Anderson gave her farewell concert at the Academy
of Music.

688
Weinraub, Bernard. "Marian Anderson Sings Finale, But Cry
     Is Bravo, Not Farewell." The New York Times. 19 April,
     1965, pp. 1, 38.

At Marian Anderson's farewell concert at Carnegie Hall,

the entire audience of 2,900, led by two elderly women, stood and cheered. She gave a two hour concert and after three encores, she left the stage with a bouquet or roses and a bouquet of mums. There was an ovation which lasted one half hour.

"A LINCOLN PORTRAIT"
READINGS

689
Bloomfield, Arthur. Oakland Symphony Springs Curious Pro-
    gram." The San Francisco Examiner. 25 March, 1970, pp. 42.

Miss Anderson appeared with the Oakland Symphony. She
read "Lincoln Portrait."

690
Commanday, Robert. "Eloquent Lincoln Portrait." The San
    Francisco Chronicle. 26 March, 1970, pp. 44.

Marian Anderson did an eloquent reading of Abe Lincoln's
words in "Lincoln Portrait" with the Oakland Symphony.

691
Duckworth, Manly. " 'Portrait' Performance Moving." The
    Orlando Sentinel Star. 17 January, 1966, pp. 6D.

Marian Anderson read "A Lincoln Portrait" with the Florida
Symphony Orchestra at Municipal Auditorium.

692
Ericson, Raymond. "Music: The Rains Came." The New York Times.
    3 August, 1966, pp. 40.

The New York Philharmonic appeared in Central Park with
Marian Anderson as soloist. After a rain storm failed to
disperse the music lovers, Marian Anderson came on to read
Copland's "A Lincoln Portrait." She drew loud applause at
the end of her reading.

693
Hertelendy, Paul. "An Unforgettable Lincoln Portrait." The
    Oakland Tribune. 25 March, 1970.

Notes Marian Anderson's superb reading of "Lincoln Portrait."

694
Hume, Paul. "Anderson, Duncan to Sing in Coming Concerts."
    The Washington Post. 18 May, 1966, pp. D5.

    Marian Anderson was to narrate Lincoln Portrait at
    Carter Barron Amphitheatre.

695
Isaacs, Jean M. "A Little Chat With A Great Lady."   The
    Indiana Post Tribune. 2 May, 1976.

    Interview with Marian Anderson before her appearance at
the North Shore Symphony as narrator of "Lincoln Portrait."

696
Isaacs, Jean M. "Marian Anderson Delights Crowd." The
    Indiana Post Tribune. 3 May, 1976, pp. B5.

    Miss Anderson received a standing ovation for her reading
of "Lincoln Portrait" at Gary West Side High School.

697
"Patriotic Works of Copland, Sousa, Gould Played at Lewis-
    ohn." The New York Times. 5 July, 1965, pp. 9.

    The Lewisohn Stadium was the scene of a "music of America"
concert on July 3rd. Marian Anderson sang and narrated
Aaron Copland's "Lincoln Portrait." Arthur Fiedler conducted
the orchestra. Miss Anderson's musical selections were
spirituals.

698
"People." The Danbury (Ct.) News-Times. 8 October, 1976,
    pp. 4.

    Miss Anderson was to do "Lincoln Portrait" at the United
Nations on October 24.

699
Sulok, Nancy. "Marian Anderson Too Busy To 'Retire'."
    The South Bend (Ind.) Tribune. 16 February, 1975, pp. 1.

    Miss Anderson was in South Bend to narrate "Lincoln
Portrait" with the South Bend Symphony Orchestra. She said
she was too busy to retire.

SEVENTY-FIFTH

BIRTHDAY SALUTE

700
"Celebrates 75th Birthday." <u>The New York Times</u>. 28 February,
    1977, pp. 1

    Pictures Marian Anderson and Rosalyn Carter at Carnegie
Hall before the benefit concert in honor of Miss Anderson's
75th birthday.

701
Fraser, C. Gerald. "A National Treasure is Saluted at 75."
    <u>The New York Times</u>. 25 February, 1977.

    A benefit concert honoring Marian Anderson's 75th birth-
day was to be held at Carnegie Hall. A short biographical
sketch follows.

702
Fraser, C. Gerald. "A National Treasure is Saluted At 75."
    <u>The New York Times Biographical Service</u>. February, 1977,
    pp. 177-178.

    Noted the 75th birthday celebration for Marian Anderson
at Carnegie Hall.

703
"Notes On People." <u>The New York Times</u>. 17 February, 1977,
    pp. 76.

    Rosalyn Carter agreed to be a patron for Marian Anderson's
75th birthday salute at Carnegie Hall. She was to sit with
Miss Anderson at the benefit concert sponsored by the Young
Audiences, and organization devoted to introducing young
people to classical music, theatre and dance. Leontyne
Price, Clamma Dale and Shirley Verrett were to perform.

704
Quindlen, Anna. "Marian Anderson Honored At 75 By Carnegie
    Hall Concert." <u>The New York Times</u>. 28 February, 1977,

pp. 24.

Miss Anderson was stirred by the grand tribute given in
honor of her 75th birthday. She and Mrs. Carter sat together
during the concert. She was given two awards: The Handel
Medallion for her cultural contributions and the United
Nations Peace Prize for her tenure as delegate to the UN.
Miss Anderson was also told of a resolution to have the
Treasury Department strike a gold medal in her honor.

705
Trescott, Jacqueline. "What I Had Was Singing." The Washing-
    ton Post. 1 March, 1977, pp. B-1, B-9.

Marian Anderson celebrated her seventy-fifth birthday
at Carnegie Hall. She was one of the best contraltos in
the world and retired in 1965 after thirty odd years. Miss
Anderson said "what I had was singing and if my career has
been of some consequence, then that's my contribution."

706
"Tribute and Medal to Marian Anderson." Pan Pipes of Sigma
    Alpha Iota. Vol. 69, May, 1977, pp. 15.

Tribute to Miss Anderson on her 75th birthday at Carnegie
Hall. She sang "Ave Maria" and was awarded a special Congressional medal presented by Mrs. Jimmy Carter.

707
"Two First Ladies Meet." The New York Times. 28 February,
    1977.

Picture of Marian Anderson and Mrs. Jimmy Carter at
Carnegie Hall.

CONCERTS IN
U.S. AND ABROAD

<u>1916</u>

708
"A Singer." <u>The Crisis</u>. Vol. 12, October, 1916, pp. 281.

Marian Anderson was one of the leading singers with the People's Choral Society in the rendition of Handel's "Messiah" at the Musical Fund Hall in Philadelphia. Miss Anderson was a high school student and the Society had contributed $144 toward a scholarship for her.

<u>1921</u>

709
"Marian Anderson." <u>New York Age</u>. 24 December, 1921, pp. 5.

Miss Anderson appeared at Carnegie Hall in Woodward's Music Festival.

<u>1923</u>

710
"Marian Anderson Heard With Philharmonic Society." <u>The Pittsburgh Courier</u>. 22 December, 1923, pp. 12.

Miss Anderson was a soloist at the Academy of Music. The applause was so loud and continuous that she was recalled many times. The conductor, Josef Pasternack, was pleased with his new protege.

711
"Marian Anderson To Sing With Orchestra Phila. Philharmonic." <u>New York Age</u>. 22 December, 1923, pp. 6.

Miss Anderson was to be the soloist with the Philadelphia Philharmonic Society.

1924

712
"The Horizon." The Crisis. Vol. 27, February, 1924, pp. 184.

Marian Anderson has appeared in Philadelphia with the Philharmonic Orchestra and also sang and recorded with the Victor Talking Machine Company.

713
"Marian Anderson In Recital In New York." New York Age. 23 February, 1924, pp. 7.

Miss Anderson sang at the Renaissance Casino. A list of her songs is given.

714
"Marian Anderson Is Heard In Pleasing Program In New York." New York Age. 3 May, 1924, pp. 7.

Miss Anderson appeared at the Renaissance Casino and at Town Hall. It was suggested that she devote more time to developing her latent talents because these concerts showed no material improvements, had failed to reach new heights of interpretation and her performance was stilted and constrained.

715
"Marian Anderson Sang Spirituals At Bellevue-Stratton." New York Age. 26 January, 1924, pp. 6.

The Matinee Musical Club of Philadelphia presented Miss Anderson and Harry T. Burleigh at the Bellevue-Stratton Hotel.

716
"Marian Anderson Sings." The Pittsburgh Courier. 3 May, 1924, pp. 1.

Miss Anderson gave her debut recital at the Town Hall in New York.

717
"Miss Marian Anderson Thrills Audience." Norfolk Journal and Guide. 26 January, 1924, pp. 10.

Miss Anderson appeared at Zion Baptist Church. She sang in Italian, German, French and English.

1925

718
"The Horizon." The Crisis. Vol. 30, October, 1925, pp. 291-292.

Marian Anderson appeared with the Philharmonic Orchestra at New York City College. Over 75,000 were present. She had been chosen over three hundred competing singers.

719
"Marian Anderson Gets Big Ovation In New York City."
    Norfolk Journal And Guide. 5 September, 1925, pp. 6.

Miss Anderson appeared as solo artist with the New York
Philharmonic Orchestra before 7,500 people.

720
"Marian Anderson Sings At J. C. Smith." Norfolk Journal And
    Guide. 19 December, 1925, pp. 10.

On December 3rd, over 1,000 people were at J. C. Smith
College in Charlotte, N. C. to hear Marian Anderson.   She
sang in German, Italian, French and English.

721
"Miss Anderson Makes Big Hit In North Carolina." Norfolk
    Journal And Guide. 5 December, 1925, pp. 15.

A & T College presented Miss Anderson in concert.   She
performed a varied program to a capacity crowd.

722
"Negro Contralto Sings at Stadium." The Eagle. 27 August,
    1925.

Marian Anderson sang with the Philharmonic Orchestra and
was the one contralto chosen by the National Music League
to appear with the orchestra.

1926

723
"Yesterday in Negro History. Jet. Vol. 21, December 7, 1961,
    pp. 11.

Noted that on December 7, 1926, Marian Anderson made her
professional debut in an AKA sorority sponsored concert.

1927

724
"Marian Anderson In Recital Here on Monday Night."   Norfolk
    Journal And Guide. 8 January, 1927, pp. 3.

Miss Anderson was to sing in a recital on the 10th.

725
"Marian Anderson Thrills Audience at First Baptist." Norfolk
    Journal And Guide. 15 January, 1927, pp. 2.

Even a heavy snowstorm did not keep patrons from coming
to hear Marian Anderson at First Baptist Church in Norfolk.

726
"Miss Anderson In Recital Here On January 10." Norfolk
    Journal and Guide. 1 January, 1927, pp. 5.

    Miss Anderson was to appear at the First Baptist Church
in Norfolk on Monday night.

1928

727
"Along The Color Line." The Crisis. Vol. 35, December, 1928,
    pp. 409.

    During last season Marian Anderson studied in London
where she appeared at a concert with the London Philharmonic Orchestra. She later toured America.

728
"Survey of The Month." Opportunity. Vol. 6, September, 1928
    pp. 280.

    Marian Anderson appeared in a concert in London where
she did several songs by British composer, Sir Roger Quilter.
He accompanied the singer.

1929

729
"Along The Color Line." The Crisis. Vol. 36, February, 1929,
    pp. 52-53.

    Marian Anderson made her first New York appearance in
December, 1928. Her international fame was expanding
rapidly and she toured Europe during the past season.

1930

730
Gaul, Harvey. "Music." The Pittsburgh Post Gazette. 30
    April, 1930, pp. 10.

    Miss Anderson was sponsored in concert by the AKA soro-
rity.

731
"Marian Anderson, Contralto, Sings At Carnegie Hall." The
    New York Evening Sun. 3 March, 1930.

    Miss Anderson sang a varied program of French, Italian
and Russian songs. William King accompanied her.

732
"Marian Anderson Delights Audience." The New York Times.
    3 March, 1930.

    Miss Anderson's program at Carnegie Hall consisted of
well chosen lyrics from Italian, German, French and Ameri-

can composers, plus a group of Negro spirituals. William
King accompanied her.

733
"Marian Anderson Sings." The New York Herald-Tribune. 3
   March, 1930.

Notes Marian Anderson's concert at Carnegie Hall. It
was noted that her diction in German and Italian needed
some revision.

734
"Marian Anderson Triumphs In Berlin." Tuskegee Messenger.
   Vol. 6, October 28, November 8, 1930, pp. 3.

The Berlin fans were so thrilled with Miss Anderson's
performance that they cheered wildly, threw flowers at her
feet and refused to leave after her performance. Her final
bow call was done in semi darkness.

735
"Miss Anderson Talented Artist, Gave Difficult Program Of
   Lyric Music." The Washington (Pa.) Daily Reporter. 28
   March, 1930.

Miss Anderson sang at the YWCA. She showed an artist's
refinement of style and taste. William King accompanied her.

736
"Music." The Philadelphia Public Ledger. 18 May, 1930.

Miss Anderson sang at the second annual National Negro
Music Festival at the Academy of Music. The festival was
arranged by the American Interracial Peace Committee.

737
"Recitals." The New Yorker. March 15, 1930, pp. 67-68.

Noted Marian Anderson's recitals at Carnegie Hall. She
was at her best in florid songs.

1931

738
"Along The Color Line." The Crisis. Vol. 38, July, 1931.
   pp. 235.

Marian Anderson sang in twenty-six concerts in 1931
covering fifteen states. She had just sailed for Europe
where she would study and give a four month fall concert
tour.

739
"Marian Anderson Pleases Audience." Tuskegee Messenger.
   Vol. 7, March 14-28, 1931, pp. 8.

Miss Anderson appeared at Tuskegee Institute and had to give six encores. People came from as far as one hundred miles to hear her.

1932

740
"Marian Anderson." The New York Times. 3 April, 1932, Sec. 8, pp. 9.

Miss Anderson was to appear with the Hall Johnson Negro Choir at Carnegie Hall.

741
"Marian Anderson." Southern Workman. Vol. 61, March, 1932, pp. 141.

Miss Anderson appeared in Ogden Hall at Hampton Institute. She sang in German, Italian, and English. Noted the wide display of range, power and beauty in her voice and her perfect enunciation and artistic interpretation.

742
"Marian Anderson With Choir." The New York Times. 6 April, 1932, pp. 22.

Miss Anderson and Hall Johnson's Negro Choir sang to a huge audience at Carnegie Hall. Miss Anderson sang a classical repertoire, including Mozart, Listz, Verdi, Tchaikovsky, and Griffes. Her singing was sensitive, controlled and deeply understanding of the music she sang.

1933

743
Kerby, Damon, "Noted Singer's Spiritual Depth." The St. Louis Post-Dispatch. 22 March, 1933, pp. 3D.

Miss Anderson said faith made her career possible. She was in St. Louis for a recital at Municipal Auditorium.

1934

744
Coverley, Roy de. "Marian Anderson in Denmark." Opportunity. Vol. 12, September, 1934, pp. 270-271.

Miss Anderson performed a charity concert in Denmark after highly priced artists were banned from singing there. She sang in six languages and her flawless technique left the audience filled with emotion.

745
Edwards, Thyra. "Marian Anderson Makes Too Much Money, So Denmark Bank Puts Ban on Great Diva." The Pittsburgh Courier. 10 February, 1934, pp. 8.

Noted that Denmark, Sweden and Finland have made Miss
Anderson a national idol. The National Bank of Denmark
refused to allow her to do more than one concert for pay.

746
"Marian Anderson Is Rebuked by Danish Nation Bankers." The
    California News. 15 February, 1934.

Miss Anderson was a huge success in Denmark, Sweden, and
Finland. She came over in September and was to return home
by Christmas, but was still there and would not return until
the next fall.

747
"Ovation To Negro Singer." The New York Times. 8 December,
    1934, pp. 19.

Marian Anderson was cheered by hundreds at the Reforma-
tion Hall in Geneva. Her program consisted of classics in
German, French, Finnish and some spirituals.

748
"To Attend Musicians' Confab Here in August." The Pittsburgh
    Courier. 7 July, 1934.

Picture of Marian Anderson who was to attend the annual
Musicians' Conference in August.

1935

749
Cooper, Opal. "Marian Anderson: 'Priestess of Art'." The
    Afro American. 23 February, 1935.

Miss Anderson was the foremost American singer in Europe.
She had a busy schedule and gave 120 concerts in a six month
period in Scandinavia.

750
"Marian Anderson Heard." New York Times. 22 November, 1935,
    pp. 19.

Miss Anderson appeared at the Vienna Concert Hall. She
performed Schubert, Monteverdi and Sibelius. Because of
the sell out crowd, a second performance was scheduled for
the next week.

751
"Music Patrons Are Entranced By Her Voice." The Norfolk
    Journal and Guide. 8 September, 1935.

Marian Anderson was called the "greatest of all American singers" by Europeans during her recital at the
Mozarteam in Austria.

752
Peyser, Herbert F. "Double Bill In Vienna." The New York
    Times. 10 March, 1935, Sec. 8, pp. 5.

The sensation of the music season in Vienna was the
debut of Marian Anderson. It was noted that her art of
song, the emotional, mystical and spiritual elements of
her nature, lend her work the character of a consecration.

1936

753
Barry, Edward. "Famed Colored Singer Charms Audience Here."
    The Chicago Daily Tribune. 27 January, 1936, pp. 11.

Marian Anderson sang at the Old Auditorium. Her voice
was flexible, capable of sustained power on one hand and
dainty and delicate on the other. There was sincerity
and selflessness in her interpretations and her manner was
charming.

754
"Colored Contralto." Time. Vol. 27, January 13, 1936, pp.
    35-36.

Marian Anderson gave a superb performance at Town Hall
in New York despite a broken foot. A short biographical
sketch follows.

755
Downes, Olin. "Marian Anderson In Second Recital." New York
    Times. 21 January, 1936, pp. 27.

Miss Anderson gave her second New York recital at Carnegie Hall. The audience was so thrilled with her performance that she had to do several encores.

756
Eversman, Alice. "Marian Anderson Sings Varied Program
    Superbly." The Washington Star. 19 February, 1936.

Miss Anderson sang at the Armstrong High School Auditorium
sponsored by Howard University School of Music.

757
Gunn, Glenn Dillard. "Song Makes History." The Chicago
    Herald Examiner. 27 January, 1936, pp. 12.

Marian Anderson gave the closing concert in a series
entitled, "The History and Enjoyment of Music," sponsored
by Northwestern University. She sang at the Auditorium
Theater. She did songs by Handel, Schubert, Sibelius and
a group of spirituals.

758
Howell, Ruth. "Dusky Marian Anderson Sings a Superb Recital."
The Washington Daily News. 19 February, 1936.

Miss Anderson sang at Armstrong High School to a capacity
crowd.

759
"Marian Anderson." Opportunity. Vol. 14, January, 1936,
    pp. 5.

Congratulates Miss Anderson on her triumphant return to
the U. S. She also received loud praises at her concert at
Town Hall in New York.

760
"Marian Anderson Holds Audience Spellbound In Best Program
    Of Season." The Utica Daily Press. 11 February, 1936.

Miss Anderson sang at Majestic Theater. Noted that her
voice, her stage appeal, her delivery, and her interpretation were superb. Kosti Vehanen accompanied her.

761
"Marian Anderson In Recital." New York Times. 10 March,
    1936, pp. 26.

Miss Anderson made her third appearance in three months
at Carnegie Hall. She sang to a capacity crowd and earned
their unstinted responsiveness with her varied and stirring
program.

762
"New York Endorses Europe's Opinion Of A Negro Contralto."
    Newsweek. Vol. 7, January 11, 1936, pp. 28.

During her first United States recital in four years,
the audience at Town Hall upheld the European opinion that
Miss Anderson was one of the greatest singers of the day.
She had also broken her foot and had to perform in a cast.

763
Sanborn, Pitts. "Rosa Ponselle As Carmen." The Christian
    Science Monitor. 7 January, 1936.

Noted that Marian Anderson's appearance on December 30th
was varied and engrossing. Her voice has an extraordinary
resource in power, tone, color and range.

764
"Singer Will Return Here." The Boston Chronicle. 19 December,
    1936.

Marian Anderson was to appear in a second concert at
Symphony Hall on January 31st.

765
"Survey of the Month - Music." <u>Opportunity</u>. Vol. 14, Jan-
    uary, 1936, pp. 31.

Marian Anderson appeared at the New York Town Hall on
December 30th in her first American recital in four years.

766
"They Brought Marian Anderson Home To Sing." <u>The Philadel-
    phia Independent</u>. 26 January, 1936, pp. 15.

The AKA's sponsored Miss Anderson in a concert in
Philadelphia.

<u>1937</u>

767
"Captures Boston Audience." <u>Boston Guardian</u>. 6 February,
    1937, pp. 1, 4.

Miss Anderson appeared at Symphony Hall in a recital in
honor of the boys and girls at Calhoun School in Calhoun,
Georgia. She displayed a majesty of power and integrity of
artistic control.

768
"Carnegie Hall Crowd Thrilled by Contralto." <u>The New York
    Amsterdam News</u>, 10 April, 1937.

Showing great versatility, Marian Anderson had the
audience yelling "bravos" and "repeats" during her concert
at Carnegie Hall.

769
"Crowd Hears Concert Diva At Princeton." <u>The New York
    Amsterdam News</u>. 24 April, 1937.

Marian Anderson did several encores when she performed
at Princeton University.

770
"Marian Anderson." <u>New York Times</u>. 28 March, 1937, Section
    10, pp. 5.

Pictures Miss Anderson who was to appear in a recital
on Friday.

771
"Marian Anderson In Closing Concert." <u>New York Times</u>. 13
    May, 1937, pp. 30.

Miss Anderson gave her final song recital of the season
at Carnegie Hall. She began with early classical arias,
a group of German lieders, pieces by Sodero, Bianchini and
Respighi and a final selection of spirituals.

772
"Marian Anderson Sings." The World Telegram. 13 May, 1937.

Miss Anderson performed at Carnegie Hall in her last New York recital of the season.

773
"Marian Anderson Sings Here Tuesday Evening." The Washington Star. 4 April, 1937.

Miss Anderson was to be presented in a recital at Armstrong High School sponsored by Howard University School of Music.

774
"Marian Anderson Would Open Way For Others To Follow." The Boston Chronicle. 16 January, 1937.

Miss Anderson was to do a benefit performance for the Calhoun School.

775
"Queen's Hall Recital." The Evening Standard. 11 December, 1937, pp. 10.

Marian Anderson was in recital at Queen's Hall. She did songs by Handel, Brahms, Schubert, Schumann, Sielius, and Negro spirituals.

776
"Singer Given Ovation on Return Visit." The Washington Star. 7 April, 1937.

Marian Anderson was sponsored by Howard University in a concert at Armstrong High School. There was ovations after each number she sang.

777
"Song Group In Anderson Engagement." The Washington Star. 3 April, 1937.

Miss Anderson was to appear in recital at the Armstrong High School as part of the Howard University School of Music concert series. A list of the selections she was to sing is included. Kosti Vehanen was to accompany her.

778
Straus, Noel. "Marian Anderson Delights Hearers." New York Times. 3 April, 1937, pp. 17.

Miss Anderson was most impressive as an interpreter during her concert at Carnegie Hall. She was in outstanding vocal shape and her singing was heightened by the sincerity and directness of her approach.

1938

779
"Anderson Sails Wednesday." The New York Herald Tribune.
    12 June, 1938.

Marian Anderson was to sail on the Normandie for a month's
vacation on the Riveria, after which she was to go on her
second South America tour.

780
Berlack-Boozer, Thelma. "Marian Anderson Superb in Concert."
The New York Amsterdam News. 23 April, 1938.

Miss Anderson was to close her New York performance at
Carnegie Hall on May 8.

781
Buchalter, Helen. "Marian Anderson Sings in Superb Recital."
The Washington Daily News. 10 May, 1938.

Miss Anderson sang at the Rialto Theatre. From the very
moment she began to sing, she carried the listeners into a
journey in song that left them spellbound long after the
last sound had died away.

782
"Delaney Sees Miss Anderson Off to Paris." The Afro Ameri-
    can. 2 July, 1938.

Hubert T. Delaney, romantically linked to Marian Anderson, was on hand to see her off on her trip to Paris.

783
Eversman, Alice. "Marian Anderson Heard in Splendid Concert."
The Washington Star. 10 May, 1938.

Notes Miss Anderson's warm, pleasable and expressive voice
at her recent appearance at the Rialto Theatre.

784
" 'First Lady' of Song Delights Vast Audience." The Guar-
    dian. 10 December, 1938.

Over 3,000 heard Marian Anderson sing at Symphony Hall.
The selections she sang were also listed.

785
Kellogg, Grayce. "Marian Superb - New York!" The Pittsburgh
    Courier. 17 December, 1938, pp. 9.

Miss Anderson gave her first New York recital of the
season at Carnegie Hall. Her accompanist, Kosti Vehanen,
had composed three compositions especially for Miss Anderson.

786
"Marian Anderson." The New York Times. 10 April, 1938, Sec.
    10, pp. 5.

Pictured Miss Anderson who was to sing in the final
Hurok Carnegie Hall series.

787
"Marian Anderson." The New York Times. 29 May, 1938, Sec.
    10, pp. 8.

Miss Anderson was to sing over station WJZ.

788
"Marian Anderson Back For Engagements in America." The New
    York Amsterdam News. 3 December, 1938.

Marian Anderson's mother was at the pier in New York to
greet her daughter after a successful European tour.

789
"Marian Anderson Delights Farewell Academy Audience." The
    Philadelphia Tribune. 2 June, 1938.

Miss Anderson made her final season appearance at the
Academy of Music. A near capacity crowd was present.

790
"Marian Anderson Farewell Recital, Academy Tonight." The
    Philadelphia Tribune. 26 May, 1938.

Miss Anderson planned a new and varied program designed
to show her exceptional ability and vertuosity when she
gave her farewell recital at the Academy of Music.

791
"Marian Anderson Heard." The New York Times. 14 April, 1938,
    pp. 27.

Miss Anderson gave her fourth recital at Carnegie Hall.
It was the final concert in the Hurok Carnegie Hall Series.
She was accompanied by Kosti Vehanen.

792
"Marian Anderson Heard In Recital." The New York Times. 9
    May, 1938, pp. 13.

Miss Anderson gave her final recital of the season at
Carnegie Hall. It was her second appearance there and her
fifth in the city this season. She did numbers by Handel,
Scarlatti, Bizet, Schubert, Massenet, Grieg, Vehanen, Ravel
and a group of Negro spirituals. She had to sing several
encores.

793
"Marian Anderson in Song Recital." The Washington Star.

8 May, 1938.

Miss Anderson was to appear at the Rialto Theatre.   The
program selection are included.

794
"Marian Anderson Orchestra Soloist in Brahms Cycle." The
    Camden (N.J.) Courier. 9 December, 1938.

Miss Anderson was to make her first appearance in Camden
as a soloist with the Philadelphia Orchestra on December
16-17 and 20.   She planned a varied program.

795
"Marian Anderson Returns." The New York Times. 25 November,
    1938, pp. 18.

Miss Anderson returned from Europe on the French liner
Normandie to begin her winter concert season in Buffalo.
She had given twenty concerts in South America and then
went to the south of France to rest and rehearse for the
upcoming season.

796
"Marian Anderson Scales Heights at Carnegie Hall." The
    Washington Tribune. 17 December, 1938.

Miss Anderson sang English, Italian, German, and French
songs, plus spirituals in her performance at Carnegie Hall.

797
"Marian Anderson Sings." The New York Times. 7 December,
    1938, pp. 26.

Miss Anderson gave her first New York recital of the
season.   It was the third event in the Hurok Carnegie Hall
series.   Her diverse program ranged from Purcell, Veracini,
Carissimi, Bach, Schubert, Ravel, Vehanen to a group of
spirituals.

798
"Marian Anderson Thrills D. C. Audience in Recital." The
    Afro American. 14 May, 1938.

Howard University sponsored Miss Anderson in a recital
at the Rialto Theatre.

799
"Marian Anderson To Air." The Afro American. 10 December,
    1938.

Miss Anderson was to make her fifth appearance with the
Magic Key Orchestra on NBC - Blue Network.

800
"Marian Anderson to Appear in Hub." The Boston Post. 4

October, 1938.

Miss Anderson was to appear in Aaron Richmond's Boston Series at Symphony Hall.

801
"Marian Anderson to Present New Program in 'Farewell'."
The Philadelphia Tribune. 5 May, 1938.

A new and varied program designed to show Miss Anderson's exceptional ability and virtuosity was planned for her farewell recital at the Academy of Music.

802
"Marian Anderson Triumphs." The Dallas Express. 19 March, 1938, pp. 1, 2.

Miss Anderson sang at McFarlin Auditorium. Her poise, musicianship, dignity and deep feeling were greatly appreciated by the capacity crowd.

803
"Marian Anderson Will Give Farewell Recital Here Tonight." The Philadelphia Record. 26 May, 1938.

Miss Anderson was to do a farewell performance in Philadelphia before going to Washington, D. C. and then to Europe.

804
"Marian Anderson Wins Acclaim For Concert in Buenos Aires." Opportunity. Vol. 16, March, 1938, pp. 89.

Miss Anderson received the greatest acclaim than any artist from the people of Buenos Aires during her concert tour. She was signed to return the next winter.

805
"Marian Anderson's Recital." The New York Times. 31 March, 1938, pp. 14.

Miss Anderson appeared at Town Hall in the 8th and final event in the Town Hall endowment series. She had to repeat several encores. Her singing had dignity and simplicity, tenderness and nobility, passion and humanity.

806
"Miss Anderson in Recital." The Guardian. 8 January, 1938.

Miss Anderson was beginning her third American Concert Tour with a recital at Symphony Hall.

807
"Music of the Times: News and Current Comment." The New York Times. 4 December, 1938, Sec. 10, pp. 11.

Pictures Marian Anderson who was to do her first recital of the season the following Tuesday.

808
Peyser, Herbert F. "Active Paris Season." The New York Times. 11 December, 1938, Sec. 10, pp. 9.

Noted that Marian Anderson's concert in Paris was a huge success. Future concerts were to be held in a larger place which would be more acoustically fit for Miss Anderson's needs.

809
Peyser, Herbert F. "Emil Sauer at 75." The New York Times. 6 February, 1938, Sec. 10, pp. 8.

It was noted that one of the best recitals in Vienna during the past weeks was one by Marian Anderson. She was heard twice in two different halls within a few days.

810
Sanborn, Pitts. "Praise for Recital by Marian Anderson." The New York World Telegram. 7 December, 1938.

Making her first New York appearance of the season, Miss Anderson gave a distinguished performance at Carnegie Hall.

811
Schalk, Toki. "Marian Superb - Boston.!" The Pittsburgh Courier. 17 December, 1938, pp. 9.

Miss Anderson appeared at Symphony Hall in Boston. There were over three thousand in attendance. Her program included numbers by Purcell, Veracini, Bach, Bantok, Ravel, etc, as well as spirituals arranged by Burleigh, Boatner and Brown.

812
"Spirituals To Feature Marian Anderson's Farewell Concert." The Philadelphia Tribune. 12 May, 1938.

Miss Anderson was to include a group of spirituals on her farewell recital at the Academy of Music.

813
"Texas Daily Praises Marian Anderson." The Crisis. Vol. 45, October, 1938, pp. 340.

The recital of Miss Anderson in Dallas received great acclaim from the music critics of the Dallas daily papers. Excerpts from the Dallas Morning News are included.

814
"Thomas Here Today." The Buffalo Courier Express. 20 November, 1938.

In citing upcoming events in Buffalo, it was announced

that Marian Anderson would sing at the Buffalo Conservatory.

1939

815
"Anderson Here Thursday." The Philadelphia Inquirer. 3 Dec-
    ember, 1939.

Marian Anderson was to appear at the Academy of Music in
Philadelphia.

816
"Anderson in Pawtucket." The Providence (R.I.) Journal. 12
    November, 1939.

List of selections to be sung by Marian Anderson when she
would appear at Pawtucket High School.

817
"As Brown Thrust Was In Springfield." The Atlanta Daily
    World. 21 June, 1939.

Miss Anderson was in Springfield in connection with the
premiere of the movie Young Mr. Lincoln. She was denied
hotel accomodations and stayed with friends. She placed
a wreath at Lincoln's tomb.

818
"At Syria Mosque Sunday." The Pittsburgh Courier. 21 January,
    1939, pp. 1.

Pictures Marian Anderson who was to appear for the first
time at the Syria Mosque in Pittsburgh.

819
Berlack-Boozer, Thelma. "Miss Anderson Sets 2 Records." The
    New York Amsterdam News. 3 June, 1939, pp. 12.

Miss Anderson sang twice in one week for New York audiences and set two new records. She was the first individual
artist to sell out the Hall of Music at the New York World's
Fair. She also sang to a standing room only crowd at Carnegie Hall in her fourth and final appearance there for the
season. Both concerts had to turn away patrons.

820
Berlack-Boozer, Thelma. "Singer Works Overtime To Please
    Crowd." The New York Amsterdam News. 22 April, 1939, pp.
    12.

Marian Anderson extended her Carnegie Hall concert by
fifteen minutes. A list of persons at the concert is
given. It was also learned that she had made contributions
to the NAACP, YMCA, Urban League and International Committee
on African Affairs.

821
Brown, Lydia T. "Marian Anderson." The Washington Afro
    American. 14 January, 1939, pp. II.

Miss Anderson made her second New York recital at Carnegie
Hall. The striking character and prevailing beauty of the
singer's marvelous voice, and the improved technique in the
lieder songs proved that she is a first rate artist.

822
"Diva Achieves New Vocal Conquests." The St. Louis Argus.
    20 January, 1939.

New Yorkers had enjoyed Marian Anderson so much that she
had been scheduled for the season's third concert in April.

823
Downes, Olin. "Marian Anderson In Recital Here." The New
    York Times. 7 January, 1939, pp. 7.

Miss Anderson gave her second recital of the season at
Carnegie Hall. She sang music by the classic masters as
an interpreter who has fully grasped and deeply felt the
import of the song. She sang the Negro spirituals with
extraordinary distinction.

824
"It Happened In Memphis." The Washington News. 4 April, 1939.

Miss Anderson sang at the Memphis Municipal Auditorium.
It was noted that this southern city which also had DAR
chapters, felt it a matter of course that Miss Anderson
should sing there.

825
Johnson, Lillian. "No Other Concert Singer Has Ever Done
    This Before." The Afro American. 17 December, 1939.

Miss Anderson was to undertake a 26,000 mile, coast-to-
coast, concert tour doing seventy concerts. Sixty-seven
of the concert cities had been sold out for five months in
advance.

826
"La Anderson On Air Memorial Day." The California Eagle.
    25 May, 1939.

Miss Anderson was to appear on Mutual radio in Springfield, Illinois. Over 60 Mutual stations would hear the
broadcast.

827
"Marian Anderson." The New York Times. 12 March, 1939, Sec.
    11, pp. 10.

Miss Anderson was to sing on radio station WEAF.

828
"Marian Anderson." The New York Times. 26 November, 1939,
    Sec. 9, pp. 10.

Miss Anderson was to appear over station WABC with a
symphony orchestra and twenty-six voice mixed chorus direct-
ed by Wilfred Pelletier in Detroit. Lists the selections
to be done on the program.

829
"Marian Anderson." The New York Times. 17 December, 1939,
    Sec. 9, pp. 9.

For the second time within a month, Marian Anderson was
to sing to a packed house at Carnegie Hall.

830
"Marian Anderson Arrives At Dallas To Begin Tour of Texas
    Cities." The Pittsburgh Courier. 25 March, 1939, pp. 23.

Miss Anderson arrived in Dallas to sing at Southern
Methodist University. She had been in Forth Worth and was
to also make appearances in Waco, Austin, San Antonio, and
Houston.

831
"Marian Anderson At Carnegie Hall Jan. 6." The Pittsburgh
    Courier. 7 January, 1939, pp. 20.

Miss Anderson was to make her second appearance at Carnegie Hall.

832
"Marian Anderson Coming Here in Civic Music Association
    Concert." The Sandusky (Ohio) Star Journal. 22 November,
    1939.

Miss Anderson was to appear December 9th at the first of
the Civic Music Association concerts.

833
"Marian Anderson Heard." The New York Times. 30 November,
    1939, pp. 18.

Miss Anderson's program at Carnegie Hall contained few
of her traditional songs. Instead, she did songs of Spain
by Pable Esteve, Jose Bassa, Fernando Obradores and Enri-
que Grandus. Then she did songs of France by Saint-Saens,
Faure and Bachelet. She did a Russian song by Tchaikovsky
and then American songs by Horatio Parker, Herbert Bedford,
Florence Price and Samuel Barber. She ended with spirituals
by Boatner and William Heilman. Her voice was in fine form
and she sang with a suggestion of tremendous power in reserve.

834
"Marian Anderson Heard at World Movie Premiere." The
    Chicago Defender. 3 June, 1939.

Miss Anderson sang at the world premiere of Young Mr.
Lincoln in Springfield, Illinois.

835
"Marian Anderson Heard Over Ether." The Norfolk Journal and
    Guide. 2 December, 1939, pp. 19.

Miss Anderson was heard over a coast to coast network
from Detroit. She sang four songs on a symphonic program
conducted by William Pelletier. A twenty-six voice mixed
choir served as the background.

836
"Marian Anderson In Fourth Recital." The New York Times.
    26 May, 1939, pp. 21

Miss Anderson gave her fourth Carnegie Hall recital of
the season. She sang music by Handel, Schubert, Tchaikos-
ky, and Tcherepnin and a group of Negro spirituals. She
also did a number composed by her pianist, Kosti Vehanen.
Her last appearance of the season was to be at the New York
World's Fair.

837
"Marian Anderson In Recital." The Pittsburgh Courier. 18
    February, 1939, pp. 7.

Marian Anderson appeared at the Philharmonic Symphony in
Los Angeles. A brief biographical sketch is included.

838
"Marian Anderson in Recital April 13." The Philadelphia
    Inquirer. 26 February, 1939.

Miss Anderson was to appear at the Academy of Music.
She was awarded a Doctorate of Music from Howard University
in June, 1938 and had just been announced winner of the
1938 Spingarn Medal.

839
"Marian Anderson Near Top in Singing Appeal." The Fort
    Washington Morning Star-Telegram. 12 March, 1939.

Miss Anderson was to appear at the municipal auditorium
sponsored by the Fort Worth Civic Music Association.

840
"Marian Anderson to Be Honored in City Tonight." The New
    York Daily Worker. 16 April, 1939.

Miss Anderson was to be honored at the Essex House
after her Carnegie Hall concert.

841
"Marian Anderson To Present Varied Program." The Atlanta
    American. 2 April, 1939.

Miss Anderson was to appear at City Auditorium in
Atlanta as part of her fourth transcontinental tour.

842
"Marian Anderson Wins Ovation Here." The New York Times. 17
    April, 1939, pp. 12.

At her fourth recital of the season at Carnegie Hall,
Miss Anderson received a prolonged ovation from the capacity
crowd. With her last song the crowd remainded seated shout-
ing for more. It was not until the pianist closed the piano
did they begin to leave.

843
"Marian Anderson's Laminous, Brown Eyes." The Pittsburgh
    Courier. 28 January, 1939, pp. 8.

It was noted that Marian Anderson blessed the city of
Pittsburgh with a great show of her lovely voice in an
exquisitely chosen program of songs from Schubert, Pernell,
Verancini, Vehenen, Greig, and Burleigh.

844
McRae, Cora. "Many Stand To Hear Marian Anderson In Audi-
    torium Concert." The Houston Chronicle. 24 March, 1939.

City Auditorium was the scene of Marian Anderson's concert. It was her third appearance in three years. She
sang with perfect breath control. Her program showed the
tremendous range of her voice.

845
"Miss Anderson On May 30 Broadcast." The Norfolk Journal
    and Guide. 27 May, 1939, pp. 16.

Miss Anderson was to sing Memorial Day over station WOR
in Springfield, Illinois. More than sixty stations were
to air the broadcast.

846
"Miss Anderson on Mutual Air Network Today." The Atlanta
    Daily World. 30 May, 1939.

Miss Anderson was to broadcast from Springfield, Illinois
to over 60 mutual network stations.

847
"Miss Anderson Sings With Philadelphia." The Norfolk Jour-
    nal and Guide. 29 July, 1939, pp. 16.

A recording of the Marian Anderson concert with the
Philadelphia Symphony was released by Victor Record Co.
The album was entitled "Songs of Brahms."

848
"Miss Anderson Springs Surprise; Confused Critics Only
    Lukewarm." The Norfolk Journal and Guide. 9 December,
    1939, pp. 18.

Critics claimed that Miss Anderson had rendered too
many numbers that were relatively unfamiliar. She did
songs of Spanish, French and Russian composers, plus her
usual spirituals. Kosti Vehenan was the pianist.

849
"Noted Singer To Appear." The Detroit Free Press. 10 Decem-
    ber, 1939.

Marian Anderson was to sing with the Detroit Symphony
Orchestra on Thursday and Friday in the Masonic Temple.

850
"Popular Contralto To Give Concert in Richmond, Ind." The
    Dayton News. 5 March, 1939.

On her fourth transcontinental tour, Marian Anderson
was scheduled to appear in Richmond, Indiana on May 16th.

851
Vennell, Bill. "Marian Anderson Captivates Houston With
    Golden Notes." The Houston Press, 24 March, 1939, pp. 24.

More than 5,000 were at the Marian Anderson concert at
City Auditorium. Her program covered almost as much range
as her voice. She had to do four encores. She was accompanied by Kosti Vehanen.

852
" 'Young Mr. Lincoln' Had Its Premiere." The New York Times.
    31 May, 1939, pp. 26.

A distinguished audience was on hand to hear Marian
Anderson as she sang at the world premiere of "Young Mr.
Lincoln," a 20th Century Fox film based on the life of
Abraham Lincoln.

1940

853
"Anderson Called 'Greatest Singer'." The Philadelphia Tribune.
    9 May, 1940.

Miss Anderson was to make her third and final recital of
the 1939-40 season at the Academy of Music. Miss Anderson
is acclaimed as just about the greatest singer in the field.

854
"At Lewisohn Stadium." The New York Times. 14 July, 1940,
    Sec. 9, pp. 5.

Marian Anderson was to make her first appearance since
1925 as soloist on Saturday night at the Lewisohn Stadium.

855
"A Finnish Pianist And An American Singer." The Rockford
    (Ill.) Morning Star. 19 April, 1940.

Shows Marian Anderson and her pianist, Kosti Vehanen.
They were at the Shrine Temple for a concert.

856
"5,500 Hear Anderson." The New York Times. 30 March, 1940,
    pp. 10.

A capacity audience of 5,500 were at the White Plains
County Center to hear Marian Anderson. This was her first
appearance there. She did songs by Handel, Scarlatti,
Bizet, Schubert and Verdi, closing with Negro spirituals.
Kosti Vehanen was her accompanist.

857
"La Anderson in Hostess Role." The New York Amsterdam News.
    6 April, 1940.

Pictures of Miss Anderson at a dinner in which she
announced that proceeds from her Carnegie Hall concert
would go to the National Urban League, the NAACP, the YMCA
National Council and the International Committee on African
Affairs.

858
"La Anderson Scores Again." The New York Amsterdam News.
    6 Apri, 1940.

Miss Anderson made two appearances in New York. She
sang at Carnegie Hall and at the Brooklyn Academy of Music.

859
Lewis, Leon. "Pastors Back Fight on N. O. Auditorium." The
    Chicago Defender. 20 April, 1940.

The Interdominational Ministerial Alliance reversed its
previous action and backed the NAACP in their fight to get
better seating arrangements for Blacks at the upcoming
Marian Anderson concert.

860
Lewis, Leon. "Public Ignores N. O. Discrimination Fight To
    Hear Marian Anderson Sing." The Chicago Defender. 20
    April, 1940.

Local newspapers and organizations refused to join the
NAACP in their fight for downstairs seating for Blacks at
the upcoming Marian Anderson concert, citing that those
seats were better than those offered Blacks in other
southern cities.

861
"Marian Anderson." The Afro American. 6 April, 1940.

Miss Anderson is shown after her concert in Newark,
New Jersey. More than 4,000 persons were in attendance.

862
"Marian Anderson." The New York Times. 2 June, 1940, Sec.
9, pp. 5.

The Essex County Symphony Society in Newark was to begin
their outdoor concerts. Marian Anderson was to be the
soloist with Alexander Smallens conducting.

863
"Marian Anderson Heard." The New York Times. 25 March, 1940,
pp. 10.

The audience demanded several encores during Miss Anderson's fourth Carnegie Hall recital. She did songs by Handel, Carissini, Beethoven and Dvorak. She concluded with
Negro spirituals. Kosti Vehanen accompanied her.

864
"Marian Anderson In Final Recital." The New York Times. 27
May, 1940, pp. 22.

Miss Anderson made her fifth and final appearance at
Carnegie Hall. Her recital was for the benefit of four
organizations. The NAACP, The National Urban League, The
International Committee on African Affairs, and the Division of Colored Work of the National Council of the Y.M.C.A.
She did German lieder, Finnish songs, aria, and Negro spirituals. Kosti Vehanen accompanied her.

865
"Marian Anderson to Sing Here Thursday, Jan. 18; Began
'Career' When Eight." The Elmira (N.Y.) Star Gazette.
8 January, 1940.

The Elmira Community Concert Association sponsored Miss
Anderson at the Keeney Theatre. A short biographical
sketch is included.

866
"Marian Anderson's Recital." The New York Times. 3 January,
1940, pp. 16.

Miss Anderson performed in the fourth event in the Hurok
Carnegie Hall Concert Series. It was her third recital of
the season at the Hall. There were encores throughout the
program with added songs at the end. Kosti Vehanen accompanied her.

867
"Marian Anderson's Recital." The New York Times. 21 October,
1940, pp. 21.

Miss Anderson gave her first New York recital of the
season at Carnegie Hall. She sang many folk and contempo-
rary songs of other lands, especially Finland. She also
introduced Latin American songs into her program by singing three Brazilian songs. She did her usual numbers by
the masters. She had to do four encores. Franz Rupp
accompanied her.

868
"Negro Singer Making Third Tour of South." The Little Rock
    Democrat. 28 April, 1940.

Miss Anderson was to appear at the Robinson Memorial
Auditorium on May 15th. When she finished this tour, she
was to go to South America. Her repertoire consisted of
more than 250 songs in five languages.

869
"Recital Tomorrow To Assist Nurseries." The New York Times.
    30 November, 1940, pp. 18.

Marian Anderson was to do a benefit recital to aid the
National Association of Day Nurseries. The funds would be
used to give the services of the association to day nurseries throughout the country.

870
"Recitals Will Aid Charity." The New York Times. 29 Septem-
    ber, 1940, Sec. 2, pp. 3.

Marian Anderson was to do two concerts at Carnegie Hall
to aid two charities. Her October 20th concert was to benefit the Greenwich House Music School and her December 1st
concert was to benefit the National Association of Day
Nurseries.

871
"Rockford Pays Tribute To a Great Lady of The Concert Stage."
    The Rockford (Ill.) Morning Star. 19 April, 1940, pp. 14.

Miss Anderson sang at Shrine Temple. The gifted ling-
uist sang in German, Italian and French. She showed versatility as an interpreter of the composer's intentions and
moods.

872
"Throng At 2nd Recital By Marian Anderson." The New York
    Times. 2 December, 1940, pp. 18.

There was a sold-out house and two hundred standees at
Miss Anderson's recital to benefit the National Association
of Day Nurseries. She was not in as good voice as when
she performed in October. The program was entirely in
French and English except for one German song. She had to
do two more spirituals and "Ave Maria" as her encore.

873
Turner, Irvine I. "Marian Anderson Sails for Honolulu." The Afro American. 15 May, 1940.

Miss Anderson was to do six concerts in Honolulu. Upon her return, she would do engagements in Philadelphia and New York and then go on a two month vacation.

1941

874
"Barbours Are Patrons for Song Recital." The Red Bank (N.J.) Standard. 5 April, 1941.

Notes some of the notable people who would attend the Marian Anderson recital at the New Jersey College for Women.

875
"La Anderson Here Again January 12." The Philadelphia Tribune. 22 November, 1941.

Miss Anderson was scheduled to appear at the Academy of Music in Philadelphia in January.

876
"Marian Anderson Recital." The New York Times. 8 January, 1941, pp. 8.

Marian Anderson gave her third Carnegie Hall recital of the season. It was the fifth event in the Hurok Carnegie Hall series. She performed songs by Durante, Gluck, Bassani, Monteverdi, Handel, Han Wetzler, Quilter and did Negro spirituals by Brown, Johnson, Burleigh and Hayes.

877
"Marian Anderson To Sing Here This Evening." The Southwestern (El Paso, Texas) Torch. 8 February, 1941, pp. 1.

Miss Anderson was to sing at Liberty Hall. A list of her selections was included. This issue was dedicated to her.

878
"Negro Singer To Appear Here, Began Career In Obscure Choir." The El Paso (Texas) Times. 2 February, 1941, pp. 11.

Miss Anderson was to sing at Liberty Hall on February 8. Brief biographical sketch is included.

879
Poindexter, J. W. "Atlantic City Turns Out For Famed Diva." The Philadelphia Tribune. 21 August, 1941.

Miss Anderson appeared in the main auditorium at Atlantic City where over 5,000 turned out to hear her. She performed a varied program.

1942

880
"American Way - A Soldier Of Song With Military Background."
  The Paterson (N.J.) Evening News. 7 April, 1942, pp. 1.

Pictures Miss Anderson at her concert at Eastside High
School under the auspices of the YM-YWHA.

881
"Even Soldier Weeps When Marian Anderson Sings." The Paterson (N.J.) Morning Call. 7 April, 1942, pp. 1.

A soldier openly cried when Miss Anderson sang, "The
Old Folks At Home" during her concert at Eastside High
School.

882
"Marian Anderson." The New York Times. 4 January, 1942, Sec.
  10, pp. 7

Pictures Marian Anderson who was to appear at Carnegie
Hall.

883
"Marian Anderson." The New York Times. 1 November, 1942,
  Sec. 8, pp. 6.

Pictures Miss Anderson who was to sing at the Town Hall
Endowment Fund concert.

884
"Marian Anderson Conquers Paterson." The Paterson (N.J.)
  Morning Call. 7 April, 1942, pp. 1, 22.

Miss Anderson sang at Eastside High School in the final
concert of the YM-YWHA music series for 1942. She sang
six encores.

885
"Marian Anderson Heard At Auditorium." The New York Times.
  17 July, 1942, pp. 18.

Marian Anderson appeared with the New York Philharmonic
Symphony Orchestra. She sang three arias in the body of
the program and sang two encores with the orchestra. Finally she and her accompanist, Franz Rupp, were left on
stage and the recital continued.

886
"Marian Anderson Presents Varied Song Program." The Washington Star. 8 January, 1942.

There was a sold-out performance by Marian Anderson at
Constitution Hall.

887
Nadell, Louis. "Marian Anderson Captivates Capacity East-
    side Audience." The Paterson (N.J.) Evening News. 7
    April, 1942, pp. 25.

Miss Anderson presented a varied program. She did
songs by Handel, Bizet, Massanet, Schubert, Quilter, Rachmaninoff and a group of spirituals.

888
"Over 3,000 Expected For Anderson Recital." The Cedar Falls
    (Iowa) Daily Record. 21 March, 1942.

Miss Anderson was to sing at the Iowa State Teacher's
College on April 20. The concert would benefit the War
Relief Benefit Fund.

889
Prouty, Will. "Miss Anderson Thrills Throng." The Asbury
    Park (N.J.) Sunday Press. 9 August, 1942, pp. 1, 11.

Nearly 4,000 heard Miss Anderson in concert at the Ocean
Grove Auditorium. She often sings the work of composers
perfected in the art of bel canto. The St. Paul's Methodist Church sponsored the concert. Franz Rupp accompanied
her.

890
"Season Is Concluded By Marian Anderson." The New York
    Times. 11 May, 1942, pp. 18.

The 1941-42 musical season of Miss Anderson came to a
close with her third and final recital at Carnegie Hall.
She brought sincerity, distinction and imaginative insight
into every work, although she had been in voice on previous occasions. She did selections by Haydn, Handel, Mit-
tler and Griffes.

891
"Song Recital Aids China, Seals Pact." The Washington Post.
    8 January, 1942.

Miss Anderson did a recital at Constitution Hall for the
benefit of United China Relief.

892
Taubman, Howard. "Marian Anderson At Carnegie Hall." The
    New York Times. 6 January, 1942, pp. 26.

Noted that Miss Anderson was at her greatest in songs of
profound compassion and soaring estasy; she can also sing
a light, lyrical song with grace and sweetness. The utter
sincerity and dignity of this artist had no finer summation
than the rapt and exquisite grandeur of her singing of
"Crucifixion," which was the highlight of the evening.

893
Taubman, Howard. "Music." The New York Times. 5 November, 1942, pp. 34.

Marian Anderson sang at the thirteenth Town Hall Endowment Fund concert. Her voice was in rare form as she was intent on the most searching expression of the music and was able to probe new depths through sensitive molding of phrases and vocal color. She did selections by Purcell, Hayden, Schubert, Dubussy, Faure and did several spirituals. Her crowning finish was when she sang "Crucifixion." She had to do several encores and insisted that her accompanist, Franz Rupp, share the applause.

1943

894
"Concert and Opera Asides." The New York Times. 7 March, 1943, Sec. 2, pp. 7.

Miss Anderson made two appearances in San Francisco. She sang at the Civil Auditorium to a crowd of 10,000. Two days later she gave a noon concert at the Marinship Yards in Sausalito to a few hundred workers.

895
"Famed Singer To Give Concert In Nashville, January 20." Lebanon (Tenn.) Democrat. 14 January, 1943.

Miss Anderson was on her eighth transcontinental trip and would appear in Nashville on January 20th. It was also noted that she had set up an annual award for the most talented young artist.

896
"Many Notables on Patron List for Concert." The Washington Star. 5 January, 1943.

List of patrons for the United China Relief Benefit concert given by Marian Anderson at Constitution Hall.

897
"Marian Anderson." Pulse. Vol. 1, March, 1943, pp. 18.

Noted the upcoming appearance of Marian Anderson at Constitution Hall.

898
"Marian Anderson At Last Sings In D.A.R.'s Hall." Life. Vol. 14, January 25, 1943, pp. 100.

On January 7th Marian Anderson sang at Constitution Hall which four years earlier had denied her an appearance. 3,800 people were in attendance with no seating segregation.

899
"Marian Anderson At Metropolitan." The New York Times. 12
    April, 1943, pp. 27.

    Miss Anderson appeared for the first time at the Metro-
politan Opera House. It was her third recital of the season. She performed Handel and Bach arias, along with a
group of Negro spirituals.

900
"Marian Anderson Off To Mexico." The New York Times. 6 May,
    1943, pp. 25.

    Miss Anderson left for a five week tour of Mexico. Her
first concert was set for May 14th at the Palacio de bellas
Artes in Mexico City.

901
"Marian Anderson Sings For Great Lakes Trainees." The Norfolk
    Journal & Guide." 18 December, 1943.

    Miss Anderson sang for the three Negro regiments at Great
Lakes Naval Training station. More than 3,000 sailors heard
her performance.

902
"Marian Anderson To Sing." The New York Times. 4 January,
    1943, pp. 10.

    Marian Anderson was to sing at the Interior Department
for the formal presentation of the mural commemorating her
Lincoln Memorial concert in 1939. The mural was painted
by Mitchell Jamieson and was chosen after a national competition.

903
"Mexicans Hear Marian Anderson." The New York Times. 20 May,
    1943, pp. 27.

    Miss Anderson sang to a full house for her Mexican debut.
More than 2,000 people were in attendance.

904
"Mrs. Roosevelt Hears Marian Anderson Sing in D.A.R. Hall
    For China Relief Fund." The New York Times. 8 January,
    1943.

    Mrs. Roosevelt entertained a box party at the United
China Relief Benefit concert given by Marian Anderson.

905
"Opera and Concert Asides." The New York Times. 11 April,
    1943, Sec. 2, pp. 5.

    Miss Anderson sang at a camp for Black soldiers near
Seattle. She ended the recital with "Sometimes I Feel Like

A Motherless Child" afterwhich the bugler sounded retreat and the flag was lowered.

906
Taubman, Howard. "35th N. Y. Recital By Miss Anderson." The New York Times. 4 November, 1943, pp. 28.

Miss Anderson performed at Carnegie Hall. It was her 35th New York recital since her debut in 1925. She sang Italian and French songs and a group of Negro spirituals. One was aware of the sincerity and concentration in which she sang. She gave several encores for the capacity crowd.

907
"3,000 In Audience At Anderson Recital." The New York Times. 5 January, 1943, pp. 15.

Miss Anderson appeared at Carnegie Hall in her first recital of the season. She was assisted by William Primrose and accompained by Franz Rupp. In the early part of her program, her vocalism was disturbed by tremolo. She sang with sincerity, imagination and tender feeling. She did two encores and then asked the audience to join in singing the National Anthem. She finally had to sing "Ave Maria" before the audience would leave.

1944

908
"Conductors and Soloists on Stadium Programs This Week." The New York Times. 9 July, 1944, Sec. 2, pp. 4.

Pictures Marian Anderson who was to sing at the Lewisohn Stadium with Russian conductor Efrem Kurtz of the Kansas City Philharmonic.

909
Diton, Carl. "Marian Anderson Thrills A Packed Audience In Carnegie Hall Concert." The Negro. Vol. 1, Winter, 1943 1944, pp. 48.

Miss Anderson's talents showed that she was ready for an operatic performance. Her concert was a departure from mere vocal display to a rich emotional declamation.

910
"Marian Anderson Heard." The New York Times. 4 January, 1944, pp. 15.

Miss Anderson gave her second and final recital of the season at Carnegie Hall. She presented a new program performing songs by Hayden, Beethoven, Strauss, Wagner, Schalit, etc. and concluded by doing four Negro spirituals. The crowd joined her in the National Anthem but stopped to listen to her remarkable musical technique.

911

"Marian Anderson Heard By Throng." The New York Times. 11
   July, 1944, pp. 18.

The largest audience of the season turned out to Lewisohn Stadium to hear Marian Anderson sing with the Philharmonic Symphony. Her contributions to the program were
delivered with her usual superlative musicianship and understanding. She gave an encore and had to take ten curtain
calls before the audience would leave.

912

"Marian Anderson Receives Ovation." The New York Times. 13
   November, 1944, pp. 15.

Miss Anderson received several ovations during her
Carnegie Hall recital. She reached new peaks in her
art. Her musical interpretations plumbed depths and
spread out into splendor and touched exquisite delicacy.

913

"Ormandy Presents Brahms Program." The New York Times. 12
   April, 1944, pp. 17.

Marian Anderson was soloist as the Philadelphia Orchestra, under the direction of Eugene Ormandy, closed its
New York season with an all Brahms program. She sang two
selections and was assisted by a small men's choir from the
Westminster Choir. Miss Anderson sang with devotion to
the music and simplicity of delivery.

1945

914

"Anderson Recital on Dec. 21." The New York Times. 16
   November, 1945, pp. 16.

The Marian Anderson recital which had been scheduled for
November 11th at Carnegie Hall was rescheduled for December
21. The singer had become ill and was forced to postpone
her performance.

915

"Marian Anderson." The New York Times. 29 April, 1945, Sec.
   2, pp. 4.

Pictures Miss Anderson who was to be heard in recital
at the Metropolitan Opera House.

916

"Marian Anderson Heard." The New York Times. 31 December,
   1945, pp. 15.

Miss Anderson gave a recital at Carnegie Hall commemorating her triumphant return from Europe ten years ago. She
sang the same program as she did ten years ago, entirely
in German and Italian and some Negro spirituals.

917
"Marian Anderson Heard In Recital." The New York Times.
    22 November, 1945, pp. 17.

    Miss Anderson performed her postponed recital at Carne-
gie Hall. She did mostly new songs. It was noted that she
could sense the style of any composition, deliver it with
taste and imbue it with meaning.

918
"Marian Anderson Recital." The New York Times. 30 April,
    1945, pp. 13.

    At her only Metropolitan Opera recital of the season,
Miss Anderson sang to a capacity crowd. She opened with
numbers by Bach and Handel. She did numbers by Granados
and de Falla in Spanish and a number in English by Rachmaninoff. She closed with a group of spirituals. Franz Rupp
was the accompanist.

919
"Marian Anderson Recital Dec. 30." The New York Times. 26
    October, 1945, pp. 16.

    Miss Anderson was to celebrate the 10th anniversary of
her return to the United States with a recital on December
30th. She went to Europe in 1930 and upon her return in
1935 gave a recital at Town Hall. In honor of the occasion,
she was to sing the identical program she sang 10 years ago.

920
"Marian Anderson To Sing In Chaffey Auditorium." The
    (Pomona, Calif.) Progress. 12 February, 1945.

    Miss Anderson was to appear at Chaffey Auditorium. A
list of her selections and a biographical sketch is included.

921
"Miss Anderson Sings Tonight at Carnegie." The Newark Star-
    Ledger. 30 December, 1945.

    Marian Anderson was to sing at Carnegie Hall in celebra-
tion of her return from a European concert tour.

922
"Miss Anderson To Sing Here Thurs., April 5." The Philadel-
    phia Independent. 31 March, 1945.

    Miss Anderson was scheduled to sing in her native city
of Philadelphia at the Academy of Music.

923
"A New Study of Marian Anderson." The New York Times. 21
    April, 1945, Sec. 2, pp. 5.

Pictures of Miss Anderson who was to give her final recital of the season at the Metropolitan Opera House.

924
"Noted Singer Goes Over Big In Gym Concert." The Fort
   Logan (Colo.) News and Views. 27 January, 1945, pp. 1.

Miss Anderson sang to over five hundred soldiers at the
Fort Logan gym.

925
Schulte, Carol. "Robeson, Anderson Visit Russ." The San
   Diego (High School) Russ. 23 February, 1945, pp. 5.

Miss Anderson appeared at Russ Auditorium of February 8.

926
"Sell Out For Marian Anderson." The New York Times. 8
   January, 1945, pp. 15.

Miss Anderson made her third appearance at Constitution
Hall before a sold-out house. She sang several new numbers
including materials by Schumann, John Weldon, James Hook,
Frieda Sarsen, Christopher Thomas and Harman Sigmande. She
also did arias by Bach and Donizetti and a group of Negro
spirituals.

1946

927
"Anderson's Ten Years." Newsweek. Vol. 27, January 7, 1946,
   pp. 68.

Miss Anderson marked the 10th anniversary of her debut
at Town Hall in New York (December 30, 1935) with a performance at Carnegie Hall. During those ten years, she had
become a triumphant symbol of American Black achievement.

928
Downes, Olin. "Music of Negroes Concert Feature." The New
   York Times. 5 April, 1946, pp. 19.

Marian Anderson was soloist with the Philharmonic Orchestra at Carnegie Hall. The program was highly representative
of the Negro element and influence in American music. It
was felt that Miss Anderson was a singer primarily for the
recital platform. Although her rich voice fascinated the
ear and her musicianship and sincerity were outstanding,
she did not sing with the same ease as when accompanied
by a pianist.

929
Kastendieck, Miles. "Marian Anderson Anniversary." The
   Christian Science Monitor. 5 January, 1946.

Miss Anderson sang at the tenth anniversary of her debut

at Town Hall, December 30, 1935. Since that first appearance, she has toured the U.S. and Europe and has become a
national institution.

930
"Marian Anderson Ends Season." The New York Times. 29
    April, 1946, pp. 25.

Miss Anderson gave her final recital of the season at
the Metropolitan Opera House. Her program featured the
music of Handel, Scarlatti, Haydn, Schubert, Thomas, Griffes, Sadero and Ravel, closing with a group of Negro spirituals. Franz Rupp was the accompanist.

931
"A New Study of Marian Anderson." The New York Times. 21
    April, 1946.

Pictured Miss Anderson who was to sing in her final recital of the season.

932
Straus, Noel. "Marian Anderson In Fine Vocal Form." The
    New York Times. 11 November, 1946, pp. 44.

Miss Anderson sang at Carnegie Hall. She did the
early classics, English lyrics and Negro spirituals.

1947

933
Blalock, John V. "Marian Anderson In Recital At North
    Carolina College." The Durham Morning Herald. 15 Novem-
    ber, 1947, pp. 3.

Miss Anderson performed to a capacity crowd at B. N. Duke
Auditorium. She made use of her extraordinary vocal equipment. The most effective part of her program was the Schubert lieder with her voice being flexible enough to bring
out the subtle and sometimes elusive lines of the lieder.
Franz Rupp accompanied Miss Anderson.

934
Kolodin, Irving. "Marian Anderson in Carnegie Hall." The
    New York Sun. 12 November, 1947.

Miss Anderson suffered several vocal lapses in her concert at Carnegie Hall. She was said to be suffering from
a cold.

935
"Marian Anderson." The New York Times. 22 June, 1947, Sec.
    2, pp. 7.

Miss Anderson was to appear at the Lewisohn Stadium
with Leonard Bernstein conducting.

936
"Marian Anderson Soloist." The New York Times. 24 June,
   1947, pp. 26.

More than 8500 people were out to hear Miss Anderson
in the opening concert of the outdoor summer series at
Robin Hood Dell. She was accompanied by the 90 piece Dell
orchestra.

937
"State Honors Marian Anderson." The New York Times. 22
   January, 1947, pp. 21.

Miss Anderson was invited to sing the Star Spangled
Banner at a joint session of the House and Senate of the
Connecticut Legislature on Abraham Lincoln's birthday.

938
Straus, Noel. "Stadium Throng Cheers Anderson." The New
   York Times. 27 June, 1947, pp. 15.

Almost 20,000 attended the Marian Anderson concert with
the Philharmonic Symphony Orchestra at the Lewisohn Stadium.
Leonard Bernstein was the conductor. Miss Anderson was at
her best, her tones being luscious, round, freely emitted
and under perfect control. She had to do five more songs
after receiving an extraordinary ovation.

939
"3,700 Throng Recital By Marian Anderson." The New York
   Times. 7 April, 1947, pp. 18.

Miss Anderson gave an Easter concert at the Metropolitan
Opera House. It was her second and final New York appearance of the season. She sang many selections that were in
keeping with the occasion. Franz Rupp accompanied her on
the piano.

1950

940
"Berlin Ovation Given To Marian Anderson." The New York
   Times. 5 June, 1950, pp. 20.

A mixed Allied and German audience filled the 2,000
seats at the Titania Palast to hear Marian Anderson. The
audience was so enthused with the German part of the program that they gave a thirty minute ovation after the program. She did five groups of songs which displayed her
voice in all its flexibility and beauty.

941
"Griffis Honors Miss Anderson." The New York Times. 20
   August, 1950, pp. 52.

Marian Anderson was appearing at the Colon Theatre in

Buenos Aires.   Stanton Griffis, U. S. Ambassador to Argentina, gave a reception in her honor at the Embassy.

942
"Marian Anderson Scores In Recital." The New York Times.
   16 January, 1950, pp. 18.

2,700 were in attendance as Marian Anderson gave her
first concert of the season at Carnegie Hall.   She sang
with a conviction that few could match.   Franz Rupp provided excellent support to her concert.

943
"1,200 Queue Up To Hear Marian Anderson Sing." The New York
   Times. 29 May, 1950, pp. 11.

Marian Anderson twice turned away from a huge audience
to sing to the 1,200 people seated on narrow benches in
the gallery behind the rostrum at the Royal Albert Hall in
London.   This was their only chance to hear her this season.
The crowd had been lined up all day to get inside the hall.

944
"Touring Europe." The Christian Science Monitor. 27 May,
   1950.

Picture of Marian Anderson who was to start a tour of
England, France, Belgium, Italy and Switzerland.

1951

945
"American Contralto." The New York Times. 25 March, 1951,
   Sec. 2, pp. 7.

Pictures Marian Anderson at her home in Connecticut
studying a large sheaf of scores.   She was to appear at
Carnegie Hall tonight.

946
"Marian Anderson at Carnegie Hall." The New York Times. 27
   March, 1951.

Some 2,700 people heard Miss Anderson at her only New
York recital of the season.

947
"Marian Anderson In San Juan." The New York Times. 1 May,
   1951, pp. 34.

Miss Anderson was the luncheon guest of Governor and
Mrs. Luis Munoz Marin.   She was to do an evening concert
which would begin her South American concert tour in
Caracus, Venezuela.   She was to return to New York on June
10th.

948
"Recitals: Marian Anderson, Contralto, Carnegie Hall, March
    25." Musical America. Vol. 71, April, 1951, pp. 18, 20.

Miss Anderson performed her only New York recital of the
season at Carnegie Hall. She began with one of Mozart's
most demanding pieces but sang it with admirable breath control and great feeling. She also included folk songs which
she sang with ease and she did the spirituals in her own
imcomparable fashion. Franz Rupp accompanied her.

1952

949
"In Recital Wednesday." The Detroit News. 2 March, 1952.

Marian Anderson was to appear in concert at the Masonic
Auditorium.

950
"Marian Anderson Sings At Hunter." The New York Times. 7
    April, 1952, pp. 20.

2,200 people packed the Hunter College auditorium to
hear Miss Anderson. It was her only New York recital of
the season. In the selections from the standard repertoire,
she showed her ability to submerge herself in different
characters, to understand their feelings and to project
them with a power transcending the barriers of language.
In the spirituals, she showed her religious faith and the
depth of her sincerity.

951
Marian Anderson Sings to Mixed Florida Audience." Jet   Vol.
    1, February 7, 1952, pp. 5.

This was the first time a Black sang before unsegregated
audience in Florida state history.

952
"Marian Anderson's T.V. Debut." Our World. Vol. 7, August,
    1952, pp. 22-24.

Miss Anderson made her debut on television on Toast of
The Town.

953
"New York Recitals: Marian Anderson, Contralto, Carnegie
    Hall, Jan. 15." Musical America. Vol. 70, February, 1952,
    pp. 272.

This was Miss Anderson's first New York recital of the
season. She did her usual repertoire and brought a serene
dignity of presence and a dedicated concentration of her
vocal and spiritual resources. Franz Rupp accompanied her.

954
"250 White Persons in Florida Get Refunds at Marian Ander-
    son Recital in Armory." The New York Times. 25 January,
    1952.

Because Miss Anderson had a clause in her contract against
segregated audiences, 250 whites were refunded their money
for her concert since mixed audiences were contrary to
local customs.

955
"Unsegregated Miamians to Hear Marian Anderson." The Washing-
    ton Star. 25 January, 1952.

Miss Anderson was to sing before an unsegregated audience
in Miami. The County Commissioner agreed to the arrange-
ment as long as white purchasers knew beforehand.

1953

956
"Anderson Ban Is Off." The New York Times. 4 March, 1953,
    pp. 29.

Miss Anderson was to make her first commercial appearance
at Constitution Hall since the DAR barred her from appearing
there is 1939. She was to give a concert at the hall March
14th under the sponsorship of the American University Concert Series. She has sung at the hall twice since the 1939
ban but they were benefit performances.

957
"Anderson Ban Lifted." The New York Times. 13 November,
    1953, pp. 24.

It was announced that the Lyric Theatre in Baltimore had
lifted its ban on Marian Anderson. She was to appear there
next January. The management did not disclose why the ban
was lifted. The theatre does not have a policy of segregated audiences but previously had allowed only white
artists to perform there.

958
"Anderson In Baltimore." Musical America. Vol. 73, November
    15, 1953, pp. 12.

Previously banned from appearing at the Lyric Theater
in Baltimore, it was announced that she would sing there
after all. The management reversed its stand "as an expression of its own appreciation of the artistic standing of
Miss Anderson."

959
"Constitution Hall." Variety. Vol. 190, March 18, 1953,
    pp. 56.

Marian Anderson sang at Constitution Hall on March 14. This was her first concert there in a regular commercial concert.

960
Gunn, Glenn Dillard. "Marian Anderson's New Visit Recalls Dramatic History." The Washington Times Herald. 8 March, 1953.

Notes that Miss Anderson would appear at Constitution Hall. She made national headlines in 1939 when the D.A.R. refused to let her sing at the auditorium. Gives a brief account of her illustrous career both in the United States and abroad.

961
Gunn, Glenn Dillard. "Sell-Out House Hails Anderson Concert Here." The Washington Times Herald. 15 March, 1953.

Marian Anderson sang to a sold-out house when she appeared at Constitution Hall from which she had previously been banned from singing fourteen years before.

962
Hume, Paul. "Marian Anderson Displays Her Unique Gifts in Recital." The Washington Post. 15 March, 1953.

Miss Anderson appeared at Constitution Hall.

963
"Japan Sees Marian Anderson." Our World. Vol. 8, November, 1953, pp. 27-31.

Japan's highest honor for cultural contribution, "the Yushuko medal," was awarded to Marian Anderson after her sixth concert in Toyko. This concert benefited the Japanese Red Cross and ended a month long tour of Japan. The seventeen concerts also took her to hospitals in the war zone of Korea.

964
"Marian Anderson Barred From Baltimore Stage." Jet Vol. 4, October 8, 1953, pp. 57.

The Lyric Theatre refused to book Miss Anderson although it did not have segregated audiences.

965
"Marian Anderson Free To Play Lyric, Balto; Board In Face-Saver." Variety. Vol. 192, November 18, 1953, pp. 73.

It was noted that Miss Anderson may become the first Black to perform at Lyric Theater as a result of a resolution passed by the executive board of the theater. An earlier refusal to allow her to sing drew negative responses from the press and theater patrons.

966
"Marian Anderson In Tokyo." The New York Times. 28 April,
    1953, pp. 9.

Miss Anderson arrived in Tokyo for a series of concerts
under the sponsorship of the Japanese Broadcasting Corporation.

967
"Marian Anderson Leaves For Latin American Tour." Jet. Vol.
    4, December 3, 1953, pp. 62.

Miss Anderson was to tour eight Latin American countries
and return to the U. S. in January, 1954 for her January 8th
concert at Baltimore's Lyric Theatre.

968
"Marian Anderson Presents Recital." The New York Times. 6
    April, 1953.

Miss Anderson gave her only New York concert of the season.

969
"Marian Anderson Scores 2 'Firsts' in Kansas City." Jet
    Vol. 3, February 26, 1953, pp. 53.

Miss Anderson became the first Negro to sing with the
Kansas City, Mo. Philharmonic Orchestra and also became
the first artist to sing to sold-out houses for two concerts
on consecutive nights.

970
"Marian Anderson Sings In Seoul." The New York Times. 31
    May, 1953, pp. 3.

After performing in Pusan on May 29th, Miss Anderson
flew to Seoul to perform for Allied soldiers. A crowd of
5,000 jammed the yard of the Korean hospital where she
sang.

971
"Marian Anderson Steps In For Ailing Horowitz In Mpls;
    Only 8 Ask Out." Variety. Vol. 190, March 18, 1953, pp.
    56.

Miss Anderson performed at Northrup Auditorium when
Vladimer Horowitz became ill. Only eight patrons asked
to have refunds on their tickets.

972
"Marian Anderson To Tour Caribbean, Honor Queen." Jet Vol.
    4, October 22, 1953, pp. 12.

Miss Anderson toured the Caribbean and Central America
in honor of the visit of Queen Elizabeth II to the British
Colonies.

973
"Miss Anderson Sings To Royalty." The New York Times. 24
    May, 1953, pp. 22.

    Miss Anderson sang spirituals and German lieder before
the Empress Nagako of Japan and her two children. This was
the first time a Black had been a guest in the imperial
court's 2,600 year history.

974
"Stage Date Refused To Marian Anderson." The New York Times.
    24 September, 1953, 1953, pp. 39.

    The Lyric Theatre in Baltimore refused to book Marian
Anderson for an appearance there. The booking was sought
by Baltimore Fellowship, Inc., an interracial, interfaith
organization. They were told there were no dates open and
refused to discuss their segregation policies.

975
Straus, Noel. "Marian Anderson Presents Recital." The New
    York Times. 6 April, 1953, pp. 22.

    Miss Anderson gave her only New York recital of the sea-
son at the Metropolitan Opera House. The first half of her
program was devoted to selections of Handel, Schubert and
Verdi. In a group of English songs, Miss Anderson's voice
was at its best. The final selection of spirituals was
delivered with deep religious fervor.

1954

976
"Marian Anderson Is Heard At Hunter In Her Only Recital
    Here This Season." The New York Times. 25 January, 1954,
    pp. 14.

    Miss Anderson gave her only recital of the season at
Hunter College Assembly to a crowd of over 2,200. She did
the usual numbers by Bach, Schubert, Schumann and Saint-
Saens. Each of her selections emerges as a small, self-
contained drama, which is freshly conceived and tellingly
projected. Her voice did not achieve the same tonal glory
as in her earlier days.

977
"South of the Border." The Black Dispatch. 15 May, 1954.

    Pictures Miss Anderson as she prepares to leave for
Buenos Aires. She planned to do concerts in principal
cities in Brazil, Argentina and Uruguay.

978
Thorpe, Day. "Marian Anderson's Recital Shows Great Voice
    Has Fagged." The Washington Star. 31 March, 1954.

Ms. Thorpe felt that at 46, Miss Anderson's voice had
began to fail.   In the high registers, her voice was thin
and forced and many of her songs were sung out of tune.

1955

979
"Anderson Due Back At Met Next Season; Off Soon On Her
    First Tour of Israel." Variety. Vol. 197, January 19,
    1955, pp. 71.

Miss Anderson would return to the Metropolitan Opera
next season.   She was to leave for a concert tour of Israel.

980
"Anderson Repeats Metropolitan Success In Philadelphia."
    Musical America. Vol. 75, March, 1955, pp. 18, 45.

Miss Anderson appeared with the Metropolitan Opera in
Philadelphia as Ulrica in "A Masked Ball."   She was more
assured and effective than she had been when she made her
debut at the Met on January 7th.

981
"Carnegie Hall-Marian Anderson." Musical Courier. Vol. 152,
    December 15, 1955, pp. 12.

Miss Anderson opened her program at Carnegie Hall with a
group of Mozart songs, songs by Schubert, Ulrica's aria
from "A Masked Ball," and a group of English songs and
spirituals.   Noted that the inner glow which permeates her
singing was the communicative medium between herself and
her audience.

982
"Discussing Music Benefit for Youth Program." The New York
    Times. 30 October, 1955.

Miss Anderson was present at a tea party to discuss her
upcoming concert at Morningside Community Center to aid
Harlem youths.

983
Dowdy, Dosha and Rene Devries. "The National Scene - Chicago."
    Musical Courier. Vol. 151, January 1, 1955, pp. 24.

In her December 5th appearance at Orchestra Hall, Marian
Anderson did Listz's aria, "Jeanne d'Arc Au Bucher." It was
a difficult number, but she displayed warm and fiery accents
and created an exciting dramatic scene.

984
Gradenwitz, Peter. "Israel." Musical Courier. Vol. 151,
    June 28, 1955, pp. 27-28.

The Israel Philharmonic Orchestra began a ten week tour

of Europe. The last series of the concerts was the best
with Marian Anderson as soloist. She had been bothered
with a cold during earlier concerts. Her great personality
and excellent musical performance pleased the huge audience.
She sang "Alto Rhapsody" with the Tel-Avi Chamber Chorus,
done in Hebrew.

985
"Marian Anderson Grown In Stature." The New York Times. 5
    November, 1955, pp. 23.

Miss Anderson appeared at Carnegie Hall. She no longer
relied on the sheer sensuous appeal of her voice or its
physical weight or agility. She can chisel the phases of
a song with the delicacy of a cameo. She communicated her
style with breath-taking delicacy. Franz Rupp was her
accompanist.

986
"Marian Anderson In Israel." The New York Times. 28 March,
    1955, pp. 23.

Miss Anderson arrived in Israel for several weeks to
sing with the Israeli Philharmonic Orchestra.

987
"Marian Anderson Sings Second Time At White House." Musical
    America. Vol. 75, February 15, 1955, pp. 186.

President Eisenhower invited Marian Anderson to sing at
the White House at a banquet on January 26th for President
Paul E. Magloire of Haiti. She was also made an honorary
citizen of Tennessee when she sang there on January 17th.
She was give a citation and golden keys to the city.

988
"Miss Anderson Sings In Paris." The New York Times. 8 June
    1955, pp. 26.

Miss Anderson and the Israel Philharmonic Orchestra,
under Paul Klecki, gave a concert at a public theatre on
June 6th. She sang pieces by Brahms in German. It was the
orchestra's third Paris appearance in its current European
tour.

989
Redewill, Frances H. "The National Scene - San Francisco."
    Musical Courier. Vol. 151, March, 1955, pp. 33.

Miss Anderson appeared at the Opera House. Her greatest
appeal was still her spirituals. She included Spanish
numbers in her long program. Franz Rupp accompanied her.

990
Schabas, Ezra. "The National Scene - Toronto." Musical
    Courier. Vol. 151, April, 1955, pp. 34.

Noted that in Miss Anderson's recital at the Eaton Auditorium, she was suffering from a throat disorder which damaged her intonation. Still, the audience was moved by her vocal quality. She included music by Purcell, Schubert, a Spanish group and four Negro spiritiuals.

991
"Sings Here Sunday." The Washington Star. 16 March, 1955.

Marian Anderson was to appear at Constitution Hall.

1956

992
Biancolli, Louis. "Marian Anderson To Sing At Stadium." The New York World Telegram. 1 June, 1956.

Miss Anderson was to open the season for the Lewisohn Stadium. In tribute to her Metropolitan Opera debut, she would do a song from that production.

993
Hickman, C. Sharpless. "The National Scene - Los Angeles." Musical Courier. Vol. 154, August, 1956, pp. 14.

Eugene Normandy led the Philadelphia Orchestra at the 35th opening of the Hollywood Bowl. Marian Anderson was one of the soloists. She was in magnificent voice and received many ovations during her program.

994
"In My Opinion - The London Concert World." Musical Opinion. Vol. 80, December, 1956, pp. 135-136.

Marian Anderson appeared at Festival Hall in London on October 28. She did works of Schubert, Monteverdi, Scott, Dvorak, Verdi, Dougherty and spirituals. Franz Rupp accompanied her.

995
Lowens, Irving. "Anderson Singing Falls Short of Old Mastery." The Washington Star. 2 April, 1956.

Notes that Miss Anderson's recent concerts were marred by insecurity of pitch, forced tone, or interpretive gaucheries.

996
"Marian Anderson In Berlin." The New York Times. 24 October, 1956, pp. 42.

Miss Anderson began a European tour which was to take her to London, Switzerland and Belgium. She had just sang to a full house at the High School for Music in West Berlin.

997
"Marian Anderson Off On Tour." The New York Times. 15 Sept-

ember, 1956, pp. 10.

Miss Anderson left for Stockholm, Sweden to begin a ten
week European tour. She was to sing in Norway, Denmark,
Finland, West Germany, the Netherlands, France, England,
and Portugal, returning to New York in early December.

998
"The National Scene-Chicago." Musical Courier. Vol. 153,
    February, 1956, pp. 85.

Marian Anderson gave her annual recital at Orchestra
Hall on January 8th. This was a benefit for the Maude E.
Smith Nursery School. She did generous offerings from
Mozart and Schubert, songs by Swanson, Hindemith, Verdi,
Dougherty, spirituals and did added encores.

999
"The National Scene-Chicago." Musical Courier. Vol. 154,
    August, 1956, pp. 9.

The Ravinia Festival's 21st season began June 26th with
Marian Anderson as soloist with the Chicago Symphony Orches-
tra. The program was all-Brahms and the orchestra and Miss
Anderson were in top form.

1000
"Peerce Going To Soviet." The New York Times. 7 April, 1956,
    pp. 13.

Sol Hurok announced that Jan Peerce would do a concert
in the Soviet Union. He also announced that he had made
plans for Marian Anderson to appear in Moscow if she could
fit that city into her European tour schedule.

1001
"Recitals - Marian Anderson." London Musical Events. Vol.
    11. December, 1956, pp. 68.

Marian Anderson appeared at Festival Hall after a four
year absence from London. She remains supreme in her interpretation of Negro spirituals, but she was no longer able
to control her voice and her intonations were faulty.

1002
Taubman, Howard. "Music: Agreeable Opening At Lewisohn
    Stadium." The New York Times. 19 June, 1956, pp. 25.

The Lewisohn Stadium opened their thirty-ninth season
with Pierre Monteux conducting the Stadium Symphony Orchestra with Marian Anderson as soloist. 15,000 attended the
concert. She sang her usual repertoire as well as three
operatic arias and a group of Negro spirituals. Miss
Anderson has to do two encores before the audience would
leave.

1957

1003
"Ceylon Hails Marian Anderson." The New York Times. 8 November, 1957, pp. 22.

   Miss Anderson received wide acclaim in Ceylon. She gave her first performance in Colombo before the Ceylonese Governor General Sir Oliver Goonetilleke and American Ambassador and Mrs. Maxwell Gluck. She was to do two more concerts before leaving for Bombay.

1004
"Grace Rainey Rogers Auditorium Recital." Musical America. Vol. 77, March, 1957, pp. 37.

   Marian Anderson sang at the Metropolitan Museum of Art. Her voice was excellent as she sang a program of familiar music. At the end of the Strauss group, she had to give an encore. Audience applause delayed the recital some five minutes.

1005
"Marian Anderson In Bangkok." The New York Times. 21 October. 1957, pp. 37.

   Miss Anderson gave a Royal Command concert before King Phumiphon, Premier Pote Sarasis and the diplomatic corps.

1006
"Marian Anderson In Bombay." The New York Times. 14 November, 1957, pp. 41.

   Miss Anderson packed the Regent Theatre for her concert in Bombay. Her voice was also relayed to Bombay's Cooperage Football Ground where another 10,000 heard her.

1007
"Miss Anderson Sings In India." The New York Times. 18 November, 1957, pp. 37.

   The largest auditorium in New Delhi was filled to capacity to hear Marian Anderson. The program was held at the Vighyan Bhavan (Conference Hall) with Prime Minister Nehru attending.

1008
"Recitals In New York - Marian Anderson, Contralto." Musical America. Vol. 77, March, 1957, pp. 37.

   Miss Anderson appeared February 1 at Grace Rainey Rogers Auditorium. The audience applauded so long at the end of the Straus group, that she gave an encore. She was in excellent voice for the program of familiar music.

1009
Rosenthal, A. M. "Marian Anderson A Sellout In India." The
New York Times. 17 November, 1957, pp. 35.

Marian Anderson's concert in New Delhi was sold out weeks
before she arrived. The 1,200 tickets were sold rapidly
with 400 being reserved for students.

1010
"10,000 Hear Marian Anderson." The New York Times. 22 November, 1957, pp. 18.

Miss Anderson sang spirituals at Mohandas K. Gandhi's
memorial before a crowd of 10,000.

1011
"U Nu Hails Marian Anderson." The New York Times. 21 October,
1957, pp. 28.

Marian Anderson appeared in Burma and the crowd cheered
for ten minutes after her performance. Premier Nu asked
to be presented to the singer. She was on a Far Eastern
tour sponsored by the State Department and the American
National Theatre and Academy.

1012
"U. S. Singer In Taipei." The New York Times. 30 October,
1957, pp. 5.

Pictures Marian Anderson with Mme. Chen Cheng, wife of
Nationalist China's Vice President. She gave concerts at
Normal University in Taipei and Taipei City Hall.

1013
Van Olinda, Edgar S. "Marian Anderson Returning To Albany."
The Albany (N.Y.) Times-Union. 11 January, 1957.

Miss Anderson was to appear in concert at Temple Israel
on January 30.

1958

1014
Hume, Paul. "Marian Anderson Represents Far More Than Music
Alone." The Washington Post. 31 March, 1958.

Miss Anderson sang at Constitution Hall. Notes that no
singer can encompass all that Miss Anderson has brought
about in her career.

1015
Taubman, Howard. "Cold War On The Cultural Front." The New
York Times Magazine. 13 April, 1958, pp. 12-13, 107-108.

Many American artists attended the Brussels World's Fair.
It was noted that in India, Marian Anderson stood before

the Gandhi Memorial shrine singing 'Lead Kindly Light' with such sincerity and dignity, that the crowd felt Americans shared their emotions for their late leader.

1959

1016
"Anderson Hailed In Virgin Islands." Musical America. Vol. 79, July, 1959, pp. 35.

Marian Anderson appeared as the final artist on the St. Thomas Civic Music Association's concert series. A capacity crowd stood in tribute as she received the most enthusiastic and heartwarming welcome of any artist appearing in St. Thomas.

1017
Biancolli, Louis. "Marian Anderson Sings At Carnegie." The New York World Telegram. 30 March, 1959.

Miss Anderson put her whole self into her recital at Carnegie Hall which made the program a personal message for those in attendance.   There was a greater intensity and a new dramatic urgency.

1018
Bongard, David. "Marian Anderson Fans Fill Philharmonic Auditorium." The Los Angeles Herald and Express. 16 March, 1959.

Miss Anderson sang at Philharmonic Hall. Her tonal voice functioned beautifully from a variety of resonance levels. The entire program was warm and neat.

1019
Dwyer, John. "2,750 Applaud Personality, Artistry of Marian Anderson." The Buffalo Evening News. 1 April, 1959.

Miss Anderson appeared at Kleinhans Hall. This was the conclusion of the Zorah Berry-Buffalo Philharmonic series.

1020
Hawthorne, Frances. "Marian Anderson Holds 2,500 Spellbound in Concert." The Iowa Bystander. 16 April, 1959.

In her 3rd Des Moines concert recital, Miss Anderson was heard by more than 2,500 people at the KRNT Theatre.

1021
Kolodin, Irving. "Music To My Ears; Anderson." The Saturday Review. Vol. 42, April 11, 1959, pp. 51.

Mr. Kolodin felt that Marian Anderson's voice at a recent appearance at Carnegie Hall was only a vague suggestion of its former self. Her voice had very little of the discipline associated with her artistry.

1022
"Marian Anderson." Musical Courier. Vol. 159, May, 1959, pp.
   16.

   Miss Anderson gave her single Manhattan recital. She
performed songs by Mozart, Schubert, Strauss, Sibelius,
Rachmaninoff and Negro spirituals. She displayed warm
dignity and personal magnetism. She had some difficulty
staying in pitch and her vocal resources were not always re-
sponsive to her emotions. She gave the large audience two
encores. Franz Rupp accompanied her.

1023
"Marian Gets Top TV Spot." The Philadelphia Tribune. 18
   April, 1959.

   Marian Anderson was to appear in a Coca-Cola Company
television special. She was the first to be signed for the
specials.

1024
"Miss Marian Anderson Will Sing With Symphony Orch. Feb. 28-
   Mar. 1." The St. Louis American. 19 February, 1959.

   Miss Anderson was to appear with the St. Louis Symphony
Orchestra at Kiel Auditorium.

1025
Morin, Raymond. "Music." The Worcester Daily Telegram. 17
   April, 1959.

   Marian Anderson appeared at the University of Connecticut.

1026
"Recitals In New York - Marian Anderson..Contralto." Musical
   America. Vol. 79, April, 1959, pp. 40.

   This Easter Sunday concert at Carnegie Hall was Miss
Anderson's only Manhattan appearance of the season. Her
voice was not as flexible as it once was, but she sang with
dedication. She did the music of Schubert, Mozart, Strauss,
and two new songs by Johann Ahle and James Hook. She was
as compelling as ever when she sang four Negro spirituals.

1027
"Sings at Clarke College in Dubuque." The Bystander. 26
   February, 1959.

   Marian Anderson was to make her first appearance in
Debuque at Clark College.

1960

1028
"America's Great Contralto." The California Eagle. 3 March,
   1960.

Miss Anderson was scheduled to sing at Santa Monica Civic Autitorium on March 17 and at the Philharmonic on March 19.

1029
Durham, Lowell. "Marian Anderson Thrills S. L." The Salt
    Lake City Tribune. 12 April, 1960.

Miss Anderson appeared under the auspices of the University Artists series. She was most effective in Schubert lieder and Negro spirituals.

1030
Hume, Paul. "Marian Anderson is Heard by 4000." The Washing-
    ton Post. 8 February, 1960.

Mr. Hume attended Marian Anderson's concert at Constitution Hall and sorrowfully felt that she was no longer mistress of her voice, as she suffered in diction, in phrasing and in the total effect of her song.

1031
Thorpe, Day. "4,000 Come to Hear Marian Anderson." The Wash-
    ington Star. 8 February, 1960.

Nearly 4,000 fans came to Constitution Hall to see Miss Anderson sworn in as a member of the Cultural Center Advisory Board. She also gave a concert.

1962

1032
"Marian Anderson Texas Dates All Unsegregated; Asks Churches
    To Help." Variety. Vol. 228, September 26, 1962, pp. 1.

Impresario, C. T. Johnson, wanted to bring Miss Anderson to Texas to ease racial tensions. He wanted the churches to help in promoting unsegregated audiences for the concert.

1033
"Marian Anderson Visits University." The University of Day-
    ton Alumnus. Spring, 1962, pp. 6-7.

Some 2,000 heard Marian Anderson when she sang at the University of Dayton.

1963

1034
"Anderson and Cliburn Due." The Houston Chronicle. 24
    February, 1963, pp. 14.

Miss Anderson was to sing at City Auditorium.

1035
Bustin, John. "Fabled Contralto Wins Bravos Here." The Austin
    (Texas) American. 26 February, 1963, pp. 5.

Marian Anderson appeared at Municipal Auditorium. She sang a wide variety of songs.

1036
Cronk, Sue. "It'll Be Her Second Trip To The Lincoln Memorial." The Washington Post. 27 August, 1963.

Noted that Mrs. Harold Ickes would join the March on Washington for Jobs and Freedom. It was her husband, then Secretary of the Interior, who made it possible for Marian Anderson to sing at Lincoln Memorial in 1939.

1037
"Singer Welcomed Here." The Albany (N.Y.) Times Union. 11 February, 1963.

Marian Anderson was welcomed at Temple Israel for a concert.

1038
Talese, Gay. "5,000 Here Attend Kennedy Tribute." The New York Times. 3 December, 1963, pp. 1.

5,000 were at City Hall Plaza to pay tribute to the late President Kennedy. Marian Anderson sang at the tribute.

1039
Van Olinda, Edgar. "1,500 Enthralled By Marian Anderson." The Albany (N.Y.) Times Union. 11 February, 1963, pp. 7.

Miss Anderson gave a concert at Temple Israel. Marian Anderson Day was observed during her visit.

1965

1040
Gilroy, Harry. "Marian Anderson Will Sing At Benefit In Paris." The New York Times. 15 September, 1965, pp. 40.

On September 28th, Marian Anderson was to suspend her retirement to give a program of Negro spirituals at Sainte Chapelle, a Gothic Church in Paris. The concert was to be in behalf of the World Festival of Negro Arts to be held in Senegal the following April. She was to do a thirty minute program and receive $10,000.

1041
Kamm, Henry. "Marian Anderson Enthralls Paris." The New York Times. 29 September, 1965, pp. 6.

Miss Anderson sang at Sainte Chapelle. Patrons paid $100 for the recital and a movie. She sang sixteen spirituals. The concert was the opening fund-raiser for the World Festival of Negro Arts to be held in Senegal. President Leopold Senghor of Senegal was in the audience.

1042
"White House Lists Events for Arts Festival Monday." The
   Washington Star. 10 June, 1965.

Miss Anderson was to perform at the First Festival of
American Arts.

1968

1043
Hughes, Allen. "Village Setting Enhances Music." The New
   York Times. 1 July, 1968.

Marian Anderson appeared at the Waterloo Village Music
Festival in New Jersey.

REVIEWS

AND CRITICISM

1044
Crawford, Marc. "Should Marian Anderson Retire?" Ebony. Vol.
   15, June, 1960, pp. 77-78, 80-81.

Many music critics felt that Miss Aderson should retire
while she was still on top.

1045
"Eisler Holds U. S. May Have To Leave." The New York Times.
   12 June, 1950, pp. 11.

Gerhart Eisler, head of the Information Department of the
East German Democratic Republic, announced that there was no
room in Europe for American Imperalists. He also asserted
that Marian Anderson had endorsed a communist petition to
ban the atomic bomb. Miss Anderson denied signing any such
petition.

1046
Hancock, Dean G. B. "Dean Would Enjoy Anderson Concerts
   More If Accompanist Were Not White." The Philadelphia
   Independent. 18 August, 1940.

Mr. Hancock wondered why Marian Anderson had a white
accompanist and whether there were any Blacks who could do
the job as well.

1047
Miller, Joy. "Criticism Hurts Her Deeply." The Washington
   Star. 22 September, 1963.

A profile of the great contralto and says that because
she never worked militantly for Civil rights, she was criti-
cised by the Black community, which hurt her deeply. She
was one of 31 to receive the Presidential Medal of Freedom.

1048
"Marian Anderson's Voice Failing, Declare Top U. S. Music
    Critics." Jet. Vol. 5, April 22, 1954, pp. 56-57.

After eighteen years on the concert stage, some critics felt that Miss Anderson's voice was showing signs of
wear and tear and her voice had lost some of its quality and
much of its control.

1049
Thompson, Dorothy. "A Tribute to Marian Anderson." The Wash-
    ington Star. 3 February, 1958.

Criticism of an article by Robert Shayon who wrote about
Miss Anderson's tour of Asia as being a propaganda trip
sponsored by the State Department. The author felt that
Miss Anderson was a messenger of humanity and her singing
conveys human values by attitude and action.

1050
"Warns Marian Anderson." The New York Times. 10 January,
    1951, pp. 32.

Miss Anderson was asked by the Richmond NAACP to cancel
her engagement at the Mosque if audiences were to be segregated. The NAACP also advised her that they would urge
people not to attend if the audience was segregated.

MISCELLANEOUS
ACTIVITIES

1051
"AEMC Luncheon A Success." The Journal Advertiser. 24 July,
    1968, pp. 15.

The Danbury Chapter of Albert Einstein College of Medicine
Auxillary featured a "Luncheon With Celebrities." Marian
Anderson was in attendance.

1052
"Arriving At Washington." The New York Times. 28 August, 1963,
    pp. 1.

Shows a group of people, including Marian Anderson, arriving in Washington, D. C. for the civil rights march.

1053
"At Central Park Event." The New York Times. 24 September,
    1962, pp. 26.

Pictures Marian Anderson and Bernard Baruch at Interfaith
Day in Central Park.

1054
"Baruch Biographer Honored." The New York Times. 29 October,
    1958, pp. 32.

Marian Anderson, delegate to the U. N., presented the
National Council of Women's book award to Margaret Coit for
her biography of Bernard Baruch.

1055
"Booker T. Washington Launched." The New York Times. 30
    September, 1942, pp. 25.

Marian Anderson and Mary McLeod Bethune officiated at
the launching of the Liberty freighter, Booker T. Washington.
The ship was to be commanded by the only licenced Black sea

captain in the American merchant marine, Stephen Mulzac.

1056
Carmody, Deirdre. "Hurok Rites Fill Carnegie Hall." The New
    York Times. 9 March, 1974, pp. 32.

More than 2,600 mourners attended the funeral of Sol
Hurok. The eulogy was delivered by Marian Anderson, whom
Mr. Hurok had discovered in Paris in 1935.

1057
Carmody, Deirdre. "Patriotism On Parade As City Bicentennial
    Gala Begins." The New York Times. 23 May, 1975, pp. 1, 42.

New York opened its official Bicentennial celebration.
Marian Anderson was one of the speakers. She read "An
American Tribute" as the All City Chorus sang the "Battle
Hymn of the Republic."

1058
"Carnegie Hall Is Bought By City; Philharmonic Will Stay
    There." The New York Times. 1 July, 1960, pp. 27.

Carnegie Hall was purchased by the city of New York. It
was going to be purchased by private business interests,
which would have forced the New York Philharmonic, the Boston
Symphony and the Philadelphia Orchestra to have their concerts elsewhere. Marian Anderson was on hand for the ceremony in which the city acquired the title to the hall.

1059
"Carver Is Yard's Fourteenth Polaris Sub." The Shipyard News
    and Views. Vol. 5, Spetember, 1965, pp. I.

Marian Anderson christened the USS George Washington
Carver in Newport News, Virginia.

1060
"City Gives Luncheon To Ghana Head." The New York Herald
    Tribune. 29 July, 1958.

Ghana Prime Minister, Kwame Nkrumah, was given a luncheon
during his visit. He met Marian Anderson, who was a delegate
to the United Nations.

1061
Conn, Stephen R. "Leontyne Price Sings To Assist Children
    At Harlem Arts School." The New York Times. 9 December,
    1967, pp. 58.

"An Evening With Leontyne Price" was a benefit concert
for the Harlem School of the Arts. After the concert, a
buffet dinner was served with Marian Anderson attending the
affair.

1062
Cummings, Judith. "Marian Anderson Is Back For A Banquet
    For Harlem Dancers." The New York Times. 25 March, 1978,
    pp. 21.

    Miss Anderson was to do a program at the St. Paul's
Chapel at Columbia University to benefit the Dance Theater
of Harlem.

1063
Damron, Robert. "Polaris Sub Carver Is Launched." The Hampton
    (Va.) Times Herald. 14 August, 1965, pp. 1, 9.

    Marian Anderson christened the USS George Washington
Carver at the Newport News Shipbuilding and Dry Dock Company.

1064
"Danbury Hospital Ball Takes Guest On Ride Into Future."
    The Danbury (Ct.) News-Times. 4 November, 1969.

    Marian Anderson was a guest at the Danbury Hospital ball.

1065
Delvin, Ruthanne. "Singer Asks End To Hate And War." The
    Hartford (Ct.) Times. 22 March, 1970, pp. 5B.

    Unable to attend a banquet to make her a life member of
the Connecticut Music Education Association, Marian Anderson
sent a message to the group for "increased national understanding."

1066
"Eisenhower Picks 34 to Help Plan Cultural Center." The New
    York Times. 12 April, 1959, pp. 79.

    President Eisenhower picked a thirty-four member advisory
committee to help plan a national cultural center in Washington, D. C. Marian Anderson was one of the committee
members chosen by the president.

1067
Ericson, Raymond. "Notes: An Arts Center To Celebrate Charles
    Ives." The New York Times. 19 February, 1978, Sec. 2,
    pp. 15.

    There were plans to establish a $11 million Charles Ives
Performing Arts Center. Marian Anderson was on the committee
which was to plan for a facility near the Connecticut State
College.

1068
Farrington, Dorothy. "Concert Artist Conducts Letter Lobby
    For Arts." The Danbury (Ct.) News-Times. 16 February,
    1970.

Marian Anderson was conducting a letter lobby campaign to secure more federal funds for the National Arts and Humanities Foundation.

1069
"14 Trustees Are Appointed To Eleanor Roosevelt Fund." The New York Times. 25 May, 1965, pp. 29.

President Johnson reappointed fourteen trustees of the Eleanor Roosevelt Fund. Marian Anderson was one of those reappointed for a six year term.

1070
"First Lady Begins Last Official Trip." The New York Times. 23 November, 1968, pp. 38.

Lady Bird Johnson began her last official cross country trip as First Lady. Accompanying here were members of the National Council on The Arts, including Marian Anderson.

1071
"Great Negro Contralto In Rotorua." The Rotorua (New Zealand) Post. 2 July, 1962.

Miss Anderson and her accompanist were on holiday in Rotorua.

1072
Henahan, Donal. "Mostel Wields No Mean Baton." The New York Times. 28 April, 1969, pp. 37.

Zero Mostel made his debut with the Symphony of The New World. Marian Anderson was on hand to speak in behalf of the integrated orchestra's mission.

1073
"H-H-H Hellos." The Washington Post. 17 May, 1966.

Hubert H. Humphrey greeted Marian Anderson and others at the reception for the U. S. Committee for Refugees.

1074
Hubbard, Scott. "Guests Enjoy Musical Reception." The Wilmington (Del.) Evening Journal. 8 May, 1972, pp. 25.

Marian Anderson was one of the guests at the Delaware Art Museum reception.

1075
Hughes, Allen. "Concert By Israel Philharmonic Marks 3 Toscanini Occasions." The New York Times. 23 January, 1967, pp. 28.

The American Israel Cultural Foundation sponsored the Israel Philharmonic at Carnegie Hall in a memorial to Arturo Tuscanini. Marian Anderson narrated "Joseph and

His Brothers," a cantana which was sung by four soloists.
This alternation of narration and singing was smooth. Miss
Anderson's reading was dignified and moving.

1076
"Hunger Fighters." The New York Times. 23 November, 1961,
     pp. 17.

     Pictures President Kennedy greeting members of the Free-
dom From Hunger Foundation at the White House. Marian Anderson was a founding member of the foundation.

1077
"Ives Fan." The Danbury (Ct.) News-Times. 5 July, 1974,
     pp. 13.

     Pictures Marian Anderson and Mayor Ducibella at the
Charles Ives concert.

1078
"Johnson Appoints 8 To Council On Arts." The New York Times.
     13 December, 1966, pp. 58.

     Marian Anderson was one of the new members appointed to
the National Council on The Arts by President Johnson. The
council decides where money to develop the arts should go.

1079
"Man of The Moment Meets The Guests." The New York Post.
     20 January, 1965, pp. 66.

     Pictures President Johnson greeting Marian Anderson. She
was wearing the Presidential Freedom Medal presented to her
last year.

1080
"Marian Anderson Addresses Friends of The Symphonette."
     The Danbury (Ct.) News-Times. 10 August, 1970, pp. 24.

     Miss Anderson spoke at a luncheon sponsored by the
Firends of the Symphonette to benefit the Ridgefield
Symphonette Orchestra.

1081
"Marian Anderson Calls On Kennedy At White House." The New
     York Times. 23 March, 1962, pp. 26.

     Miss Anderson visited the White House and exchanged
mementos with President Kennedy. She gave him a copy of
her latest record, "Spirituals," and he gave her a reproduction of the Inauguration emblem. Miss Anderson was to
perform at the State Department that night.

1082
"Marian Anderson Heads Chest's Special Gifts Group." The
     Albany (N.Y.) News-Times. 7 October, 1960.

Miss Anderson was named as special gifts chairman of the Danbury, Connecticut Community Chest drive.

1083
"Marian Anderson Honorary Head." The University of Hartford Observer. Vol. 3, October, 1976, pp. 1, 6.

Miss Anderson was named honorary chairman of the 1976 Committee for Musical Wednesdays at the University of Hartford College of Music.

1084
"Marian Anderson Lights Way For Millions of Persecuted." The Toronto Daily Star. 11 December, 1962, pp. 29.

Miss Anderson received a copy of the Ontario Human Rights Code and lit a candle for those imprisioned throughout the world solely for their beliefs. She also received an honorary degree from Queen's University.

1085
"Marian Anderson Named To Connecticut Arts Post." The New York Times. 22 July, 1965, pp. 23.

Governor John J. Dempsey appointed Marian Anderson to the newly created State Commission On The Arts. The commission had an appropriation of $50,000 for the next biennium.

1086
"Marian Anderson To Aid College Fund." The Wilmington (Del.) News. 5 October, 1965, pp. 13.

Miss Anderson was to appear at a reception to raise funds for the United Negro College Fund.

1087
"Marian Anderson To Lecture." The Rockford (Ill.) Register Republic. 11 October, 1967.

Miss Anderson was to lecture at Guilford High School.

1088
"Marian Anderson To Speak at U of M." The Bronze Reporter. 30 May, 1959.

Miss Anderson was to be the spring commencement speaker at the University of Michigan.

1089
"Marian Anderson To Top New World Symph's Gala." Variety. Vol. 254, April 23, 1969, pp. 59.

Miss Anderson was to preside over the "Spring Gala Benefit Concert" sponsored by the Symphony of The New World.

1090
"Marian Anderson's Visit to CIM Resembles A Tour By A Queen."
    The Cleveland Plain Dealer. 1 June, 1972.

Miss Anderson visited the Cleveland Institute of Music.

1091
McGarey, Mary. "Marian Anderson Sings A Lecture of Love."
    The Columbus Dispatch. 13 February, 1976.

Miss Anderson lectured at the Ohio Theater. She gave
an inspiring message of faith and love. It was a recollec-
tion of her life and career.

1092
"Memorial To Tolstoy." The New York Times. 17 November, 1960,
    pp. 35.

Marian Anderson was one of a committee of seventy organized to commemorate the 50th anniversary of the death of
Russian writer, Leo Tolstoy. A concert was planned, featuring his favorite music and excerpts from his writing.

1093
Mink, Ken. "Marian Tells of Leap From 50-Cent Concerts."
    The Dayton Daily News. 19 October, 1967.

Miss Anderson spoke of her career at the Dayton Junior
League.

1094
"Miss Anderson Backed." The New York Times. 15 July, 1958,
    pp. 7.

Rep. Lester Holtzman of Queens wrote to President Eisenhower asking him to consider Marian Anderson for the newly
created post of Assistant Secretary of State for African
Affairs. He cited her recent Asian tour and her ability to
be a goodwill ambassador.

1095
"Miss Anderson Calls On The Andersons." The New York Times.
    29 September, 1952, pp. 5.

Marian Anderson visited in Copenhagen with Mrs. Eugenie
Anderson, who was U. S. Ambassador to Denmark.

1096
"Miss Anderson In Haiti." The New York Times. 31 December,
    1953, pp. 10.

Miss Anderson and Ralph Bunche were among the guests at
the 150th anniversary of Haiti's independence from France.
The two day celebration was to end with a formal banquet.

1097
"Miss Anderson Joins Board." The New York Times. 11 May,
    1965, pp. 35.

Marian Anderson was elected as a trustee of the Brooklyn
Institute of Arts and Sciences.

1098
"N.A.A.C.P. Warned Fight Is Not Won." The New York Times.
    7 December, 1959, pp. 21.

Roy Wilkins, Executive Secretary of the NAACP, was guest
speaker at a fund raising dinner. Marian Anderson was one
of the guests of honor at the dinner.

1099
"Negro Singer Urged For Job." The Long Island (N.Y.) Star
    Journal. 15 July, 1958, pp. 5.

Congressman Lester Holtzman urged President Eisenhower
to name Marian Anderson as Assistant Secretary of State
for African Affairs.

1100
Orr, Robin. "A Luncheon With Marian Anderson." The Oakland
    Tribune. 24 March, 1970.

Miss Anderson was guest of honor at a luncheon sponsored
by the Oakland Symphony Guild.

1101
Orr, Robin. "A Salute To Marian Anderson." The Oakland
    Tribune. 22 March, 1970.

Miss Anderson was to be the guest of honor at the Oakland Symphony Guild meeting at Mills College.

1102
"Panel Will Study Connecticut Arts." The New York Times.
    28 July, 1963, pp. 64.

Marian Anderson was named to a fifteen member committee
to survey art facilities in Connecticut.

1103
"A Presidential Appointee." The Washington Post. 8 February
    1960.

Picture of Marian Anderson being sworn in as an advisory
member of Washington's Cultural Center.

1104
"Retired Concert Singer Here For Lecture Tonight." The Rock-
    ford (Ill.) Morning Sun. 11 October, 1967.

Marian Anderson was to speak at Guilford High School sponsored by Rock Valley College. She was to talk about her "philosophy of life."

1105
Robertson, Nan. "Descendents of John Adams Delights First
    Lady." The New York Times. 10 June, 1967, pp. 16.

Lady Bird Johnson was on tour in Quincy, Massachusetts. She was honored at a dinner and one of the special guests was Marian Anderson.

1106
Robertson, Nan. "Nixons Attend Concert At Kennedy Hall."
    The New York Times. 10 September, 1971, pp. 40.

Marian Anderson sat in the presidential box along with the Nixon family and Mrs. Dwight Eisenhower as the National Symphony Orchestra performed at the Kennedy Center.

1107
"Rockefeller Says Girl Scouts Help Curb Delinquency." The
    New York Times. 15 October, 1959, pp. 41.

Gov. Rockefeller spoke at a meeting of the Greater New York Council's annual fund-raiser for the Girl Scouts. Marian Anderson and Sam Levinson were made honorary members. The honorary members were cited for their "good deeds throughout the year," were given scout pins and saluted the scouts for their work.

1108
"Romulo Praises Red Cross Role." The New York Times. 9 May,
    1961, pp. 32.

Some 4,500 delegates attended a three day Red Cross convention in Cincinnati. Marian Anderson was elected as one of the new members-at-large to their Board of Governors.

1109
"Salvation Army Lists Campaign Leaders." The Danbury (Ct.)
    News-Times. 6 February, 1975, pp. 10.

Marian Anderson was one of the honorary chairpersons for the Salvation Army's building fund.

1110
Shenker, Israel. "Scholars Dissent The 'New Revolution'."
    The New York Times. 24 October, 1969, pp. 43.

An audience gathered at the Pierre Hotel to hear those whom Brandeis University had given honorary degrees during the past years. Each guest spoke on "The University and The New Revolution." Marian Anderson said her heart went out to the militant students as well as this nation. "Both are worth saving," she insisted.

1111
Shepard, Richard F. "105 U. S. Negro Artists Prepare For Senegal Arts Fete In April." The New York Times. 11 February, 1966, pp. 36.

105 American delegates, including Marian Anderson, were to lead the U. S. representation to the First World Festival of Negro Arts in Senegal in April. The AID and USIA was to help pay the expenses of the artists.

1112
"Singer Aids Musicians." The New York Times. 12 May, 1955, pp. 33.

Marian Anderson endowed a scholarship fund in Tel Aviv after her first tour of Israel. The American fund for Israel Institutions would administer the funds to aid young musicians. This was the second fund established by the singer. The Marian Anderson Scholarship Fund had awarded $27,000 in scholarships to fifty-four U. S. singers.

1113
"Singer Praises Opera House." The Seattle Post Intelligence. 16 March, 1962.

Marian Anderson praised the new Seattle Opera House at the World's Fair.

1114
"Singer To Sponsor Ship." The New York Times. 21 September, 1942, pp. 17.

The Booker T. Washington Ship Launching Committee announced that Marian Anderson would be on hand at the official launching of the Booker T. Washington freighter at the Wilmington Yard of the California Shipbuilding Corporation. Mrs. Portia Washington Pittman, his only living daughter, and a granddaughter were to be present along with several prominent Blacks.

1115
Spiegel, Irving. "S. Hurok Honored For Cultural Aids." The New York Times. 25 January, 1961, pp. 4.

Marian Anderson was one of the artists who paid tribute to Sol Hurok when New York city and the American-Israel Cultural Foundation honored him at a $150 a plate concert dinner. He was honored for "distinguished service in the cause of cultural exchange."

1116
Sullivan, Dan. "Marion Freschl, 70, Feted By Her 'Alumni'." The New York Times. 10 January, 1966, pp. 14.

Marian Anderson was the master of ceremonies at a party honoring her former voice teacher. Several of Marion Fres-

chl's 'alumni' were present with testimonials and gifts.
Miss Anderson said that Miss Freschl "went far beyond being
a 'teacher' to her students."

1117
"Ten Leaders Back Breezy Point Park." The New York Times.
4 October, 1962, pp. 49.

Marian Anderson was one of the leaders trying to convert
the Breezy Point area of the Rockaway, Queens, into a vast
waterfront park. The leaders wanted to preserve the more
than 1,000 acres for recreation space.

1118
Thinnes, Tom. "Kids Meet A Great Lady." The Kalamazoo (Mich.)
Gazette. 14 October, 1975; pp. Al, A3.

Marian Anderson visited Northglade School to talk to
the students.

1119
"Tribute to Hurok." The New York Post. 10 May, 1967, pp. 2.

Marian Anderson was at a dinner in honor of Sol Hurok,
who was her manager.

1120
"Wirtz and Marian Anderson Help Christen Submarine." The New
York Times. 15 August, 1965, pp. 39.

The polaris submarine, George Washington Carver, the
first nuclear vessel to be named for a Black, was christened
at the Newport News Shipbuilding and Dry Dock Company by
Marian Anderson.

1121
"Women Leaders Appeal To Khrushchev On Bomb." The New York
Times. 28 October, 1961, pp. 6.

Four women, one of which was Marian Anderson, who had
been delegates to the U. N., appealed to Premier Khrushchev
to stop Soviet plans to explode a fifty megaton bomb. They
sent a cablegram urging him to "stop such a senseless demonstration of instruments of slaughter."

3
AWARDS
AND HONORS

AWARDS

Bok Award

1122
Carter, Elmer A. "The Bok Award." Opportunity. Vol. 19,
    April, 1941, pp. 99.

This editorial noted that Marian Anderson received the
Bok Award. This award is given to the Philadelphian who
has contributed a service to advance the larger interest
of Philadelphia. The editorial expressed thanks to the
trustees of the Bok Award for presenting the award to a
Black.

1123
Charity Gets $10,000 Award Won by Marian Anderson." The
    Washington Star. 18 March, 1941.

Miss Anderson gave her $10,000 Bok Award to needy but
talented youngsters.

1124
"Marian Anderson, Negro Contralto, Receives the Philadelphia
    Award." The Philadelphia Tribune. 18 March, 1941.

Miss Anderson returned to her home city to receive the
Philadelphia Award known as the Bok Award. The award carried
a $10,000 prize and is awarded to a Philadelphian who has
contributed most to the city.

1125
"Marian Anderson Receives Coveted Philadelphia Bok Award."
    Opportunity. Vol. 19, April, 1941, pp. 120.

On March 17th, Miss Anderson received the Bok Award of
$10,000 at the Academy of Music. She was awarded as the
person who had done the most for Philadelphia during the
past year. The award was founded in 1921 by Edward W. Bok.

1126
"Marian Anderson Receives The Bok Award, Highest Honor That
    Philadelphia Bestows." The New York Times. 18 March, 1941,
    pp. 26.

Miss Anderson received the Bok Award as the person who
had done the most for the Philadelphia community during
the past year. Miss Anderson said the $10,000 award "shall
enable some poor, unfortunate but nevertheless very talented
people to do something for which they have dreamed of all
their young lives."

1127
"Second Woman To Get Award." The Philadelphia Tribune. 18
    March, 1941.

Marian Anderson was the second woman to receive the
Philadelphia Award since it was founded in 1921 by Edward
Bok. In 1934, Dr. Lucy Wilson, president of the South
Philadelphia High School for Girls where Miss Anderson
attended, received the award.

1128
"Success Story." The New York Times. 19 March, 1941, pp. 20.

Notes that a poor Black girl from Philadelphia won the
Bok Award. Marian Anderson scrubbed porches as a girl to
help her mother and went on to become a world famous contralto.

1129
"To Marian Anderson." The Camden Post. 19 March, 1941.

Notes the presentation of the Edward W. Bok Award to
Miss Anderson.

1130
"The Woman Who Is A Symbol." The Brown American. Vol. 4,
    April, 1941, pp. 2.

Notes that Miss Anderson won Philadelphia's Bok Award.
She was considered a symbol of American democracy.

Church Awards

1131
"Church Honors Miss Anderson." The New York Times. 19 Octo-
    ber, 1959, pp. 32.

Miss Anderson received the Rector's Award at St. Philip's
Protestant Episcopal Church in New York. The award was an
antique silver cross, hand-fashioned in England about a
century ago. It was awarded to her as "an outward symbol
of inward grace." Speaking to the Women's Day congregation,
Miss Anderson urged each woman to realize her own potential.

1132
"Churchwoman Of Year." The Catholic Transcript. 7 July, 1967,
    pp. 1.

Shows Marian Anderson presenting the Churchwoman of The
Year Award to Mrs. Marcus Kilch. She was last year's winner.

1133
"Notes On People." The New York Times. 1 September, 1973,
    pp. 22.

The 1973 Family of Man awards for excellence went to
Marian Anderson and Dr. Kenneth B. Clark. The awards were
sponsored by the Council of Churches of New York City.

1134
"2 Faiths Honor Miss Anderson." The New York Times. 21
    February, 1957, pp. 24.

The National Conference of Christians and Jews bestowed
the Brotherhood Award on Marian Anderson. The selection
was based on the "simplicity, dignity, and graciousness"
in her autobiography, My Lord, What A Morning.

1135
"Two Honored By Baptists." The New York Times. 8 May, 1959,
    pp. 28.

Marian Anderson and Rev. Dr. Harry Emerson were recipients
of the Baptist Century Awards by the Empire State Baptist
Missionary Convention.

Congressional Gold Medal

1136
Graustark, Barbara. "Newsmakers." Newsweek. Vol. 92, Oct-
    ober 30, 1978, pp. 37.

Marian Anderson received a Congressional gold medal. The
award saluted her "unselfish devotion to the promotion of
the arts..."

1137
"Honor Marian Anderson." Variety. Vol. 286, March 16, 1977,
    pp. 2.

President Carter signed a proclamation to award a special
gold medal to Miss Anderson for her "distinguished career,"
her devotion to the promotion of the arts, her support for
humanitarian causes, world peace and musical achievements.

Gimbel National Award

1138
"Marian Anderson, Dr. Mudd Get Gimbel Awards." The Phila-
    delphia Inquirer. 7 January, 1959.

Miss Anderson was one of the recipients of the Gimbel Award.

1139
"Marian Anderson Receives Award." The Washington Post. 7 January, 1959.

Miss Anderson received the Gimbel National Award and was declared as a "spokeswoman for American democracy." The award consisted of a scroll and $2,500.

1140
"Marian Anderson Receives Gimbel National Award." The St. Louis American." 8 January, 1959.

The Gimbel National Award was presented to Miss Anderson. It is given to recognize women for their service to humanity. Miss Anderson received along with a gold embossed scroll, a $2,500 check.

1141
"2 Women Honored." The New York Times. 7 January, 1959, pp. 66.

Marian Anderson and Dr. Emily Mudd received the Gimbel Awards for 1958. Miss Anderson received the $2,500 national award. She was the fifth national winner and the first Black to be honored in the twenty-seven year history of the award.

Golden Heart Award

1142
Fox, Tom. "A Warm Glow Surrounds Her." The Philadelphia Inquirer. 5 February, 1976.

Marian Anderson was in Philadelphia to receive the Golden Heart award from the Chapel of the Four Chaplains.

1143
Seltzer, Ruth. "Marian Anderson Honored By Chapel of Four Chaplains." The Philadelphia Inquirer. 5 February, 1976, pp. 2D.

Miss Anderson was to receive the Golden Heart award at the 25th anniversary dinner of the Chapel of Four Chaplains.

Liberian Order Of African Redemption

1144
Marian Anderson Given Highest Liberian Award." The Afro American. 18 December, 1943.

The highest award of the Republic of Liberia, The Liberian Order of African Redemption, was awarded to Miss Anderson. More than 1,000 witnessed the presentation and Mrs.

Franklin D. Roosevelt was one of the many speakers praising
Miss Anderson's work.

1145
"Marian Anderson Given Highest Liberian Award." The Negro.
    Vol 1, February/March, 1944, pp. 24.

The Liberian Order of African Redemption, the highest
award of the Republic of Liberia was awarded to Miss Anderson by Walter Walker, on behalf of Liberian President,
Edwin Barelay.

1146
"Marian Anderson Receives Award." Pulse. Vol. 2, February,
    1944, pp. 10.

Miss Anderson was awarded the Order of African Redemption, the highest award of the Republic of Liberia. It
was awarded for her efforts toward international good-will.

1147
"Miss Anderson Honored." The New York Times. 13 December,
    1943, pp. 18.

Miss Anderson was awarded the Order of African Redemption,
the highest honor of the Republic of Liberia. The Award
was made by the Consul General for Liberia, Walter Walker
on behalf of Liberian president, Edwin Barclay.

Hall of Fame

1148
Bernstein, Paula. "Great Women of U. S. Given Own Shrine."
    The Philadelphia Tribune. 11 June, 1975.

Marian Anderson was among the first twenty women inducted
into the Women's Hall of Fame in Seneca Falls, New York.

1149
Darnton, John. "Rallies Muted As Women End Suffrage Cele-
    bration." The New York Times. 27 August, 1973, pp. 59.

Marian Anderson was one of twenty women inducted into
the new Women's Hall of Fame in Seneca Falls, New York.
It was the 53rd anniversary of the women's suffrage movement. Miss Anderson was unable to attend the festivities.

1150
"Miss Anderson Inducted In Birmingham Hall of Fame." Jet.
    Vol. 42, June 15, 1972, pp. 62.

Miss Anderson was the only Black among the six persons
inducted into the American Arts Hall of Fame. The induct-
ion was part of the 1972 Festival of Arts.

1151
"Three Black Women Earn Place in New Hall of Fame." Jet.
    Vol. 44, September 13, 1973, pp. 7.

Marian Anderson was one of the three Black women chosen
as members of the Women's Hall of Fame in Seneca Falls,
New York. This was the site of the first women's rights
convention. Miss Anderson was the only living Black woman
chosen. The other two were Harriet Tubman and Mary McLeod
Bethune.

Litteris et Artibus

1152
"Sweden Honors Marian Anderson." The New York Times. 7
    September, 1952, pp. 79.

The Swedish government awarded Miss Anderson the "Litteris
et Artibus" award, which is reserved for top artists and
scientists.

1153
"Swedish King Gives Marian Anderson Rare Medal." Jet. Vol.
    2, September 18, 1952, pp. 15.

King Gustav of Sweden, presented Miss Anderson with the
Litteris et Artibus decoration which included a gold medal.

Lord And Taylor Award

1154
"Lord and Taylor Honors 11 For Work Overseas." The New York
    Herald Tribune. 8 May, 1958, pp. 14.

Marian Anderson was among those honored by Lord and Taylor.

1155
"Store Honors 'Unofficial Ambassadors' 6 Individuals and 4
    Companies Named." The New York Times. 8 May, 1958, pp. 22.

Lord & Taylor honored six individuals and four stores
at their 21st award luncheon. Marian Anderson was one of
the recipients. It was noted that "with a spirit that
soars to the melody of the greatest of human qualities, she
creates by her own trust and love of America, a new understanding of our country for the people of the world."

Miscellaneous Awards

1156
"Anderson, Marian," in Winners: The Blue Ribbon Encyclopedia
    of Awards, by Claire Walter. New York: Facts On File,
    1978, 731p., pp. 10, 13, 15.

Noted that Miss Anderson has won the following awards:
Presidential Medal of Freedom (1963), the Spingarn Medal

(1939), and the Ladies Home Journal, Woman of The Year Award
(1977).

1157
"Chaos Is Feared By Oppenheimer." The New York Times. 23 May,
    1956, pp. 21.

Dr. J. Robert Oppenheimer and Marian Anderson received
awards for distinguished service to the principles of
American democracy at a dinner marking the eleventh anniversary of Roosevelt University. Miss Anderson's award,
presented by Marshall Field, praised her as a "great spokes-
man of a universal language."

1158
Cheshire, Maxine. "Marian Anderson Gets an Obbligato." The
    Washington Post. 24 March, 1962.

Marian Anderson met with President Kennedy and received
an Inauguration Medal.

1159
"Citizen Award Given To Marian Anderson." The New York Times.
    27 December, 1964, pp. 57.

The New Haven Register announced that they had established
a Connecticut Citizen of The Year Award and had selected
Marian Anderson as the first recipient. The person is
chosen on the basis of service or outstanding personal accom-
plishment. It was felt that Miss Anderson had "devoted a
lifetime to music, to good citizenship and to expression of
the noblest ideals of her race and country."

1160
Courier Award." The New York Courier. 24 April, 1965, pp. 1.

At her farewell concert, Marian Anderson was given a
plaque from the New York Courier for "excellent musical
achievement."

1161
"Educator Assails Capsuel Courses." The New York Times. 2
    March, 1957, pp. 16.

At the annual book awards of the Secondary Education
Board, Marian Anderson received an award for her autobiography, My Lord, What A Morning. The board was holding
their 31st conference.

1162
"Finland's Award to Noted Singer Highest Honor." The Norfolk
    Journal & Guide. 24 September, 1947.

The Finnish Government awarded the Order of the White
Rose, their highest honor to Marian Anderson for her contribution to culture and art.

1163
"Honors Marian Anderson Philadelphia High School." The
    Afro American. 21 March, 1936.

Miss Anderson received a silver trophy from Northeast
High School in recognition of her international success
and for courtesies she has extended the school in recent
visits.

1164
"In The World of Music." The New York Times. 17 September,
    1944, Sec. 2, pp. 4.

Marian Anderson received the silver cup for the highest
attendance record of any solo concert artist at the Hollywood Bowl during the past season. Her first appearance at
the bowl on July 18th broke a ten year record when 20,000
attended the concert.

1165
Kohler, Saul. "Shafer Pledges Drive To Return States To
    'A Meaningful Role'." The Philadelphia Inquirer. 7
    January, 1967, pp. 23.

Marian Anderson was one of the recipients of the
Pennsylvania Awards for Excellence.

1166
Madden, John. "Mourning Cuts Audience; Archbishop At Concert;
    Betty Allen Scores." Variety. Vol. 250, April 10, 1968,
    pp. 55.

The National Association of Negro Musicians held its
third annual benefit concert at Lincoln Center's Philharmonic Hall. The concert was also a tribute to the late
Martin Luther King, Jr. Marian Anderson was awarded the
Association's first Humanitarian Award.

1167
"Marian Anderson Given Medal, College Celebrates Centennial."
    The Syracuse (N.Y.) Herald-Journal. 25 September, 1967,
    pp. 17.

Miss Anderson received a special centennial medal and
citation from Cortland College. Later she and the Syracuse Symphony presented a gala concert.

1168
"Marian Anderson Honored." The Chicago Tribune. 9 July, 1966.

Miss Anderson accepted a medal of merit from Chicago's
Mayor Daley.

1169
"Marian Anderson Honored For Civil Rights Efforts At Opening
    of Station WVNJ." The New York Times. 20 December, 1948,

pp. 44.

Miss Anderson received a plaque in recognition of her efforts for equal civil rights at the formal opening of station WVNJ in Newark. The plaque was presented by Mrs. Parker O. Griffith, a vice president of the Newark Broadcasting Corporation. The plaque said the contralto "Through the art of song and living has done more than any other living person to advance the crusade for equal opportunity, freedom of expression and mutual cooperation in America."

1170
"Marian Anderson Receives SAI Certificate of Merit." Pan
    Pipes of Sigma Alpha Iota. Vol. 54, November, 1961, pp.
    10-11.

Miss Anderson was awarded the Sigma Alpha Iota certificate of merit as an expression "for her gifts of great service to the music profession, for her contribution to the cultural life of this country and for her encouragement of international understanding through music."

1171
"Marian Anderson Scholarship Established by Roosevelt U."
    The Crusader. 28 November, 1964.

At her farewell concert at Orchestra Hall, the Roosevelt University Women's Scholarship Association planned to present her with a citation and established a Marian Anderson scholarship. The presentation was to take place at a champagne dinner.

1172
"Medina Will Get Page One Award." The New York Times. 19
    March, 1958, pp. 28.

The New York Newspaper Guild awarded Marian Anderson a special public affairs award. The award cited Miss Anderson for conducting "her life and career in a way that has reflected glory on her country, race and profession."

1173
"Miss Anderson Gets Award for Aid To Youth." The Afro
    American. 4 December, 1943.

Marian Anderson won the merit award of the New York Youth Committee for her work with young music students.

1174
"Negroes Are Urged to Aid Rights Fight." The New York Times.
    23 August, 1955, pp. 20.

At the fifty-sixth annual convention of the Improved Benevolent and Protective Order of Elks of the World, Marian Anderson received the order's Elijah Lovejoy Medal for outstanding contributions in interracial relations.

1175
"Notes On People." The New York Times. 1 November, 1978,
   pp. 21.

The first Annual Kennedy Center Honors was to be awarded
on December 3rd. Marian Anderson was to be one of the
five recipients honored for "their significant contributions
to American culture through the performing arts."

1176
"Philadelphia Hails Famed Marian Anderson." The Philadelphia
   Tribune. 23 January, 1965.

The city of Philadelphia paid tribute to Marian Anderson
on January 15 in the Mayor's Reception Room. An inscribed
Liberty Bell was presented to her in appreciation of the
fame she brought to the city.

1177
Ross, Nancy L. "U. S. Gold Medallions To Be Sold Mid-June
   By Public Mail Order." The Washington Post. 11 February,
   1980, pp. D9.

The first U. S. gold piece in fifty years was to be
produced for sale by mid June. One million medallions
containing ½ troy ounce of gold was to bear the likeness
of Marian Anderson. Another coin was also to be minted
honoring another American.

1178
"Service Award." The Waterbury (Ct.) Republican. 10 November,
   1975, pp. 5.

Marian Anderson received an award from the Waterbury
Chapter of Links, Inc.

1179
"Singer Honorary Texan." The Houston Post. 26 February, 1963.

Marian Anderson was in Austin for a concert. She was
presented with a certificate making her an honorary Texas
citizen.

1180
"Singer Honored For Civil Liberties Work." The Cleveland
   Call & Post. 3 September, 1955.

The Elks presented Marian Anderson with their medal
for outstanding achievement in the field of music.

1181
"Singer To Be Honored." The New York Times. 8 October, 1955,
   pp. 12.

Marian Anderson was chosen to receive the distinguished
public service award from the Connecticut Bar Association.
The award, a sterling silver bowl, was to be presented to
her October 18th at a banquet closing the association's
annual meeting.

1182
Spiegel, Irving. "Health Research Urged By Folsom." The New
    York Times. 5 May, 1958, pp. 48.

Marian Anderson was among those receiving awards at the
3rd annual commemorative dinner of the Albert Einstein College
of Medicine of Yeshiva University. The 1958 Albert Einstein Award For Citizenship consisted of a commemorative medallion bearing a bas relief of the late professor and carries
a $1,000 prize.

1183
"To Honor Miss Anderson, Ickes." The New York Times. 16
    April, 1946, pp. 29.

Marian Anderson and former Secretary of the Interior,
Harold Ickes, were selected to receive the 1945-46 Alpha
Medallion from the Nu Chapter, Alpha Pi Fraternity at Lincoln University. The awards were to be given at the university in a special ceremony on May 13th.

1184
"Urban League Honors Two." The New York Times. 19 December,
    1956, pp. 35.

Marian Anderson and her manager, Sol Hurok, received
silver medallions from the National Urban League for
"notable contributions to the cause of better human relations and understanding."

1185
Wilson, John S. "30 Black Musicians Get Ellington Medal At
    Yale." The New York Times. 9 October, 1972, pp. 36.

Marian Anderson was one of the musicians receiving the
Ellington Medal during Yale University's convocation. The
Conservatory Without Walls - a description and celebration
of Afro-American musical legacy. Miss Anderson was
not able to attend the ceremonies.

National Institute of Social Science Gold Medal

1186
"Hoover To Get Medal Again." The New York Times. 3 November,
    1958, pp. 24.

Marian Anderson was one of the recipients of the Gold
Medal for "distinguished service to humanity." The award was
given by the National Institute of Social Sciences.

1187
"Social Science Medals Given to Hoover and 3 Others." The
    New York Times. 14 November, 1958, pp. 12.

    Pictures the recipients of the gold medals and citations
which were presented by the National Institute of Social
Sciences. Marian Anderson was one of the recipients.

Presidential Medal Of Freedom

1188
"Accepts Award." The New York Times. 7 December, 1963, pp. 14.

    Pictures Marian Anderson receiving the Presidential Medal
of Freedom from President Johnson.

1189
"An American Honors List." The New York Times Magazine. 14
    July, 1963, Sec. 6, pp. 16.

    Marian Anderson was among those chosen to receive the
Presidential Medal of Freedom which was the nation's highest
civilian honor.

1190
Cleland, Daisy. "A Tribute to Mrs. Kennedy." The Washington
    Star. 6 December, 1963.

    Mrs. Lyndon B. Johnson and Mrs. Jackie Kennedy were on
hand for the ceremony presenting thirty-one people the
Presidential Medal of Freedom. One recipient was Marian
Anderson for her voice had "enthralled the world."

1191
"Freedom Medal Citations." The New York Times. 7 December,
    1963, pp. 14.

    The Presidential Freedom Medal to Marian Anderson read
that as "artist and citizen, she had ennobled her race and
her country while her voice has enthralled the world."

1192
Hunter, Marjorie. "President Named 31 For Freedom Medal."
    The New York Times. 5 July, 1963, pp. 1, 10.

    President Kennedy named 31 people to receive the Presiden-
tial Medal of Freedom. Marian Anderson was one of those
selected.

1193
"Marian Anderson, Dr. Ralph Bunche Among 31 Receiving
    Freedom Medal." The Crusader. 14 December, 1963.

    President Johnson was to present the Medal of Freedom
to thirty-one recipients. Marian Anderson was one of
those recipients. Her citation said that she had contri-

buted her talent to promoting peace and goodwill in the U.S.

1194
Miller, Joy. "Marian Anderson's Medal." The Sarasota Herald-
    Tribune. 22 September, 1963.

Notes that Miss Anderson was among the 31 people, three
of which are women, to receive the Presidential Medal of
Freedom. She said it was a tremendous honor. A biographical sketch follows.

1195
Wicker, Tom. "Freedom Medal Honors Kennedy." The New York
    Times. 7 December, 1963, pp. 1, 14.

Marian Anderson was among the 31 people to receive the
Presidential Freedom Medal. Also honored were the recently
slain, President Kennedy and the late Pope John XXIII.

Pro Benignitate Humana Decoration

1196
"Marian Anderson Finnish Decoration." Women United. Vol. 9,
    August, 1949, pp. 27.

Miss Anderson was awarded the Finnish decoration Pro
Benignitate Humana (For the Benefit of Humanity) on May
17th at the American Legation.

1197
"Marian Anderson Receives Finnish Decoration." The Black
    Dispatch. 28 May, 1949.

Miss Anderson was awarded the "Pro Benignitate Humana,"
a Finnish decoration.

Religious Heritage of America Award

1198
Nannes, Caspar. "700 See 3 Americans Get Religious Heritage
    Awards." The Washington Star. 24 June, 1966.

Marian Anderson was one of the recipients of the Religious Heritage of America Award. The citation said that her
voice and her humane deeds left an imprint of spiritual
values and ideals.

1199
"Outstanding Churchmen Are Honored." The Washington Post.
    24 June, 1966.

Marian Anderson was one of three persons honored at the
Religious Heritage of America dinner.

1200
"Spellman Honored By Heritage Group." The New York Times.

24 June, 1966, pp. 48.

Marian Anderson was named "Church Woman of The Year" by
the Religious Heritage of America at a dinner at the Statler
Hilton in Washington, D. C.

1201
"Spellman, Marian Anderson To Get Religious Awards." The
    Washington Post. 11 June, 1966.

Miss Anderson was among three persons chosen to receive
Religious Heritage Awards. The Church Woman of the Year
Award was given to her for being "a constant source of
religious inspiration."

Spingarn Medal

1202
"Award for Achievement is Bestowed by Presidents Wife."
    The New York Herald Tribune. 4 July, 1939.

Picture of Marian Anderson receiving the Spingarn Medal
from Mrs. Franklin D. Roosevelt.

1203
"Camera Record of NAACP Conclave Highlights." The Norfolk
    Journal and Guide. 8 July, 1939, pp. 20.

Shows several pictures of the NAACP conclave at the
Mosque Theatre in Richmond. Included are photos of Mrs.
Roosevelt presenting Marian Anderson with the NAACP's
Spingarn Medal.

1204
"Cameramen Miss Award Presented Miss Anderson." The
    Norfolk Journal & Guide. 15 July, 1939.

Newsreels of Miss Anderson receiving the Spingarn Medal
were blurred and made unfit for showing.

1205
"Fete Miss Anderson." The Washington Herald. 5 May, 1939.

Mrs. Franklin D. Roosevelt was to make the presentation
of the Spingarn Medal to Marian Anderson at the 30th annual
conference of the NAACP in Richmond.

1206
"Film On Spingarn Too Blurred." The New York Amsterdam News.
    22 July, 1939, pp. 2.

Miss Anderson had to say her thanks to so many people
that the film of her receiving the Spingarn Medal was too
blurred for showing.

1207
"First Lady Honors Marian Anderson." The New York Times. 3
    July, 1939, pp. 15.

Some 5,000 saw Mrs. Roosevelt present the 1938 Spingarn
Medal to Marian Anderson. She told Miss Anderson that
"your achievement far transcends any race or creed," and
that "she had the courage to meet many difficulties." In
accepting the medal, Miss Anderson said she appreciated the
"significance it carried."

1208
"First Lady Presents Medal For Achievement To Famed Singer."
    The Norfolk Journal and Guide. 8 July, 1939, pp. 1.

Pictures Mrs. Roosevelt presenting the 24th Spingarn
Medal to Marian Anderson.

1209
"Honor For Marian Anderson." The New York Times. 6 January,
    1943, pp. 18.

Miss Anderson received the annual citizen's award of the
Independent Order of Brith Sholom.

1210
"Marian Anderson Get Medal From 1st Lady." The New York
    Daily News. 3 July, 1939, pp. 4.

Shows Mrs. Roosevelt presenting the Spingarn Medal to
Marian Anderson.

1211
"Marian Anderson Spingarn Award Nominee." The Washington
    Tribune. 28 January, 1939.

It was announced that Miss Anderson was to receive the
Spingarn Medal for 1938. The formal statement of the
award committee and name of the committee members are
given.

1212
"Marian Anderson Winner." The New York Times. 27 January,
    1939, pp. 14.

The 1938 Spingarn Medal was awarded to Marian Anderson.
The announcement stated that "Marian Anderson has been
chosen for her special achievement in the field of music.
Equally with that achievement, which has won her world-wide
fame as one of the greatest singers of our times, is her
magnificent dignity as a human being.

1213
"Medal Winner." The New York Times. 29 January, 1939, Sec.
    4, pp. 2.

Marian Anderson was awarded one of the highest honors of her race. The NAACP honored her with the Spingarn Medal for 1938. The award is given for "the highest or noblest achievement by an American Negro."

1214
"Mrs. F. D. To Present Spingarn Medal To Miss Anderson."
The New York Amsterdam News. 6 May, 1939, pp. 2.

Mrs. Eleanor Roosevelt was to present the 24th Spingarn Medal to Marian Anderson at the close of the NAACP convention in Richmond. The ceremony was to be broadcast over radio.

1215
"Mrs. Roosevelt Honors Contralto." The New York Amsterdam
   News. 8 July, 1939, pp. 1.

Pictures Mrs. Roosevelt presenting the 24th Spingarn Medal to Marian Anderson.

1216
"Mrs. Roosevelt Presents the 24th Spingarn Medal to Miss
   Anderson." The Crisis. Vol. 46, September, 1939, pp. 267.

Picture of Mrs. Roosevelt presenting the Spingarn Medal to Miss Anderson.

1217
"Richmond Hails First Lady As N.A.A.C.P. Convention Closes."
   The Afro American. 8 July, 1939.

Pictures of Marian Anderson, and Mrs. Roosevelt at the presentation of the Spingarn Medal to Miss Anderson in Richmond, Virginia.

1218
"Spingarn Medal." The New York Amsterdam News. 28 January,
   1939, pp. 6.

Marian Anderson was chosen to receive the 1938 Spingarn Medal. The award was even more significant in that it was awarded to a woman who had been barred from singing at Constitution Hall because of her color.

1219
"Spingarn Medal Goes To Singer." The Washington Afro American. 28 January, 1939, pp. 1, 2.

It was announced that Marian Anderson would receive the 1938 Spingarn Medal. She was to receive the award on July 2nd at the annual NAACP convention. A list of other Spingarn recipients is given plus the names of the Spingarn Award Committee.

1220
"Spingarn Medal Is Presented to Miss Anderson." The New
    York Herald. 3 July, 1939.

Mrs. Roosevelt presented Marian Anderson with the
Spingarn Medal. Over 5,000 persons attended the NAACP
conference.

1221
"24th Spingarn Medal to Marian Anderson." The Crisis.
    Vol. 46, February, 1939, pp. 55.

Miss Anderson was named the recipient of the Spingarn
Medal for 1938 for her achievement in music.

1222
"24th Spingarn Medal To Marian Anderson." The Pittsburgh
    Courier. 28 January, 1939, pp. 24.

The 1938 Spingarn Medal was to be awarded to Marian
Anderson. She was chosen for her special achievement and
world-wide fame in music. Her magnificent dignity and unassuming manner also added to her esteem.

1223
"Two Great Women." The New York Amsterdam News. 8 July, 1939,
    pp. 5.

Mrs. Roosevelt presented the NAACP's Spingarn Medal to
Marian Anderson. This occasion was an indication that
democracy is not yet dead in the United States.

1224
Young, P. Bernard, Jr. "Mrs. Roosevelt and Miss Anderson
    Make History." The Norfolk Journal and Guide. 8 July,
    1939, pp. 1, 10.

In Mrs. Roosevelt's tribute to Marian Anderson, she
said, "she has rare courage, great dignity and fine modesty." Mrs. Roosevelt then presented to Marian Anderson the
24th Spingarn Medal.

Woman Of The Year

1225
"Awards and Honors." Musical Courier. Vol. 162, December,
    1960, pp. 41.

Marian Anderson was named Woman of The Year by the
women's division of the American Friends of the Hebrew
University. A reading room at the university in Jerusalem
was to be named for her.

1226
"Marian Anderson Cited." The New York Times. 8 October, 1958,
    pp. 31.

Miss Anderson was named Woman of The Year by the New York branch of the American Association of University Women. It was said that Miss Anderson is "a person who has found the key to human understanding, which is beauty and music."

1227
"Marian Anderson Cited." The New York Times. 15 November, 1960, pp. 46.

Miss Anderson was named Woman of the Year by the National Women's Division of the American Friends of the Hebrew University. She received an illuminated scroll at the group's 8th annual awards luncheon. The proceeds from the luncheon was to go toward a reading room for the U. N. documents at the university. The room would be named after Miss Anderson. She was described as "a citizen of the world who ranks as a woman of the century."

1228
"Notes On People." The New York Times. 24 May, 1977, pp. 28.

The Annual Ladies Home Journal "Woman of The Year" awards were held at Ford's Theatre in Washington, D. C. Marian Anderson was one of nine women cited. Journal readers nominated the women who were chosen by a jury of women leaders.

1229
"Women Of The Decade - Marian Anderson: Woman of The Year, 1977." Ladies Home Journal. Vol 96, November, 1979, pp. 187.

Miss Anderson was named Woman of The Year for her creative arts. A short biographical sketch is included.

1230
"Women of The Year, 1977." Ladies Home Journal. Vol. 94, June, 1977, pp. 77.

Biography of Marian Anderson who was one of the women named as 1977 Women of the Year.

HONORARY
DEGREES

American University

1231
Feinberg, Lawrence. "New AU President Vows Higher Standards."
The Washington Post. 22 October, 1976.

Marian Anderson was awarded an honorary degree at American University in Washington, D. C. in the inaugural ceremonies for the new school president.

Bethune Cookman College

1232
"New B-CC Prexy Naming Scheduled For March 18." The Daytona
Beach Morning Journal. 28 February, 1975.

Marian Anderson was to get an honorary Doctor of Letters
degree from Bethune Cookman College.

Boston University

1233
"Boston University." The Negro History Bulletin. Vol. 24,
October, 1960, pp. 20.

Marian Anderson was awarded an honorary Doctor of Music
degree from Boston University on June 5th. A short biographical sketch is included.

1234
"Marian Anderson Honored By Boston University." Jet. Vol.
18, June 16, 1960, pp. 21.

Boston University awarded Miss Anderson an honorary
Doctor of Music degree.

1235
"New Leader Is Urged." The New York Times. 14 June, 1960,
    pp. 40.

Boston University held its 97th commencement on June 13th.
Marian Anderson was one of eight to receive an honorary
degree.

Brandeis University

1236
"Brandeis Honors 8." The New York Times. 13 June, 1960, pp.
14.

Brandeis University conferred honorary degrees on eight
people at their commencement exercises. Marian Anderson
was one of the recipients.

Dickinson College

1237
"Miss Anderson Honored." The New York Times. 24 April, 1954,
    pp. 15.

Miss Anderson received an honorary degree of Doctor of
Humane Letters at Dickinson College on the eve of her departure for a South American concert tour. Dickinson
College president, Dr. William E. Edel, told Miss Anderson
that "you have been to other cultures and peoples a representative of America at its best."

Duke University

1238
"Honorary Degree." Jet. Vol. 47, November 14, 1974, pp. 25.

Marian Anderson, 70, received a Doctor of Humane Letters
degree from Duke University.

1239
"Marian Anderson." Music Journal. Vol. 32, December, 1974,
    pp. 35.

Pictures Marian Anderson and Duke president Terry Sanford,
as he reads the citation accompanying her Doctor of Humane
Letters degree.

1240
"Musical Honors." Stero Review. August, 1974, pp. 68.

Pictures Marian Anderson who was to get an honorary degree from Duke University.

Ewha Women's University (Seoul)

1241
"Marian Anderson Honored." The New York Times. 25 September,
    1957, pp. 23.

Marian Anderson received an honorary Doctor of Music
degree from Ewha Women's University in Seoul. She was
lauded for her "contribution through music to human culture"
and her promotion of "understanding and sympathy among
peoples."

Fordham University

1242
Terte, Robert H. "Spellman Seeks Anti-Smut Group." The New
    York Times. 11 June, 1964, pp. 18.

Marian Anderson received an honorary Doctor of Humane
Letters degree at Fordham University's 119th commencement
exercises.

Hahnemann Medical College

1243
"Marian Anderson." The Philadelphia Inquirer. 7 June, 1963,
    pp. 29.

Miss Anderson received an honorary degree from Hahnemann
Medical College.

Howard University

1244
"Marian Anderson Nearly Mobbed by 700 Well-Wishers at H. U.
    Exercises." The Washington Tribune. 18 June, 1938.

Miss Anderson was forced to flee after receiving an honorary Doctorate of Music degree from Howard University. She
had to rest in bed after she was almost mobbed by the well-
wishers.

1245
"Marian Anderson Receives D. Mus. Degree." The Dallas News.
    19 June, 1938.

Howard University presented Miss Anderson with a Doctorate of Music degree.

1246
"Miscellaneous Items." The Niagara Falls (N.Y.) Gazette.
    16 July, 1938.

It was noted that Marian Anderson received a Doctor of
Music degree from Howard University.

1247
"Music Notes." The New York Sun. 13 June, 1938.

Marian Anderson received an honorary degree of Doctor of Music from Howard University.

1248
"Music Notes." The New York Times. 10 June, 1938.

Marian Anderson received an honorary Doctorate of Music from Howard University.

Loyola University

1249
"Dr. Anderson - 35th Time." The Danbury (Ct.) News-Times. 13 July, 1970, pp. 21.

Marian Anderson was to get an honorary degree from Loyola University.

Mills College

1250
"Mills Awards 157 Degrees." The San Francisco Chronicle. 13 June, 1966, pp. 13.

Marian Anderson received an honorary Doctor of Fine Arts degree at Mills College.

Mount Holyoke College

1251
"Degree Conferred on Marian Anderson." The New York Times. 21 June, 1958, pp. 23.

Mount Holyoke College awarded Marian Anderson an honorary Doctor of Music degree at their commencement exercises. It was said that "because your singing unites the artist's conscience with the conscience of a sensitive and deeply spiritual human being, it has been a potent influence for good will and understanding among all people."

New York University

1252
"At N.Y.U. Commencement." The New York Herald Tribune. 5 June, 1958, pp. 13.

Marian Anderson received an honorary Doctor of Music degree from New York University.

1253
"Text of Citations With N.Y.U. Degrees." The New York Times. 5 June, 1958, pp. 26.

Pictures Marian Anderson as she receives the honorary Doctor of Music degree at New York University. The text of the citations for honorary degrees conferred is given.

It said of Miss Anderson, "this woman of superlative gifts
has become almost legendary in her own lifetime."

Oberlin College

1254
"Oberlin To Mark 125th Milestone." The New York Times.
    12 October, 1958, pp. 139.

Oberlin College was to mark its 125th anniversary with
a three day convocation. Marian Anderson was to receive
an honorary Doctor of Music degree during the ceremonies.

Princeton University

1255
Fellows, Lawrence. "993 Get Degrees From Princeton." The
    New York Times. 17 June, 1959, pp. 26.

More than 2,000 were on hand to see 933 receive degrees
at Princeton University's 212th commencement. Several
honorary degrees were also given, including a Doctor of
Humanities degree to Marian Anderson. It was said of her,
"her transcendent powers of human understanding have made
her our most influential cultural ambassador to the world
at large and have added grace and strength to the American
voice in the United Nations."

Queen's University (Ontario)

1256
"23rd Honorary Degree To Marian Anderson." Variety. Vol.
    229, December 19, 1962, pp. 2.

Miss Anderson was to receive an LL.D degree from Queen's
University in Ontario on December 10th. It was to be her
first degree from a Canadian university.

Rust College

1257
"Anderson, Gregory and McNair Honored at Rust." Jet. Vol.
    47, December 19, 1974, pp. 44.

Rust College in Holly Springs, Mississippi, awarded Miss
Anderson an honorary degree at the 108th Founder's Day and
Dedicatory Service.

Smith College

1258
"Marian Anderson Honored By Smith." The New York Times. 17
    May, 1944, pp. 15.

Miss Anderson received an honorary Doctor of Music degree
from Smith College during their graduation ceremonies.

1259
"Smith Honors Miss Anderson." Headlines. Vol. 1, July, 1944,
    pp. 36.

Smith College awarded Marian Anderson an honorary Doctor
of Music degree on May 16th.

Spelman College

1260
"Honorees." Jet. Vol. 56, June 21, 1979, pp. 16.

Constance Baker Motley, Marian Anderson and Mattiwilda
Dobbs got honorary doctoral degrees at Spelman College

1261
"Marian Anderson To Receive An Honorary Degree." The New
    York Times. 19 May, 1979, pp. 12.

Miss Anderson was to receive an honorary degree from
Spelman College in Atlanta.

1262
"Star Matter." The Washington Star. 18 May, 1979, pp. A2.

Marian Anderson was to receive an honorary degree from
Spelman College.

Syracuse University

1263
"Syracuse Confers Its Degrees In Rain." The New York Times.
    30 May, 1960, pp. 31.

The program at Syracuse University's 106th commencement
was shortened due to a heavy rainstorm. Marian Anderson
was one of the recipients receiving an honorary Doctor of
Humane Letters degree.

1264
"Syracuse U. Awards Marian Anderson Degree." Jet. Vol. 18,
    June 9, 1960, pp. 45.

Miss Anderson was one of six recipients of honorary
degrees at Syracuse University's 106th Commencement. She
received a Doctor of Humane Letters degree.

Temple University

1265
"Beury Honored By Temple." The New York Times. 13 June, 1941,
    pp. 20.

At the graduation ceremonies at Temple University, six
persons received honorary degrees. Marian Anderson was
awarded a Doctor of Music degree at the June 12th ceremony.

1266
"Degree For Marian Anderson." The New York Times. 25 May,
1941, pp. 13.

Miss Anderson was one of six recipients of honorary degrees from Temple University on June 12th.   She was awarded
a Doctor of Music degree.

Tulane University

1267
"People." Time. Vol 91, May 10, 1968, pp. 51.

Marian Anderson was awarded an honorary doctor of humane
letters degree from Tulane University. It was her first
degree from a southern university and the first awarded by
Tulane to a Black.

University of Bridgeport

1268
"Marian Anderson." The Danbury (Ct.) News-Times. 4 June,
1963, pp. 11.

Shows Miss Anderson receiving an honorary degree from
the University of Bridgeport.

University of Illinois

1269
"Marian Anderson Gets Doctorate." The Crusader. 8 August,
1964.

Miss Anderson received an honorary doctorate of music
degree from the University of Illinois.

1270
"Marian Anderson Gets Doctorate." The Philadelphia Tribune.
8 August, 1964.

The University of Illinois presented Miss Anderson an
honorary doctorate of music degree.

1271
"Marian Anderson Received Honorary Degree In Illinois." The
New York Times. 14 June, 1964, pp. 62

Miss Anderson was awarded an honorary degree from the
University of Illinois.

University of Michigan

1272
"Degree Honors Marian Anderson." The Washington Post. 15
June, 1959.

Miss Anderson came to the University of Michigan to receive an honorary degree and found that she was also to be
the main speaker.

University of Pennsylvania

1273
"U. of P. Class Told of Space Frontier." The New York Times.
    12 June, 1958, pp. 28.

Marian Anderson was one of the recipients of an honorary
degree at the 202nd commencement at the University or Pennsylvania held in Convention Hall.

Wayne State University

1274
"Degrees of Feminism." The Michigan Evening Outlook. 12
    December, 1974, pp. 16.

Wayne State University awarded Marian Anderson an honorary degree.

1275
"4 Women Due For WSU Honor." The Detroit News. 27 November,
    1974, pp. 5B.

Marian Anderson was one of four scheduled to receive an
honorary degree from Wayne State University.

1276
"Honorary Degrees." The Detroit News. 11 December, 1974.

Marian Anderson was awarded an honorary degree by Wayne
State University.

MARIAN ANDERSON AWARD

1277
"Anderson Awards Listed." The New York Times. 8 October,
    1943, pp. 22.

One hundred-two young men and women from twenty-two states
competed for the Marian Anderson awards. The winners were:
Elton Johnson, Isabelle Schapp, Rosalinde Nadel, Constance
Stokes, and Katherine Graves. An award for further study
was given to Camilla Williams, one of last year's winners.

1278
"Anderson Fund Awards." The New York Times. 26 October, 1952,
    pp. 86.

The Marian Anderson Scholarship Award was divided among
five contestants. First prize went to Shirlee Emmons.
Other winners were Betty-Lou Allen, and Judith Rasken.

1279
"Audition Winners Named." The New York Times. 11 October,
    1967, pp. 42.

The 1967 winners of the Marian Anderson Scholarship Fund
were named. Joyce Mathis won the $1,000 first prize. Other
winners were Eva Morris-Thomas and Margaret Cowie.

1280
"Contralto Gets Award." The New York Times. 13 October,
    1960, pp. 34.

Gladys Kriese won the $1,000 first prize in the Marian
Anderson Scholarship Fund competition. Other winners were
Gwendolyn Walters, Carol Toscano and Arnita Ferguson. This
was the 19th year for the awards.

1281
"Five Singers Win Prizes." The New York Times. 21 January,
    1943, pp. 25.

Two scholarships and three supplementary awards amount-
ing to $2,700 were granted in the first competition for
the Marian Anderson award. The winners from twelve states
in the East and Midwest were: Camilla Williams, William
Brown, Mildred Hill, Faye Drazin and William Smith.

1282
"Four Win Music Awards." The New York Times. 15 February,
    1951, pp. 26.

Four contestants in the Marian Anderson Scholarship Fund
drive received $1,800. They were Martha A. Flowers, Lois
Raye, Sara Mae Endich and Robert Riedel. More than $20,000
had been given out since the fund was established.

1283
"Marian Anderson Award Establishes Annual Prize For Young
    Talent." Opportunity. Vol. 20, January, 1942, pp. 25.

After Miss Anderson won the Bok Award, she stated that she
wanted to use the money to help talented youths. The Marian
Anderson Award had no fixed amount but would vary according
to the needs of the winner. It was available to anyone
(black or white) in any field of endeavor.

1284
"Marian Anderson Winners." The New York Times. 1 November
    1968, pp. 34.

Linda Matousek and Nelda Ormond were co-winners of the
$800 first prize in the Marian Anderson Scholarship Fund.

1285
"Marian Anderson's Gift." The New York Times. 22 December,
    1941, pp. 24.

The annual Marian Anderson Award was established to aid
talented young artists in pursuing their chosen careers.
The amount of the award will vary according to the need of
the student. Three trustees were selected to administer
the funds.

1286
"Marian Anderson's $10,000 Bok Award Begins Paying Dividends."
    The Philadelphia Tribune. 5 December, 1942.

Miss Anderson placed her $10,000 Bok Award in a fund to
be used by needy young people. Some selection of winners
had already been made.

1287
"Soprano, 22, Wins Prize." The New York Times. 14 October,
    1959, pp. 52.

Catherine Wallace was named as the 1959 winner of the
Marian Anderson scholarship competition. She would receive

$1,000. Other winners were Paul Huddleston, Thomas Carey
and Ann Lee. The winner of the award for previous years
winners was Helen Cox Raab.

1288
"Soprano Wins $1,000." The New York Times. 23 October, 1951,
   pp. 27.

Georgia Laster won the 1951 Marian Anderson Scholarship
Award. She was selected from 203 applicants. Other winners
were Herbert Gantt, Gloria Davy, Doris Mayes, and Jan Gabur.

1289
"Three New Yorkers Win Marian Anderson Grants." The New
   York Times. 25 October, 1963, pp. 36.

Three New Yorkers won the 22nd annual Marian Anderson
Scholarship Award. First prize of $1,000 went to Billie
Lynn Daniel. Second prize went to Maria Mastrangelo and
third prize went to Claudie Lindsey.

1290
"2 U. S. Singers Win Anderson Awards." The New York Times.
   12 October, 1961, pp. 41

One hundred forty seven contestants participated in the
20th annual Marian Anderson Scholarships. The $1,000 first
prize went to Corinne Jensen. Other winners were Alexander
Yancy, and Grace De La Cruz. Gwendolyn Walters received
the $100 gift to former scholarship winners. This year's
first prize was given in memory of Korean soprano, Young
Soon Lee, a 1959 winner who was killed in a crash while
traveling to compete in the 1960 auditions. The fund has
given out over $40,000 to twenty-seven singers of all natio-
nalities.

1291
"Two Scholarships." Etude. Vol. 61, March, 1943, pp. 145.

Two scholarships and three supplementary awards were
given in the first Annual Marian Anderson Music award.
Camilla Williams and William Brown tied for first place.
Mildred Hill, Fay Drazin and William Smith were awarded
$400 each.

1292
"2 Win Marian Anderson Singing Auditions." The New York
   Times. 12 October, 1953, pp. 31.

Madeline Chambers and McHenry Boatwright were co-winners
in the 1953 Marian Anderson Scholarship Fund. Both received
$750 for further study. Other winners were Elinor Zvenitsky,
Robert Mosley and Coletta Warren. During the past thirteen
years the fund has awarded $23,000 to young artists.

TRIBUTES
AND HONORS

1293
Barthel, Joan. "She Has The Whole World..." The New York Times. 18 April, 1965, Sec. 2, pp. 13.

Noted that Marian Anderson was not easy to interview. She seldom refers to herself as "I" preferring to speak in the third person. She is more at ease discussing what is ahead than what she has accomplished. Although she faced much rejection because of her color, she had maintained a deep sense of serenity.

1294
"Birth-Control Group Honors 4 at Start of $1 Million Drive." The New York Times. 16 November, 1967, pp. 26.

A luncheon was given to raise money for the Margaret Sanger Institute of Human Reproduction and Development. Four women were honored for their contributions to the planned parenthood movement. Two others, one of which was Marian Anderson, were also honored but were unable to attend the luncheon.

1295
"Black Arts Group To Honor 3 Oct. 8." The New York Times. 25 September, 1972, pp. 49.

Marian Anderson was one of three to be honored by the Blacks Academy of Arts and Letters. The purpose of the academy "is to help bring recognition to those whose contributions to art, literature and scholarship reflect the richness and variety of the Black experience."

1296
Chambers, Marcia. "Shirley Verrett Takes Up The Challenge." The New York Times. 22 October, 1973, pp. 44.

In this article, Miss Verrett talks about Marian Anderson and Leontyne Price who paved the way for many Black artists.

1297
Confer, Grayce B. "How Marian Anderson Blessed My Life."
  Negro Digest. Vol. 11, February, 1962, pp. 37-40.

Mrs. Confer relates how twice Marian Anderson's singing
has blessed her. While pregnant, she went to hear Miss
Anderson and waited in a long line to greet her. Mrs. Confer
had a baby girl two weeks later. Again when Mrs. Confer's
mother was ill, they heard Miss Anderson sing He's Got The
Whole World In His Hands, which cheered the mother tremendously.

1298
"First Lady Named For Aid To Negroes." The New York Times.
  14 February, 1940, pp. 13.

Mrs. Eleanor Roosevelt, Harold Ickes and Marian Anderson
were among several honored for distinguished achievement in
the improvement of race relations during 1939. The winners
were selected by a national poll conducted by the Schomburg
Collection and the Association for The Study of Negro Life
and History. Mr. Ickes was honored for granting Miss Anderson use of Constitution Hall for her Easter concert.

1299
Gallup, George E. "Mr. Kennedy Ranks First, Mrs. Johnson
  Next in Poll." The Washington Post. 25 December, 1963.

Marian Anderson ranked 10th in a poll of Most Admired
Women of 1963.

1300
"Honored At Reception." The New York Times. 17 April, 1939.
  pp. 12.

Marian Anderson was guest of honor at a reception and
dinner at the Essex House after her concert. She was
escorted by Mayor and Mrs. LaGuardia and Hubert T. Delaney,
Negro Deputy Tax Commissioner.

1301
"The House Was Full of Celebrities." The New York Amsterdam
  News. 22 April, 1939, pp. 1.

Shows Miss Anderson at the Essex House where over four
hundred celebrities had gathered for a supper in her honor.
She had appeared at Carnegie Hall earlier.

1302
Hurok, S. "Talent Isn't Enough." Etude. Vol. 67, September,
  1949, pp. 5-6.

Mr. Hurok notes that a spine-tingling sensation was his
guide in engaging an artist. He reflected on how he became
Marian Anderson's manager after hearing her sing in Paris
in 1934. He was able to guarantee her concert dates and she
made her Town Hall debut in 1935.

1303
Jarratt, Jennifer. "Marian Anderson Turns Her Talents To
Helping Others." The Detroit Free Press, 13 November,
1965, pp. 4B.

Miss Anderson was to receive several tributes at a reception in her honor sponsored by the United Negro College Fund.

1304
"Manager of The Stars." Headlines and Pictures. Vol. 3,
July, 1946, pp. 42.

Marian Anderson's manager, Sol Hurok, published his mem-
oirs. The chapter, "One In A Hundred Years" is devoted to
Marian Anderson.

1305
"Marian Anderson Among 9 Honored." The New York Times. 9
October, 1958, pp. 39.

Marian Anderson was one of nine women honored by the
Distinguished Daughters of Pennsylvania. The organization
expressed pride in her achievements in international understanding.

1306
"Marian Anderson Created For 'Ave Maria' Says La Guardia."
The New York Amsterdam News. 22 April, 1939, pp. 12.

Speaking at the supper held in Marian Anderson's honor,
New York mayor, F. H. La Guardia praised her for possessing
a voice that has no equal and for mastering the control of
it.

1307
"Marian Anderson Feted by H. U. Faculty Wives." The Washington
Afro American. 15 April, 1939.

The Howard University Faculty Wives entertained in honor
of Miss Anderson at Frazier Hall. A list of the receiving
line, outstanding guests and the hostess committee is given.

1308
"Marian Anderson Hailed By Michigan Legislature." The New
York Times. 18 February, 1965, pp. 27.

The Michigan Legislature gave Marian Anderson a commen-
datory resolution during a joint session of both Michigan
houses. The resolution lauded Miss Anderson as a great
artist, humanitarian and person and as an exponent of "all
that is best in her race."

1309
"Marian Anderson Library Gets $100,000 Boost." Jet Vol. 57,
September 20, 1979, pp. 61.

Luciano Pavarotti gave a benefit concert for the Marian Anderson Library and Music Scholarship Fund at the University of Pennsylvania. It was the highlight of Marian Anderson Day in the city.

1310
"Marian Anderson Named One of America's Ten Leading Women for 1940." The Washington Tribune. 4 January, 1941.

A committee of educators named Miss Anderson one of the ten outstanding young women of America.

1311
"Marian Anderson Often Honored." The Philadelphia Inquirer. 19 March, 1939.

Since her return from Europe four years ago, Miss Anderson has received many honors and trophies for her musical accomplishments.

1312
"Marian Anderson Ranks 1st in Poll." The Philadelphia Inquirer. 31 December, 1939.

Miss Anderson was voted the most prominent citizen and best creator of interracial goodwill for 1939. The poll was conducted by the country's newspaper reporters.

1313
"Marian Anderson Rated 10th Most Popular Woman." Jet. Vol. 25, January 9, 1964, pp. 62.

Miss Anderson rated 10th among the Gallup Poll of the women Americans most admire.

1314
"Marian Anderson Welcomed." The New York Times. 26 January, 1959, pp. 25.

Marian Anderson was welcomed as a Fellow of The American Academy of Arts and Sciences.

1315
"Marian Set Precedent On Jim Crow." The New York Amsterdam News. 27 May, 1939, pp. 20.

A suit was brought against the New Orleans Municipal Auditorium Commission for refusing to permit Black artists to appear there. It was noted that Marian Anderson set a precedent in this area when she was refused a concert at Constitution Hall.

1316
Maxwell, Elsa. "A Midnight Supper." The New York Post. 16 January, 1946, pp. 12.

In a 10th anniversary celebration, manager Sol Hurok gave Marian Anderson a supper party at Sherry's. Many people paid tribute to her.

1317
"Miss Anderson and The Opera." The New York Times. 24 March,
    1940, Sec. 9, pp. 8.

This letter to the editor from a white southerner wanted to know why Marian Anderson had not been asked to sing at the Metropolitan Opera House.

1318
"Miss Anderson In The South." The New York Times. 9 April,
    1939, Sec. 10, pp. 6.

This letter to the editor was written by a man who had seen Miss Anderson perform in Houston, Texas. 5,000 were at the Civic Auditorium with one-third being Black. Blacks were on all floors, but occupying the third to one side of the stage. Miss Anderson bowed when she came on stage and then deliberately turned to those of her race and bowed very long and low.

1319
Morgan, Alfred Lindsay. "Summer Symphony Programs On The
    Air." Etude. Vol. 65, August, 1947, pp. 430, 465.

The 4th Annual poll by Musical America magazine listed Marian Anderson as one of the solo artists winners for her guest appearance on "The Telephone Hour."

1320
"Negro History Week." The New York Times. 15 February, 1940,
    pp. 18.

The Association For The Study of Negro Life and History celebrated Negro History Week by citing several people for "distinguished achievement in the improvement of race relations in 1939." Marian Anderson was one of those honored.

1321
"Notables Greet Great Negro Singer." The Daily Worker. 18
    April, 1939.

Miss Anderson was honored at a reception by the Theatre Committee.

1322
"Notes On People." The New York Times. 9 April, 1977, pp. 38.

The University of Pennsylvania was to receive the papers and memorabilia of Marian Anderson. She gave the collection of letters, newspaper clippings, and gifts to the university primarily because it was located in Philadelphia. The Van Pelt Library was to house the collection.

1323
Novak, Benjamin J. "Opening Doors In Music." The Negro
    History Bulletin. Vol. 34, January, 1971, pp. 10-14.

In talking about the early singing artists, it cites
Marian Anderson as blazing the path and opening many doors
which had previously been closed to Blacks.

1324
"Play Site Honors Marian Anderson." The New York Times. 31
    July, 1954, pp. 15.

The Marian Anderson recreation center was formally dedicated on July 30th. The $700,000 facility was located two
blocks away from where the singer was born. The center
features an outdoor pool and a three acre playground. There
is an auditorium, gymnasium and the latest in recreation
equipment.

1325
Prattis, P. L. " 'Marian Anderson's Voice Has Virture of
    Purity'... Prattis." The Pittsburgh Courier. January,
    1939, pp. 3.

It was noted that Miss Anderson's voice has beauty of
tone, range, technical perfection and, above all, the virture of purity. Her voice has the power to meet any demand
made upon it.

1326
Prattis, P. L. "Our Marian Is Selected As One of World's
    Ten Greatest Women." Pittsburgh Courier. 14 November,
    1936.

Elsa Maxwell selected Marian Anderson as one of the ten
greatest women in the world.

1327
Price, Leontyne. "Marian Anderson," in Double Exposure, by
    Roddy McDowall, New York: Delacorte Press, 1966, 251p.,
    pp. 172-173.

Miss Price recalls how, as a child, her mother saved
money for her to attend a Marian Anderson concert in
Jackson, Mississippi. After seeing her, Miss Price was
filled with a determination to study music. Notes that the
deep appreciation of people throughout the world and in all
phases of life is legend.

1328
"Quotable." The New York Times Magazine. 27 March, 1960, Sec.
    6, pp. 12.

This letter to the New York Times Magazine on quotable
notes suggested that one by Marian Anderson be added. It
said: "As long as you keep a person down, some part of you
has to be down there to hold him down."

1329
Rouzeau, Edgar T. "Marian Anderson, Who Once Was A Flop
     With Harlemites, Now Has Them As Admirers After the Whites
     Okayed Her." The Pittsburgh Courier. 17 December, 1938,
     pp. 24.

It was remembered when only four hundred Blacks would
turn out to hear Marian Anderson. It was noted that since
whites began to recognize Miss Anderson, then Blacks in
Harlem began to go to her concerts.

1330
Runbeck, Margaret L. "I Must Keep My Color." Negro Digest.
     Vol. 9, April, 1951, pp. 65-72.

This white woman relates the reaction she received when
she kissed a Negro woman. This woman was Marian Anderson.
Ms. Runbeck goes on to discuss the tributes various people
and organizations have given to Miss Anderson and how an
illness almost caused Miss Anderson to lose her voice,
but faith in God brought her through.

1331
Schumach, Murray. "U. S. Negro Women Honored At Fair." The
     New York Times. 17 August, 1964, pp. 22.

Black women were honored at the New York World's Fair.
Among those honored was Marian Anderson. Both Governor
Rockefeller and Mayor Wagner said special tributes to her.
She was given a World's Fair Medallion by F. J. McCarthy
who said, "no one more typifies the theme of the World's
Fair, 'peace through understanding', than Marian Anderson.

1332
"Seconds Anderson Nomination." The New York Times. 14 April,
     1940, Sec. 9, pp. 8.

This letter to the editor stated that Daniel Krupp's
urgent plea to invite Marian Anderson to sing "Erda" should
be seconded by all music lovers.

1333
Toppin, Edgar A. "Breaking The Old Walls of Prejudice."
     The Christian Science Monitor. 5 June, 1969, pp. 1.

Cited Marian Anderson as one who led the way in integra-
ting her profession.

1334
"Tribute to Marian Anderson." Headlines. Vol. 1, July, 1944,
     pp. 45-46.

The theater division of the Riverdale Children's Association sponsored a reception for Marian Anderson on May 7th.
She received a manuscript of Handel's Sampson.

1335
Waters, Crystal. "Singing For Your Supper." Independent
   Woman. Vol. 15, April, 1936, pp. 106-108, 127-128.

Notes how hard it is to succeed as a singer. Cites Marian
Anderson as the season's vocal sensations.

1336
"Who's Who At Supper Reception For Marian Anderson." The New
   York Amsterdam News. 22 April, 1939, pp. 12.

Shows photos of the celebrities present at the supper
held in Miss Anderson's honor at Essex House. The dinner
was sponsored by the Theatre Arts Committee.

1337
"Women of Achievement Chosen." The Washington Post. 9 November, 1948.

Marian Anderson was one of the twelve women chosen by
Coronet Magazine as outstanding in their fields of endeavor.

PORTRAITS

AND BUST

1338

"An American Album." <u>New York Times Magazine</u>. 15 October, 1961.

Shows paintings of Marian Anderson and Franklin D. Roosevelt done by the late Enit Kaufman. The N. Y. Historical Society planned a memorial exhibition of her works.

1339

"Art Group Receives Bust of Noted Singer." <u>The New York Times</u>. 19 June, 1955, pp. 75.

An original bronze bust of Marian Anderson was presented to the Washington County Museum of Fine Arts in Hagerstown, Maryland. It was donated by Mrs. Mary Karasick. The sculpture was done by Hungarian-born sculptor, Nicolaus Koni, in Vienna. It is his interpretation of Miss Anderson singing Schubert's "Death and the Maiden."

1340

Fisher, Dorothy Canfield. "Gallery of American Leaders." <u>The New York Times Magazine</u>. 24 September, 1944, pp. 20-21, 46.

Shows a collection of American leaders done by Enit Kaufman. Among those she painted was Marian Anderson.

1341

"Gallery Refuses to Exhibit Marian Anderson Portrait." <u>The Washington Tribune</u>. 22 February, 1941.

The Corcoran Art Gallery refused to exhibit a portrait of Miss Anderson. The gallery said the portrait was below their standards for acceptance and denied race had anything to do with the refusal.

1342
"Interfaith Group Received Portrait." The New York Times.
    26 August, 1957, pp. 18.

An oil portrait of Marian Anderson was presented to the
National Conference of Christians and Jews. The portrait
was done by S. Edmund Oppenheim and was presented to the
conference by Milton H. Biow, co-chairman of the Marian
Anderson Portrait Committee.

1343
"Marian Anderson, in American Portraits, by Dorothea F.
    Fisher. New York: Holt and Company, 1946, 318p., pp.
    310-312.

Shows black and white paintings done by Enit Kaufman and
a short biographical sketch by Ms. Fisher.

1344
"Marian Anderson," in Portraits of Greatness, by Yousuf
    Karsh. New York: Nelson & Sons, 1959, 207p., pp. 16-17.

The author notes that this picture of Miss Anderson
shows a harmonious soul revealing itself in song. Mr.
Karsh had snapped several pictures of her but was not satis-
fied with them until he caught her off guard humming "The
Crucifixion."

APPENDIX

Manuscript Holdings

Amistad Research Center
   Julius Rosenwald Fund Records. 1917-1948.
   Open. Description and register
   Biographical material on several Blacks, including
   Marian Anderson

Atlanta University, Trevor Arnett Library, Negro collec-
tion
   Cullen-Jackman Memorial Collection: Miscellany. n.d.
   Open. Unpublished guide
   Includes a few bells-lettres by several prominent
   women, including Marian Anderson.

   Maud Cuney Hare Papers. 1900-1936.
   Open. Unpublished guide
   Included in this collection are photos of Marian Ander-
   son

   Southern Conference For Human Welfare Records. 1938-
   1967.
   Open. Unpublished guide
   Marian Anderson is included among the correspondents.

Chicago Historical Society
   Claude A. Barnett Papers. 1920-1967.
   Open. Inventory
   Several women in entertainment and art are included in
   the correspondence and clipping file. Marian Anderson
   is among those mentioned.

Columbia University, Rare Book and Manuscript Library
   L. S. Alexander Gumby Collection. 1800-1960.
   Open. Unpublished guide
   Scrapbooks on Marian Anderson are included in this
   collection.

Fisk University Library
  Langston Hughes Papers.   1921-
  Open.
  Several Blacks, including Marian Anderson, are cited
  in his papers.

Moorland-Spingarn Research Center, Howard University
  Marian Anderson and the D.A.R. Controversy Records.
  1939-1945.
  Open. Unpublished guide
  Correspondence, reports, broadsides, programs, press
  releases, and clippings relating to the refusal of the
  D.A.R. to allow Marian Anderson use of Constitution
  Hall for an Easter concert in 1939.

Museum of The City of New York
  Theater and Music Collection
  Restricted
  Portraits, photographs, playbills, scene designs and
  costumes of Black entertainers are in this collection.
  Materials relating to the career of Marian Anderson
  are included.

Schomburg Center for Research and Culture, New York Public
Library
  "Negro Week" Collection Papers.   1940
  Correspondence and other documents relating to "Negro
  Week" at the New York World's Fair. Miss Anderson
  performed at the fair.

Pennsylvania, University of, Van Pelt Library
  Marian Anderson Collection.
  Open. Published guide (forthcoming)
  This collection included diaries, autobiographical
  comments, promotional pamphlets, programs, reviews,
  clippings, photographs, awards, memorabilia, personal
  and general corresponcence and music (some with notes
  by Miss Anderson).

Sophia Smith Collection, Smith College
  Music
  Open
  Included in this collection is one box of original
  manuscript material relating to Marian Anderson. Rec-
  ords and letters documenting her role in the Chicago
  Youth Conference, her Far East Tour, and congratulatory
  messages on her United Nations appointment

Yale University, Sterling Memorial Library
  Spirituals and Blues Collection
  Marian Anderson is included in this collection of
  holdings of phonograph records by Black artists.

Discography

Bach
"Bach Arias and Great Songs Of Faith."
    RCA   LCT 1111   (1953)

Bennett, Robert Russell
"Songs at Eventide."
    RCA   LM/LSC 2769   (1964)

Brahms, Johannes
"Alto Rhapsody, Op. 53."
    RCA   LM 1146   (1951)
    RCA   SP-555   (1969)

"Christmas Carols."
    RCA   LM 7008   (19??)
    WDM   7008   (1952)

"Christmas Carols."
    RCA   LM/LSC 2613   (1962)

"Collector's Showcase."
    Club   99 508   (1976)

"Farewell Recital."
    RCA   LSC 2781   (1964)
    RCA   LM 2781   (1965)

"First Recordings Of Marian Anderson."
    Halo   50281   (1956)

"Golden Age of Opera Potporri - 4."
    EJS   169   (19??)

"Golden Age of Opera Potporri - 8."
    EJS   184   (19??)

"Great Combinations."
    RCA   LM 1703   (1952)

Handel.
"Three Arias."
    RCA   49-3158   (1951)

"He's Got The Whole World In His Hands."
    RCA   LM/LSC 2592   (1962)

"Jus' Keep on Singing."
    RCA   LM/LSC 2796   (1965)

"Lady From Philadelphia."
    RCA   LM 2212   (1958)

"The Lord's Prayer and Other Songs of Faith
    And Inspiration."
    RCA   VCS 7083   (1971)

Mahler, Gustav
"Kindertotenlieder (Songs on The Death of
    Infants)."
    RCA   LM 1146   (1951)

"Marian Anderson Sings."
    Varsity 6986   (19??)

"Marian Anderson Sings Christmas Carols."
    RCA   ERA 116   (19??)

"Marian Anderson Sings Great Spirituals."
    RCA   ERA 62   (19??)

"Operatic Recital."
    Royale 6001 (19??)

"Recital."
    Royale 1278 (19??)

Sarsen-Bucky, Frida
"Snoopy Cat; The Adventures of Marian
    Anderson's Cat, Snoopy."
    Folkways FC 7770   (1963)

Schubert.
"Beloved Schubert Songs."
    RCA   WDM 1530   (1951)

Schubert
"Lieder."
    RCA   49-1278   (1950)
    RCA   49-3158   (1951)

Schumann, Robert Alexander
"Der Nussbaum. The Nut Tree."
    Victor 14610   (193?)

Schumann, Robert Alexander
"Frauen Liebe Und Leben. Op. 42."
    RCA   WDM 1458   (1950)

Sibelius, Jean
"Symphony No. 6. Come Away, Death."
    Scandia SLP 569   (1972)

Siebelius, Jean
"Tapiola, Op. 112."
    Scandia SLP 557   (1971)

"Songs By Schubert, Schumann, Brahms,
    Straus, and Haydn."
    RCA   LM 2712   (1964)

"Spirituals."
```
   RCA      LM 110      (19??)
   RCA      LM 2592     (1962)
   RCA      LM 7006     (1953)
   RCA      LM 2032     (1956)
   RCA      AVMI 1735   (1976)
```

Tchaikovsky
"Jeanne D'Ark. Adieu Forets."
   Tap 311

"Treasury of Immortal Performances."
   RCA   LM 2712   (1964)

Verdi, Giuseppe
"Un Ballo In Maschera. A Masked Ball."
   RCA   LM 1911   (1955)

"When I Have Sung My Songs: The American
   Art Song, 1900-1940."
   New World Records NW 247 (1976)

INDEX